The Collapse of the Confederacy

Edited by Mark Grimsley and Brooks D. Simpson

University of Nebraska Press, Lincoln and London

© 2001 by the University of Nebraska Press
Manufactured in the United States of America
∞
Library of Congress Cataloging-in-Publication Data
The collapse of the Confederacy / edited by
Mark Grimsley and Brooks D. Simpson.
    p.   cm.–(Key issues of the Civil War era)
Includes bibliographical references and index.
ISBN 0-8032-2170-3 (cloth : alk paper)
1. Confederate States of America–History
2. Confederate states of America-Politics
and government.   3. Confederate States of
America–Social conditions.   4. United States–
History–Civil War, 1861–1865–Campaigns.
5. United States–History–Civil War,
1861–1865–Social aspects.   I. Grimsley, Mark.
II. Simpson, Brooks D.   III. Series.
E487.C67   2001
973.7'13—dc21
00–059969

Contents

Maps

The Collapse of the Confederacy

Mark Grimsley and Brooks D. Simpson

Introduction

Americans have known defeat—at Bataan, the Chosin Reservoir, and in the bitter ordeal of Vietnam—but Southerners are the only Americans ever to have confronted outright military disaster. For that reason the death of the Confederate States of America in 1865 has long fascinated Americans of every region, strongly focused on the stark question, Why did the Confederacy perish? Most responses have taken a "macro" view of the answer. That is, they have identified some fatal defect that ensured that the South would lose the struggle for national existence. The present work takes a different approach. It focuses instead on the final months of the Confederacy's life and examines the perceptions and decisions of the people who lived through that period. In that sense, it offers a "micro" view of the Confederacy's demise.

Some years ago the political scientist Fred Iklé lamented the failure of historians to examine the termination of wars with anywhere near the zeal devoted to their causes and conduct.[1] Although Iklé framed his complaint mainly in terms of civilian decision making, it applies equally to the short shrift often accorded military decisions taken by the losing side after defeat seems inevitable. In this respect, Civil War historians are as guilty as any. Practically all of them agree that after the fall of Atlanta in September 1864 and Abraham Lincoln's triumphant reelection in November, the South had no remaining chance to make good its independence. Well aware that Appomattox and Durham Station loom close at hand, their treatments of the war's final months smack strongly of denouement: the great, tragic conflict flows to its now certain end.

Certain, that is, to us, but deeply uncertain to the millions of Americans, North and South, who lived through the anxious days of early 1865. That their bid for independence was doomed was not obvious to all Southerners in early 1865. Many regarded the hour as one of grave peril for the Confederacy but no worse than the sickening reversals of spring 1862 or—harkening back to the American Revolution—the dismal winter at Valley Forge. Some even recalled the intense war weariness (now almost forgotten) that preceded the unexpected triumph at Yorktown in 1781. Even those who realized the Confederacy could not win the war believed, with some reason, that it was possible to obtain good terms for a negotiated return to the Union. Yet how to accomplish this delicate feat, and how to conserve the South's military position in the meantime?[2]

Northerners, though hopeful and increasingly confident of victory, were not certain when it would come. Many expected the fighting to drag on into late spring or summer. Others fretted lest some sudden disaster restore the military stalemate. And several high-ranking officials worried that the defeat of the Confederacy's field armies might spur Southerners to turn to large-scale guerrilla warfare of the sort that had plagued Union-occupied areas for years. Northern victory might be inevitable, but considerable doubt remained about the conditions that would obtain when it did.

The final months of the Confederacy thus offer fascinating opportunities— as a case study in war termination, as a period that shaped the initial circumstances of Reconstruction, and as a lens through which to analyze Southern society at its moment of supreme stress. Such a study can also extend the important ongoing dialogue concerning the general or macro explanations for Southern defeat.

These macro explanations often take the form of epitaphs, a conceit that goes back as far as the Civil War itself. Well before the South met defeat, the Georgia soldier-politician Robert Toombs caustically predicted that the Confederacy's tombstone would read, "Died of West Point"—a swipe at the professional officers he thought were ruining the Southern cause. Eighty years later, Bell Irvin Wiley avenged the officers by suggesting that the Confederacy "Died of Big-Man-me-ism"—a swipe at men like Robert Toombs. Noting that governors such as Joseph E. Brown of Georgia often thwarted the central government's efforts to mobilize manpower and resources, Frank Lawrence Owsley offered "Died of States' Rights" as the Confederacy's epitaph. In a similar vein, David Herbert Donald advocated "Died of Democracy."[3]

Each epitaph claimed that the rebellion perished from internal causes and implied that the South could have won the war but for fatal errors by its political and military leadership. A contrasting interpretation, however, holds that the Confederacy did not dissolve from within but was bludgeoned to death from without. Richard Nelson Current crystallized this explanation in a well-known 1960 essay. Toting up the formidable population and economic advantages enjoyed by the North, he concluded that the Confederacy barely had a chance. "Surely," he wrote, "in view of the disparity of resources, it would have taken a miracle . . . to enable the South to win. As usual, God was on the side of the heaviest battalions."[4]

This durable interpretation dominated Civil War historiography during the 1950s, 1960s, and 1970s and remains by far the most widely held opinion among lay students of the conflict. Within the academic community, it went without serious challenge until Richard E. Beringer, Herman Hattaway, Archer Jones, and William N. Still Jr. mounted a frontal assault in a provocative 1986 study, *Why the South Lost the Civil War*. These historians had their own epitaph for the Confederacy: "Died of Guilt and Failure of Will."[5] After systematically evaluating and rejecting a variety of external factors, including the North's formidable manpower base, superior manufacturing capacity, and near-complete naval command of the Atlantic Ocean, Gulf of Mexico, and inland waters, the authors suggested that Southern whites were never comfortable waging a bloody war to perpetuate slavery—this was the "guilt" part—and never generated enough popular support or nationalist sentiment to fully mobilize their society and prevail in the face of serious reversals—the "failure of will" component.

The "guilt" thesis died pretty much stillborn, but the argument that the Confederates lacked sufficient will, though criticized as tautological, nevertheless attracted considerable attention and engagement. Indeed, *Why the South Lost the Civil War* remains the most significant postmortem on Confederate defeat to emerge in the past thirty years. Most of the attention, however, has been critical. One historian thought the book "unfailingly interesting and provoking" but maintained that "not all of it is convincing and . . . some of it will strike many readers as palpably foolish." Another believed that while it succeeded in repudiating the idea that Northern superiority in numbers did not account for Confederate defeat, it was "less effective" in showing that "the real culprit was the weakness of Southern nationalism, guilt over slavery, and failure of will." Still others chided the book for "several very questionable assumptions and assertions" or simply scoffed outright. William C. Davis, for example, was incredulous that Beringer and his collaborators could believe that notwithstanding the devastation that gripped the Confederacy by 1865, the commanding Federal military posture, and the decline of the Southern resource base, the Confederacy could yet have achieved independence if its citizens had only believed. "Like Peter Pan trying to revive Tinkerbell," he wrote, "Southerners were to close their eyes, clap their hands, and 'wish real hard' for something to happen."[6]

Indeed, the "internal divisions" thesis has never gained wide acceptance among present-day historians who are closely interested in the question of Confederate defeat. A good candidate for the current orthodoxy is an interpretation advanced in James M. McPherson's deceptively brief 1992 essay "American Victory, American Defeat." Among the barrage of points McPherson made was the observation that the wartime North had internal divisions at least as serious as those in the South, so an explanation for Confederate defeat could not rest on that factor alone. Noting that Beringer and his coauthors tended to conflate "lack of will" and "loss of will," he argued that the second formulation was the correct one. The Confederates had the will to begin and sustain the fight, but they eventually lost it. And what caused them to lose it? Military reversals. That explanation, McPherson continued, "introduces external agency as a crucial explanatory factor—the agency of northern military success, especially in the eight months after August 1864." Superficially this resembled Current's argument that the North won because it had the stronger battalions. But that argument was highly deterministic, whereas McPherson emphasized the element of contingency: the possibility that key events—especially battles—might have gone differently. "To understand why the South lost, in the end, we must turn from large generalizations that imply inevitability and study instead the contingency that hung over each military campaign, each battle, each election, each decision during the war."[7]

So much for "Died of Guilt and Failure of Will." But give credit to Beringer, Hattaway, Jones, and Still: they sparked a dialogue that has remained lively for over a decade. Further, they established an agenda that most of their challengers have faithfully embraced, most recently Gary W. Gallagher in *The Confederate War: How Popular Will, Nationalism, and Military Strategy Could Not Stave Off Defeat.*[8]

Gallagher's version of the Confederacy's epitaph would read, "Killed by the North, After a Mean-Fought Fight." All things considered, he thinks the Union won the war more than the South lost it, and he thinks the Confederates hung pretty tough. It is a fresh presentation of an old thesis and takes its cue from Current's essay about the strongest batallions. "If wars are won by riches," Current argued, "there can be no question why the North eventually prevailed. The only question will be: How did the South manage to stave off defeat so long?" While not denying that the "internal divisions" thesis contains some truth, Gallagher believes it is badly overdrawn. To prove it, he offers a salvo of quotations from letters and diaries that suggest the strength of white Southerners' fidelity to their cause. These quotes are not always convincing—some of them have a "whistling through the graveyard" quality, and they seem more plentiful for the first half of the war than the second half—but overall they demonstrate his basic point, which is that it makes as much sense to explore the reasons for Confederate unity as it does to look for rifts.

Gallagher concludes his book with a call for historians to set aside the stale exploration of the factors underlying Confederate failure in favor of "the more complex and fruitful question of why white southerners fought as long as they did. The interplay among popular expectations, national strategy, performance on the battlefield, and Confederate nationalism and will offers rich opportunities for investigation."[9] *The Collapse of the Confederacy* examines the interplay of precisely these factors during the final half year of the Civil War.

The first three essays address, from different angles, a common question: If Union victory was inevitable by November 1864, why did the conflict continue for another six months? Why did Confederate leaders choose to protract the struggle until they had lost any chance to influence the terms of eventual reunion with the North—and why did so many white Southerners continue to follow them? Did they fail to understand their dire predicament? Did they believe the situation could improve? Or were they somehow paralyzed, like a cancer patient who cannot accept that the fatal diagnosis is upon him? Where the Confederacy's political leaders are concerned, the answer to the last three questions is "yes." They underestimated their country's mortal peril. They believed the situation might improve. And although they toyed with a negotiated settlement, their efforts in that direction were halting and unrealistic.

The stance of the Confederate leadership becomes more understandable when one considers the military situation that confronted the Confederacy on New Year's Day 1865. Nominally it seemed not much different from that of the previous January. The rebel government still controlled roughly the same expanse of territory. In the West, Union forces occupied all of Tennessee, much of Louisiana, and a ribbon of land bordering the Mississippi River from Memphis to Baton Rouge—holdings essentially unchanged since December 1863. Elsewhere, the central government and pro-Confederate state governments retained political control. The Trans-Mississippi states, although largely cut off from the eastern Confederacy by Union naval control of the Mississippi River, remained under the military sway of Gen. Edmund Kirby Smith and some thirty thousand Rebel troops.[10] The U.S. Navy had gained control of Mobile Bay, Alabama, in August 1864, but the city itself remained in Confederate hands. Georgia had witnessed the passage of a Federal army through the state but likewise remained largely under Confederate control.

In the eastern theater, the Union Army of the Potomac and the Army of the James—both under the direct supervision of Lt. Gen. Ulysses S. Grant—confronted Gen. Robert E. Lee's Army of Northern Virginia along a fifty-mile front at Richmond-Petersburg. A lesser Union force occupied the lower Shenandoah Valley. With those two exceptions, the Federals actually controlled very little of Virginia. And aside from a few Union enclaves along their coasts (most of which had been there since early 1862), North Carolina and South Carolina remained in Confederate hands. Charleston, South Carolina, still defied the Union navy, and Wilmington, North Carolina, still received blockade runners bearing supplies from Europe.

Just one new Union enclave had joined the rest. Located at Savannah, Georgia, it contained a Federal army under Maj. Gen. William T. Sherman. Unlike the other Northern forces that held coastal lodgments, Sherman's army had not come by sea. Instead it had marched the length of Georgia in two dramatic campaigns, seizing and burning crops, tearing up railroads, and generally creating havoc as it passed. Sherman had left no garrisons behind him: Georgia remained as Confederate after his passage as before. But his men had made the march practically unopposed, and therein lay the Confederacy's crucial difficulty: the South possessed nowhere near the military manpower to shield regions exposed to similar Union raids.

On January 1, 1865, the Confederate army had a total strength of about 155,000 men. With the exception of Lee's 60,000-man Army of Northern Virginia, no more than 25,000 of those soldiers were assembled at any given point. Most were strung out in packets of 3,000 to 10,000, unable to achieve greater concentrations because of geographical distance and the need to defend key strategic points against possible attack. By contrast, the Union strength on New Year's Day 1865 was 496,000.[11] Concentrations of 20,000, 30,000, and even 70,000 troops fairly littered the North's military perimeter. Yet the injuries these forces might inflict, though painful, could not be fatal. Union and Confederate policy makers alike understood that the locus of Confederate power was Lee's army, shielded within the Richmond-Petersburg entrenchments. Union forces totaling 120,000 stood facing Lee; they had

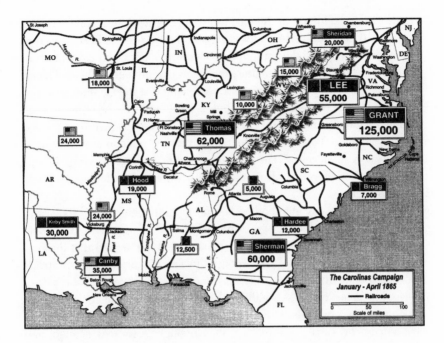

done so for nearly six months. But Lee had managed to preserve the stability of his position, and if the status quo persisted he might be able to do so indefinitely. The main danger was Sherman's army of 60,000 veterans at Savannah. If Sherman could join Grant's armies in front of Richmond-Petersburg, Lee's situation would instantly become untenable. He would have to abandon the Richmond-Petersburg defenses. Once flushed from these earthworks, his army could never survive against the combined might of Sherman and Grant.

The Confederate high command faced a second problem as well, namely, the erosion of Southern morale, both civilian and military. By early 1865, an estimated 100,000 soldiers were absent from their units without leave; hundreds more were absconding every week.[12] What to do? Some whispered that the chance for independence had already passed: the South must return to the Union on the best terms it could arrange. Others vocally maintained that the situation was far from hopeless.

In their view, the South simply needed more manpower. Some, including Jefferson Davis and Robert E. Lee, suggested the use of slaves as soldiers. That proposal, utter anathema just a year previously, now seemed an urgent necessity. At best, however, it would require months to train, equip, and field a force of slave soldiers. In the meantime, sufficient white manpower must be found. This could be done, it was argued, if deserters could be coaxed or coerced back to duty, if the conscription laws were more vigorously enforced, and if most exemptions from military service were eliminated. The *Richmond Whig* published figures in January 1865 asserting that the Confederacy contained about 460,000 white men of military age, even discounting those in occupied regions of the South. Of these, the Confederate government knew that only about 100,000 were in the ranks. Another 100,000 were estimated to be away without leave. The rest, presumably, had taken refuge in jobs that legally exempted them from the draft or were simply defying efforts to conscript them.[13]

Why were so many able-bodied Southern white males not in the army? Those within the Confederate government believed it was because the people had become disheartened. Many outsiders agreed but argued that the government itself bore much of the responsibility for the people's poor spirits. "If the government would do its duty," insisted the *Raleigh* (NC) *Conservative*, "—would manage the affairs of the Republic with the wisdom, the forecaste, the energy, the economy it should do, the people would not be lacking in devotion to the cause. . . . We have men enough, resources enough, and courage enough among our people to vanquish the foe, if we had the wisdom and forecaste in the government to bring them out."[14]

Thus, as 1865 began, Confederate politicians and opinion makers agreed that the situation was serious but did not agree that defeat was inevitable. They argued. Their debate gained added urgency when, on January 11, Francis P. Blair Sr. arrived in Richmond. The father of Lincoln's postmaster general, Blair was known to have close ties to the Union president. Ostensibly he had come to retrieve some personal papers, but everyone suspected that Blair was in town as a peace feeler, and Jefferson Davis knew it for a fact. The two men met on January 12, setting in motion a chain of events that resulted in the famous Hampton Roads peace conference on February 3. There, Lincoln and U.S. secretary of state William H. Seward met with three Confederate commissioners appointed by Davis.

Steven E. Woodworth explores this and other efforts at a negotiated settlement in "The Last Function of Government: Confederate Collapse and Negotiated Peace." The Hampton Roads conference was neither the first nor the last attempt to explore the possibility of a peace short of unconditional surrender. Each effort foundered, he believes, primarily because of the intransigence of one man, Jefferson Davis, who utterly rejected the need to seek a negotiated settlement and maneuvered effectively to short-circuit every effort at a compromise peace. Even his assent to the Hampton Roads conference was deceptive, for he deliberately set preconditions he knew the Lincoln administration could not meet. When the meeting ended without agreement, he touted its failure as a demonstration that the South could have no peace without the acceptance of reunion and emancipation—as he put it, "subjugation." The gambit worked. Many white Southerners voiced anger at Lincoln's evident determination to crush them. Their will to resist temporarily stiffened. But other Southerners continued to hope for a negotiated settlement, and peace proposals were floated in the Confederate Congress and in several states.[15]

Everyone—both those who favored peace and those committed to continuing the war—understood that the military equilibrium must be maintained. Essentially, that meant preventing Sherman from reaching Virginia and combining with Grant. Sherman had recently concluded a march through Georgia characterized by the abandonment of conventional supply lines, extensive reliance on foraging, and widespread destruction of property. It was assumed he would do the same again in the Carolinas; some generals and newspapers even correctly predicted the route he would take.[16]

How to stop him? In "Learning to Say 'Enough': Southern Generals and the Final Weeks of the Confederacy," Mark Grimsley explores the efforts of the Confederate high command to solve that difficult problem. He also shows how mindful Gens. Robert E. Lee, P. G. T. Beauregard, and Joseph E. Johnston were of the interplay between military strategy and the politics of war termination. Each, in his own way, conducted operations with a view toward the possibility of a negotiated peace and lobbied the Confederate government to accept the full implications of the South's fatal strategic position. Ultimately, one of these commanders would take a step unprecedented in American military history, a step that flew in the face of its entire tradition of civil-military relations.

The linkage between strategy and war termination was just as acute on the Northern side of the hill. Brooks D. Simpson analyzes how Abraham Lincoln, Ulysses S. Grant, and other senior Union leaders worked out the Civil War's endgame in "Facilitating Defeat: The Union High Command and the Collapse of the Confederacy." The problem they faced was not simply a matter of defeating the Confederate armies but also of doing so in a way that would foreclose the prospect of rebel guerrilla resistance and, even more important, create the best possible conditions for a true reunion between

North and South. As Simpson points out, Grant was just as aware of these considerations as Lincoln—and perhaps even more effective in finding a way to address them.

The fourth essay in this collection explores a perennial "might have been" of the Confederacy's final months: what if the Rebels had abandoned conventional military resistance once it became untenable and exercised the guerrilla option instead? The authors of *Why the South Lost* have not been alone in believing that this is an option the Confederates could and should have followed, and Jefferson Davis is widely believed to have called for its adoption after the fall of Richmond. In "Jefferson Davis and the 'Guerrilla Option': A Reexamination," William B. Feis demonstrates how historians have misunderstood the defiant president's statement of April 4, 1865, offering a stimulating, fresh assessment of the course Davis really intended for the South to pursue.

The last two essays in this collection focus on the common citizens of the Confederacy. How did they think and act during their nation's final months? For some the secessionist cause had plainly lost its legitimacy. Numerous civilians encouraged their menfolk to abandon the armed struggle. The famed diarist Mary Boykin Chesnut wrote of a woman who called out to her wayward conscript husband as a squad of soldiers hauled him back to the army: "Take it easy, Jake—you desert agin, quick as you kin—come back to your wife and children." She kept up the cry as he receded into the distance, "Desert, Jake! Desert agin, Jake!"[17] But as George C. Rable makes clear in "Despair, Hope, and Delusion: The Collapse of Confederate Morale Reexamined," the response of white Southerners to the crisis was far more complex than mere depression and alienation. A surprising number remained optimistic or at least determined. Quite a few harbored the belief that some last-minute stroke of fortune would remedy the gloomy military situation. Rable's essay has much to say about the relationship between popular will and Confederate defeat.

So too does the volume's final essay, in which Jean V. Berlin inquires, "Did Confederate Women Lose the War?" Lay students of the conflict may find the question seemingly out of left field. But most academics will instantly recognize it as the speculative ending of Drew Gilpin Faust's well-known article tracing the gradual disillusionment of Southern slaveholding women with the Confederate cause. This development was significant not only in its own right but also because, Faust pointed out, the Confederate home front was disproportionately composed of women. "And without the logistical and ideological support of the home front, the southern military effort was doomed to fail. . . . It may well have been because of its women that the South lost the Civil War."[18] Taking direct issue with Faust's thesis, Berlin finds that although Southern women endured tremendous hardship during the war, especially its final months, they focused their anger almost solely against the North and did not become dangerously alienated from the Confederate war effort.

Taken together, these essays offer proof that *the way* in which a war ends matters nearly as much as who wins and who loses. Historians are probably correct to think that after November 1864 the Confederacy had no chance to achieve independence. But it would be a mistake to conflate that reasonable conclusion with the assumption that the war was therefore bound to end as it did, with the total military capitulation of the Southern armies and the dissolution of the Confederate government. The conflict could just as plausibly have ended with a negotiated settlement; it could have been prolonged into midsummer; it could have entered—as Davis hoped—"a new phase" similar to the Fabian resistance of George Washington's Continental army. Civilian morale in the South was never so uniformly depressed as hindsight would have it, and it remained responsive, as it had always been, to changes in the political and strategic landscape. The final chapter of the war need not have been written at Appomattox and Durham Station. It follows, therefore, that the book of Reconstruction might have begun quite differently as well. An air of inevitability has clung too long to the Confederacy's final months. The passions, choices, and actions of Americans during that period still mattered, powerfully.

Notes

1. Fred Charles Iklé, *Every War Must End*, rev. ed. (New York: Columbia University Press, 1991), vii.

2. See, e.g., *Charleston (SC) Courier*, January 17, 18, 1865.

3. Quoted in Richard E. Beringer, Herman Hattaway, Archer Jones, and William N. Still Jr., *Why the South Lost the Civil War* (Athens: University of Georgia Press, 1986), 6–7.

4. Richard N. Current, "God and the Strongest Battalions," in *Why the North Won the Civil War*, ed. David Donald (Baton Rouge: Louisiana State University Press, 1960), 32.

5. Beringer et al., *Why the South Lost the Civil War*, 34.

6. Reviews of *Why the South Lost the Civil War* in *Journal of American History* 74 (1987): 523–24; *American Historical Review* 92 (1987): 748–49; *Journal of Southern History* 53 (1987): 336–38; William C. Davis, *The Cause Lost: Myths and Realities of the Confederacy* (Lawrence: University Press of Kansas, 1996), 124.

7. James M. McPherson, "American Victory, American Defeat," in *Why the Confederacy Lost*, ed. Gabor S. Boritt (New York: Oxford University Press, 1992), 34, 42.

8. Gary W. Gallagher, *The Confederate War: How Popular Will, Nationalism, and Military Strategy Could Not Stave Off Defeat* (Cambridge MA: Harvard University Press, 1997).

9. Gallagher, *Confederate War*, 153.

10. Consolidated abstract from returns of the Confederate army, ca. December 31, 1864, in *War of the Rebellion: A Compilation of the Official Records of the Union and Confederate Armies*, 128 vols. (Washington DC: U.S. Government Printing Office, 1880–1901), Ser. IV, 3; 989. Cited hereafter as OR.

11. Consolidated abstract from returns of the U.S. Army for December 31, 1864, OR, Ser. III, 4: 1034.

12. John S. Preston (Superintendent, Bureau of Conscription) to John C. Breckinridge, March 3, 1865, OR, Ser. IV, 4: 1119.

13. *Richmond Whig*, undated, reprinted in *Raleigh (NC) Daily Conservative*, January 9, 1865.

14. *Raleigh (NC) Daily Conservative*, January 5, 1865.

15. On the Hampton Roads conference, see Edward Chase Kirkland, *The Peacemakers of 1864* (1927; rpt. New York: AMS Press, 1969), 206–58; William C. Davis, *Jefferson Davis: The Man and His Hour* (New York: HarperCollins, 1991), 589–94.

16. See, e.g., Lafayette McLaws to his wife, January 12, 1865, Lafayette McLaws Papers, Southern Historical Collection, University of North Carolina at Chapel Hill.

17. Entry for March 30, 1865, in C. Vann Woodward, ed., *Mary Chesnut's Civil War* (New Haven: Yale University Press, 1981), 773.

18. Drew Gilpin Faust, "Altars of Sacrifice: Confederate Women and the Narratives of War," in *Divided Houses: Gender and the Civil War*, ed. Catherine Clinton and Nina Silber (Oxford: Oxford University Press, 1992), 199. The article originally appeared in *Journal of American History* 76 (1990): 1200–28.

Steven E. Woodworth

The Last Function of Government

Confederate Collapse and Negotiated Peace

The seven men sat around a dining-room table, looking for all the world like so many mourners at a wake. Indeed, Confederate secretary of the navy Stephen Mallory thought he and his six companions made a picture that was "the most solemnly funereal" he had ever seen. The deceased, however, was not a person but an idea. The dream of Confederate nationhood had succumbed to Northern military pressure—and perhaps other factors. It was dead, at any rate; in most minds it had been dead for quite some time.

Yet its specter continued to haunt the minds of one or two members of the meeting. President Jefferson Davis still refused to face what was by now a settled fact. "I think we can whip the enemy yet," he insisted, "if our people will turn out." It was April 11, 1865, and Robert E. Lee and the Confederacy's chief army had surrendered two days earlier. Nevertheless, the president, backed as usual by Secretary of State Judah P. Benjamin, clung to the increasingly bizarre delusion that the South could still achieve independence. Even Davis himself had to admit in later years that his opinion had been "over-sanguine." The fact was that the organized Confederate government could no longer extort even minor concessions from its foe. It would endure such conditions of peace as its now completely victorious conqueror saw fit to impose.

As the Confederate cabinet, joined by its two top remaining generals, brooded heavily through its last meeting, it was the military men who hammered home to Davis the reality of the situation. While the president stared down at a scrap of paper he held in his lap, absently folding, unfolding, and refolding it with nervous hands, Gens. Joseph E. Johnston and Pierre G. T. Beauregard stated categorically that the end had come. Further resistance was a practical impossibility. It was wormwood and gall to Davis, and at least one observer thought the generals, both of whom had carried on bitter personal feuds with the president during the war, seemed to take grim pleasure in it. Johnston, the senior of the two and the chief spokesman, later recalled how he had concluded his remarks by urging "that the President should exercise at once the only function of government still in his possession, and open negotiations for peace." In fact, it was too late even for that, and Davis began to see as much. All that would be offered them, he countered, was "a surrender at discretion."[1]

It need not have been so. Extensive opportunity had existed, even *after* the Confederacy's military options had been exhausted, for working out a negotiated peace that could have secured far better terms for the South. Lincoln was willing to make substantial concessions in exchange for an early end to hostilities, provided only that such a peace encompassed both Union and emancipation. A trail of opportunities—all somehow missed—had led to this council of despair around a dining-room table in Greensboro, North Carolina.

Several times over the past two years, even before hope of victory had vanished, some Southerners had appeared ready to explore the possibilities of a negotiated peace. In June 1863 Vice-President Alexander H. Stephens approached Davis about it. Vicksburg was already besieged and all but lost, and Lee's army was, unbeknownst to Stephens, preparing to move northward for its invasion of Pennsylvania. The vice-president suggested that as a prewar friend and political associate of Abraham Lincoln, he might be well suited to the role of negotiator. The ostensible purpose of his mission would be to discuss the conduct of the war—the exchange of prisoners and Federal actions viewed by Confederates as uncivilized. At least, thus Stephens hoped to be able to sell the idea to the rival presidents, but he had more in mind. In asking Davis's authorization, he went further and requested authority to discuss with Lincoln "any point in relation to the conduct of the war." His goal, he explained, was to bring about a peace agreement based on the "recognition of the sovereignty of the states, and the right of each . . . to determine its own destiny." That was an exceedingly ambiguous formula that could have embraced a restored Union, an independent Confederacy, or perhaps something in between. Davis rejected it out of hand, and Lincoln would have too.

Davis did not trust the short, slight, wizened Confederate vice-president, and he had reason not to. Stephens's heart had never been in the Confederate cause. He was a gifted but not quite mentally balanced Georgian whose admirable dedication to civil liberties had unfortunately led him into a fixation with the letter of the law apart from its spirit. In his fevered mind, the law was as drained of substance as his withered body seemed drained of natural vitality. That was all well and good when the game had been a punctilious defense of the rights and liberties of slaveholders and their state governments, but when secession came, Stephens had demurred. Only after the state of Georgia had declared itself out of the Union did he acquiesce. Having declared himself opposed both to the Union and to the rebellion, he chose to go with the majority in his home state.[2]

Much to the detriment of the Confederacy, however, he proved just as adept and enthusiastic in carping about its government as he had been about that of the United States. Quickly he became a thorn in the side of the Davis administration, sulking in Georgia when his duty was in Richmond and roundly denouncing Davis as a would-be tyrant and destroyer of liberty for pursuing necessary war measures.[3]

Not without reason, then, was Davis uneasy about entrusting to Stephens the responsibility of carrying out the delicate negotiations that might lead to a peace settlement. Instead, he determined to send the vice-president north in hopes of meeting with Union officials but with the strictly circumscribed task of dealing only with prisoners of war and related matters. "Your mission is simply one of humanity," he informed Stephens in written instructions issued July 2, "and has no political aspect." Stephens was unwilling to go on those terms, but Davis, perhaps eager to destroy the vice-president's possible effectiveness as a rallying point for any nascent Confederate peace movement, insisted.[4] If the public saw Stephens negotiating and no peace followed, he would be discredited as a peacemaker.

As events fell out, Stephens did not get even that far, at least not during 1863. He traveled down the Virginia peninsula to pass into Federal lines around Fort Monroe, and there his 1863 mission ended. Detained near the front lines while the authorities in Washington decided whether to receive him, Stephens waited in frustration. No one in the Federal capital seemed to believe that Stephens could indeed have come merely to discuss prisoners of war. Lincoln felt a strong personal desire to talk to his old Whig associate Stephens, but though he was usually fairly receptive to suggestions of a negotiated end to the fighting, this time he said no. Vicksburg had by then fallen and Lee's army had retreated in defeat from Gettysburg. The Rebels "will break to pieces," the president told his secretary John Hay, "if we only stand firm now." Lincoln believed it would be foolish at this juncture to enter into negotiations, the bare appearance of which would strengthen the enemy, when an early and complete victory seemed to be in prospect. In short, Confederate stock had momentarily dropped low enough to extinguish the possibility of negotiations for the time being. Even Lincoln would not talk. His cabinet members were still more adamantly opposed, trusting Stephens no more than Davis did. Secretary of State William H. Seward and Secretary of War Edwin M. Stanton both vigorously argued against any meeting with Stephens, and Lincoln had to agree. Stephens returned, and the first halting gesture toward a negotiated peace failed.[5]

The Confederacy, however, did not "break to pieces." Lee's army escaped back into Virginia. The Union army of Maj. Gen. William S. Rosecrans suffered a severe setback at Chickamauga that fall, and despite Ulysses S. Grant's dramatic victory at Chattanooga in November, it was clear that the war would continue for at least another campaigning season. Both sides had time to reflect further on the prospects of war and peace.

The issue was most pressing for Southerners, who were, after all, losing the war and at the same time suffering the worst of its hardships. Stephens continued to be an unofficial rallying point for those of them who thought the time had come to make a deal. Letters to him from prominent Confederates during the summer and fall of 1863 and into the following winter lamented Davis's intransigence and expressed hope that something might be accomplished in cooperation with "the friends of peace in the North."[6]

Stephens made no public pronouncements but collaborated with his brother Linton as well as Georgia governor Joseph E. Brown to present their ideas of negotiated peace to the Southern people. Both Linton Stephens and Joe Brown were of as doubtful a character as the Confederate vice-president. Linton shared his brother's ideological fixations but was more prone to bitter hatreds. Joe Brown's fixation was his own power. A shameless demagogue, Brown objected to any authority above himself and steadfastly obstructed nearly every effort of Jefferson Davis to prosecute the war in any way that pertained to the state of Georgia.[7]

Both Alexander and Linton Stephens had by this time begun to consider a peace that would be accompanied by a restoration of the Union. Though written correspondence between Brown and the Stephens brothers is scanty and cryptic, probably deliberately so, the governor seems to have agreed with their desires—or at least found it useful to pretend as much. He made plans to call a special session of the Georgia legislature in March 1864, and together he and Alexander Stephens worked on the speech he would send to be read in the assembly urging that after each Confederate victory the Davis administration should offer the North peace on the basis of the "great fundamental principles of the Declaration of Independence." At the same time, Linton, probably with the help of his brother, worked on a series of resolutions by which the legislature could express its approval of these same ideas. It might have been a useful means of easing the Southern populace into accepting the idea of peace and reunion.[8]

Quite accidentally, Davis did something that disrupted the whole scheme —or that allowed Brown and the Stephenses to disrupt their own scheme. In February 1864, in an unrelated matter, Davis issued a proclamation suspending the privilege of the writ of habeas corpus throughout the Confederacy. For the Georgia leaders any such move was like throwing red meat into a cage full of lions, and they almost forgot their plans for negotiated peace in their eagerness to pounce on this political tidbit. Consequently, when the Georgia legislature actually met on March 10, the long, windy, and intemperate speech read by the clerk on Brown's behalf contained more of complaint about habeas corpus suspension and of general and vituperative condemnation of the Davis administration than it did of peace. The necessarily veiled and oblique references to the possibility of negotiations were overshadowed by the shrill anti-Davis rhetoric and alarmist cries about the fate of liberty. A potential appeal to many Southerners' latent desire for peace and misapprehensions of the outcome of a war to the finish was drowned out in what could—probably accurately—be written off as a partisan political tirade.[9]

Alexander Stephens made his own speech to the legislature six days later, a three-hour address that also focused on rights, liberties, and Stephens's ideas of Richmond's abuses. Linton Stephens duly introduced his resolutions, two sets of them now—the peace resolutions and another set condemning Davis and the suspension of habeas corpus. The latter received the bulk of debate and passed by a narrow margin. The peace resolutions passed with little debate by a wide margin, a sure sign that their blandness had faded to meaninglessness in contrast to the controversial partisan issues. Another chance to begin the discussion of peace negotiations thus passed without awakening a significant response among Confederate statesmen or the Southern people.[10]

In May 1864 military operations began again with Grant's coordinated offensives in East and West. Hopes were high in the North that the war would end soon. By July, however, hope deferred had sickened the hearts of many Northerners. Sherman was stalled outside Atlanta, Grant outside Richmond.

Casualty lists were ghastly beyond all the nation's ghastly experience in the previous three years of war. The situation was sufficient to raise doubts about the possibility of a purely military conclusion to the war, and negotiation took on new appeal to many in the North.

Significantly, Lincoln was up for reelection that fall, and the military stalemate made his chances look dim. Many in both North and South saw the opposing Democratic Party as the "peace party"—not without reason. By August, Lincoln himself believed that he would be beaten, and, "unless some great change takes place, badly beaten," and that his successor would have run on a platform that would make it impossible for him to continue the war after the inauguration. The South would win.[11]

One hundred miles to the south, Jefferson Davis in Richmond was sensitive to the same political winds and hastened to spread his sails to them. Perhaps the election could be influenced so as to bring about a victory for those Northerners who favored a negotiated peace that accepted Southern independence. At any rate, the circumstances offered delightful prospects for all sorts of Confederate mischief-making. To that end, Davis launched an operation that unintentionally created the next potential opening for negotiations.

With the approval of Congress, Davis dispatched Clement C. Clay of Alabama and Jacob Thompson of Mississippi, politicians both, to join University of Virginia professor James P. Holcombe at Niagara Falls, Canada, there to pose in some vague way as diplomats while in fact actively aiding "a peace sentiment which it was understood was then active along the Border States, and particularly to give aid to a peace organization known as the 'Knights of the Golden Circle,' which flourished in the Northwestern States." Years later Davis asserted that the delegation would have "a view to negotiating with such persons in the North as might be relied upon to aid the attainment of peace," but his handling of the situation makes clear that he intended no good-faith negotiations. Clay and Thompson received no written instructions, and the president's oral directives were "suggestive and informal." In no imaginable case would Davis have sent emissaries with power to treat for peace without including very explicit written instructions. The real purpose of the mission is reflected in another of Davis's postwar statements to the effect that he sent the commissioners "to facilitate such preliminary conditions as might lead to formal negotiations between the two Governments, and they were expected to make judicious use of any political opportunity that might be presented." The "preliminary conditions" Davis had in mind no doubt included the election of a Democratic president. Any "negotiations" the commissioners might do would, in effect, be a sham aimed at discrediting Lincoln to the Northern electorate.[12]

The trio carried out the mission admirably. They cunningly managed to get into contact with a shady character named William C. "Colorado" Jewett, friend to the unstable but influential New York newspaper editor Horace Greeley, and thus, by July 12, with Greeley himself. Next they gave the flighty editor to understand—or allowed him to think—that a fully accredited, authentic Confederate government delegation waited on the north bank of the Niagara, ready to negotiate a peace settlement. That was a master stroke. The excitable Greeley was all but hysterical about the summer's military disappointments and ripe for picking by such slick Confederate operators.[13]

Greeley wrote to Lincoln urging him to pursue negotiations at once. The Northern people, he assured the president, "desire any peace consistent with the national integrity and honor"—whatever that meant—and if Lincoln would only take this opportunity he could dispel the "wide-spread conviction that the Government and its prominent supporters are not anxious for Peace." Of course, it would not do for the public to learn that the Confederacy had sought peace and Lincoln had spurned the offer out of hand. The implication was that the public would be sure to learn just that, if Lincoln did not cooperate, since Greeley would tell them himself, and as his *New York Tribune* was the most widely read newspaper in the North, he could do it. All this constituted a very astute political trap. The Confederate commissioners had done their work well.

Lincoln was no political neophyte either, and he chose his next move carefully. Agreeing in principle to the idea of negotiations, he appointed Greeley to be his agent. The newspaperman was to go to Niagara Falls, get whatever Confederates might be lurking there, ready to talk, and bring them to Washington. Specifically, the safe-conduct Greeley was authorized to offer covered "any person anywhere professing to have any proposition of Jefferson Davis in writing for peace, embracing the restoration of the union and abandonment of slavery." Greeley balked. Now *his* credibility was on the line. Lincoln insisted and, when the editor still proved reluctant, dispatched his secretary John Hay to take Greeley to Niagara Falls along with a letter, addressed, "To whom it may concern," making explicit Lincoln's offer. "Any proposition," it read, "which embraces the restoration of peace, the integrity of the whole union, and the abandonment of slavery, and which comes by and with an authority that can control the armies now at war against the United States, will be received and considered by the Executive Government of the United States, and will be met by liberal terms on other substantial and collateral points, and the bearer or bearers thereof shall have safe conduct both ways." The Confederate emissaries, of course, had no proposition of that sort and, thus compelled to put up or shut up, they had to choose the latter.

In his later years, Davis seems to have become confused about the meaning of all this. The passage of twenty years made the result seem the intention in his mind, and he wrote, "This movement, like all the others which had preceded it, was a failure." It was nothing of the sort, at least not in terms of what it was intended to accomplish. The Confederate emissaries had forced Lincoln into a politically damaging admission that emancipation was one of his essential war aims. Not all Northerners were prepared to fight for that cause, at least not at the expense the 1864 campaign was exacting. Many by this time objected even to the stipulation that Southern acceptance of reunion had to precede negotiation. Being forced to state his terms had cost Lincoln politically.

Holcombe, Clay, and Thompson, like the good politicians they were, went straight to the press and accused Lincoln of deliberately scotching negotiations by naming outrageous and unacceptable preconditions. This, they claimed, showed Northerners the need to rid themselves of Lincoln. The Democratic papers crowed predictably about Lincoln's extremism, and even the precious Greeley, in the pages of his *New York Tribune*, characterized Lincoln's response as a blunder.[14]

Yet aside from the success of a relatively minor political maneuver, the incident had revealed far broader possibilities. Lincoln could be politically maneuvered into negotiation, and the terms he was prepared to offer were as generous as the South could expect to gain short of complete victory. If the South were indeed, as Davis liked to claim, fighting not for slavery but for "constitutional liberty," the virtual blank check Lincoln offered presented a very plausible way to achieve it within the Union. If for the moment Confederate prospects looked good, any future downturn in its fortunes might heighten the appeal of gaining half a loaf by negotiations rather than none by resistance to the bitter end.

The sham negotiations on the Niagara were not the only tentative moves toward peace that summer. James F. Jacques, a Methodist preacher and now colonel of the Seventy-third Illinois, and James R. Gilmore, a free-lance journalist from Massachusetts, two otherwise rather obscure individuals acting entirely on their own, sought permission to pass through the lines and sound out Davis regarding peace. Lincoln gave them no authority but let them go. Through various byways and intermediaries they arrived at last in the office of the Confederate president. The two Northerners came right to the point. They explained that "they had no official character or authority" but believed they had a pretty good idea of the Lincoln administration's position regarding "an adjustment of the differences existing between the North and the South." Perhaps if they could get the two sides talking, something could be worked out. Jacques, Davis recalled, "expressed the ardent desire he felt, in common with the men of their army, for a restoration of peace." The Union soldiers, he assured Davis, "would go home in double-quick time if they could only see peace restored." Gilmore then chimed in with the meat of their proposal. If the Southerners would agree to return to the Union, they believed Lincoln would be willing to grant a complete amnesty to the former Rebels. The issue of slavery could then perhaps be put to a nationwide popular vote, and the majority of white Americans could thus decide its continuance as well as any other problematic issues.

Jacques and Gilmore may have had a sound grasp of Lincoln's ideas about peace, except perhaps regarding slavery, but they had a lot to learn about Davis's. They were about to start. He found them profoundly ignorant and their offer insulting, excusable only because of their good intentions. He did not want anybody's amnesty because he had not done anything wrong; the war was all the North's fault anyway. Furthermore, he did not propose "to discuss questions of state with such persons" as they were. "The war . . . must go on," Davis concluded, "till the last man of this generation falls in his tracks . . . unless you acknowledge our right to self-government." He was prepared to "see every Southern plantation sacked, and every Southern city in flames." Though he had just dismissed as outrageous the proposition that the South might give up its human chattels, he insisted the Confederacy was not fighting for slavery. "We are fighting for Independence—and that, or extermination, we will have."[15]

In July 1864 Davis was definitely reckoning they would have the former, and he was not the only one. While Lincoln was grimly observing that the issue dividing North and South, union versus disunion, was "distinct, simple, and inflexible" and that it "can only be tried by war and decided by victory," many Confederates felt increasing confidence that the victory would be theirs.[16]

Among Confederate leaders, however, ideas varied on how best to maximize their chances. Senator Benjamin H. Hill of Georgia warned that "proposals of negotiation from us, as matters now stand, are inconsistent with honor and futile for good." Instead, he advised, the Confederacy ought to announce that if the Northern voters would only dispose of Lincoln and his party, the South would be prepared to receive "honorable" peace proposals to the end of having a convention of state representatives that would establish "the most liberal relations of unity and commerce" between the two sections but, presumably, maintain Confederate independence. All that left the issue of independence, and the legitimacy and survival of the government he headed, entirely too muddled to suit Jefferson Davis, who ignored the idea.

Davis also ignored another—and similar—sally by his erratic vice-president, who had assured him back at the beginning of the Northern presidential campaign that if only the peace advocates could win in the North, any negotiation would finally have to lead to Southern independence and that Davis need have no fear that an armistice would be the first step to Confederate disintegration and the reintegration of the Southern states into the Union. That was exactly what Davis feared, and that fear led him to give short shrift to all of Stephens's continued suggestions for vague approaches to negotiations. Various members of the Confederate Congress showed an interest in the concept of negotiations, discussed and debated it, but came to no concrete conclusions.[17]

The Confederate success of the summer of 1864, bought at the price of thousands of Southern lives and seized by the tactical skill of Robert E. Lee and the courage of Confederate soldiers, was the last period of significant Southern battlefield success. It presented the South a fair opportunity to negotiate a favorable compromise peace, but it also raised Confederate hopes to the point of decreasing Southerners' willingness to do so.

As the summer waned, however, so too did the cheering prospects. On August 5, Federal naval forces took control of Mobile Bay in one of the war's most dramatic battles afloat. That might have gone unnoticed by the public—for a time, it did—but then on September 3 came the first chilling blast of the autumn of Confederate hopes. "Atlanta is ours and fairly won," an exultant William T. Sherman wired Washington from the fallen city. And so it was. Sherman's victory brought an enormous boost to Northern morale and was perhaps the largest single factor in changing Lincoln's reelection chances from questionable to probable. Lincoln might just have won anyway, but the capture of Atlanta made the Democratic platform, with its claim that the war was a failure, look very foolish indeed. Northern spirits soared. It was "the greatest event of the war," exulted New York diarist George Templeton Strong. The South was stunned. It "obscures the prospect of peace, late so bright. It will also diffuse gloom over the South," moaned the *Richmond*

Examiner, echoing Davis's assumption that "peace" meant only Southern victory. If further proof were needed that Northern victory was drawing nigh, Philip Sheridan soundly defeated Jubal Early's Confederate forces in the Shenandoah Valley on September 19 at the third battle of Winchester and again on the twenty-second at Fisher's Hill. Then on October 19 he all but finished off the Confederate army in the Valley with a stunning victory at Cedar Creek. In her diary, South Carolinian Mary Boykin Chesnut wrote, "We are going to be wiped off the earth."[18]

As awareness spread that the summer's opportunities were slipping away, peace advocates in the South shook off the political lethargy that had quieted them through the dog days and took on a new urgency in their old endeavors. Alexander Stephens issued a public letter on September 22 calling for a general convention of all the states, North and South, to discuss all disputed issues. This was an echo of the Democratic Party platform, which also called for a convention of all the states. Of course, the Democratic platform at least claimed to favor such a step as a means of restoring the Union— Stephens, of securing peace outside it. Ironically, neither Stephens nor the Democrats were probably sincere in any of this except a desire for peace. Many Southerners sensed the lack of commitment to Confederate independence in Stephens's proposal and roundly criticized him for it. Others were sympathetic. Joe Brown agreed and tried to persuade the other governors of Confederate states east of the Mississippi to join in a call for a convention— but without success.[19]

Just one week after the publication of Stephens's letter, South Carolina congressman William W. Boyce reiterated his commitment to a negotiated peace by publishing an open letter to Davis that was similar in content to Stephens's. An immediate armistice, he argued, should be followed by a convention of Northern and Southern states to negotiate a peace settlement. The reaction he received was, predictably, the same that had greeted the earlier call. The press condemned Boyce as a reconstructionist who was advocating capitulation, and public meetings in the congressman's home state denounced him. Other critics questioned the constitutionality of the entire concept, which, after all, entirely bypassed Jefferson Davis and the rest of the Confederate central government in Richmond. As far as Stephens, Brown, and their coterie were concerned, of course, that was the beauty of it. Besides, Stephens argued, the states would have to ratify any agreement that affected their status (a dead giveaway that he was thinking about some form of reunion), and therefore final authority rested with them anyway.[20]

Sternly discountenanced by Jefferson Davis and shouted down in press and public meeting, the convention-of-the-states proposal went nowhere. It was, on its face, the most bizarrely unrealistic of the peace proposals broached in the Confederacy during the last two years of the war, at least in view of Lincoln's current occupancy of the White House and the increasing probability that he would remain there beyond March 4 of the following year. He would never have acceded either to an immediate armistice—without a guarantee of reunion—or to a convention of the states that would have made his duly elected Federal government as irrelevant as the Davis regime in Richmond. Beyond such natural wartime factors as wishful thinking and lack of information, such proposals probably show a cautious and gingerly approach to the issue of negotiation. If the Southern people could once have been brought to accept the idea of negotiations that did not necessarily presuppose their triumph, they would have been much easier to reconcile to any final reasonable settlement of a war that they were in fact in the process of losing. Immediate reaction to the convention-of-the-states proposals revealed a populace that, at least in a large and extremely vocal segment, still refused to accept anything short of total victory.

It did, however, point the way to another possible mode of bringing about a negotiated settlement. For one who allowed any validity to the actions of the Southern states in seceding, Stephens's argument that the states had the final say about their status was unanswerable. The Confederate constitution made its central government very explicitly the creature of the states. The states had made the Confederacy; by all rights, then, they could unmake it. States acting on their own would also enjoy some substantial advantages when the time came to negotiate with the Federal government. The Lincoln administration would not acknowledge that there was a legitimate government for the so-called Confederate States of America. Yet, it was not likely to deny that there was, or could be, a legitimate government for any one of the states that the Confederacy had claimed as its own. Finally, a state government, unlike that of the Confederacy, would not, in negotiating for a peace with reunion, be negotiating for its own extinction. Thus separate state action was a distinct possibility as a way to end the war.

Not surprisingly, Brown and Stephens were soon considering this course. It was a natural extension of their advocacy of the convention of the states. In October 1864, Stephens wrote his brother that "should any State at any time become satisfied that the war is not waged for the purposes securing her best interest . . . she has a perfect right to withdraw, and would commit no breach of faith . . . in doing so." This was a preposterous theory of government, but it might have been a good way to get out of a bad situation.

Stephens and Brown were already dealing with a possible opportunity to exercise it. After Sherman had taken Atlanta, Unionist politician Joshua Hill of Georgia had approached him with a proposition involving the state's withdrawal from the war. Sherman took an interest in the matter and sent Hill along with Augustus R. Wright and William King, two prominent Georgians, to the state capital at Milledgeville to make Brown an offer. Another messenger carried Sherman's proposal to Stephens. If the state of Georgia would withdraw from the Confederacy, withdraw its troops from the Confederate armies, and return to a proper relationship with the Union, Sherman would keep his troops to the main highways, minimize damage, and pay for what they ate. Sherman thought it would be "a magnificent stroke of policy," and indeed it had real potential to end the war. Ulysses S. Grant, getting wind of the matter, was highly optimistic and believed that if it went through, it would "be the end of the rebellion."[21]

It was not to be. Confronted with the opportunity to take concrete action of a sort they had claimed was both expedient and legal, Stephens and Brown did nothing. The vice-president complained to friends about Sherman's informality in sending an oral rather than a written message. When the general renewed his offer, through the offices of William King, Stephens declined on the basis that he had no power.[22]

Davis was worried enough about the state of affairs in Georgia to make a visit there himself late in September in hopes of firing once again the popular enthusiasm for independence. How effective he was is questionable. His speeches tended toward shrillness and could not avoid numerous and disconcerting revelations of the magnitude of the Confederacy's truly desperate plight. Still, the preponderance of public opinion, even in Georgia, seemed to be on his side. Stephens's and Brown's brief flirtation with the idea of making a separate peace with Sherman brought down on their heads a storm of denunciation, and so beset was the Confederate vice-president that he felt compelled to have reprinted an 1834 speech of his to show that he had always been consistent on the issue of state's rights.[23]

In late November Brown delivered to the Georgia legislature another harangue against Davis, and Linton Stephens then introduced resolutions calling for a state convention to launch negotiations aimed at a separate peace. The legislature, however, influenced by a strongly worded letter from Davis, not only rejected the idea but gave the president a vote of confidence instead.

By that time, Georgia's opportunity had passed. Sherman had left Atlanta bound for Savannah and the sea and was making good his promise to Grant to "make this march and make Georgia howl."[24]

If any other Confederate state but Georgia seemed likely to begin the process of state-by-state reconciliation to the Union, aside from those already entirely overrun by Federal forces, that state was North Carolina. Considerable Unionist political strength had existed there before the war, and throughout the conflict it continued to be one of the most restive of Confederate states. By midwar the *Raleigh Standard* editor William W. Holden had become the leading spokesman of those who were at least ambivalent about the Confederacy, and during 1864 he issued calls for what amounted to little less than the seeking of a separate peace by his state and others. Yet the issue was clouded by the fact that Holden's reputation was, to put it mildly, that of a maverick. Also, his stand appeared to be and probably in large part really was simply a continuation of prewar partisan politics. If the political divisions of pre–Civil War North Carolina had brought the Confederate government an instant opposition faction in that state, they also naturally gave it a pro-Confederate party, a large party that could be counted on to fight whatever Holden proposed simply because he had proposed it and he was the political enemy. Between his own eccentricity and the built-in opposition of a two-party system, Holden was defeated in a bid for election as governor of the state, and thereafter his calls for various peace conferences and state conventions carried less weight. Still, Holden stated the situation with a clarity and forthrightness seldom if ever achieved by his fellow Confederates. In January 1865 he wrote, "If there is a strong probability that, in the end, we will be overrun and subjugated, and held down by our enemy at his mercy, would it not be wise to avoid that unspeakable evil by compromising our difficulties at once, on the best terms that can be obtained?"[25]

By that time the Southern need to negotiate a settlement was obvious—or should have been. Lincoln had been reelected, and the final military defeat of the South was as certain as anything could ever be in war. Almost incredibly, the door for a negotiated settlement remained open to Southerners if only they—or their political leaders—would avail themselves of it.

The efforts of Holden and his North Carolina peace party had not been lost on Greeley, who once again conceived an intense interest in negotiated peace and a plan for achieving it. On December 15, 1864, Greeley broached his idea in a letter to the aged patriarch of the politically powerful and influential Blair family. Francis Preston Blair Sr. had once been a newspaperman himself and, more to the point, had been a close adviser of Andrew Jackson and of other presidents since. He had also been a leader in the formation of the Republican Party. His son Montgomery had served for a time as Lincoln's postmaster general, and his other son, Frank, was then a corps commander in Sherman's army. To the elder Blair, Greeley suggested that a duly authorized envoy from Lincoln might woo North Carolina out of the Union and that Blair himself was just the man for the job. "I believe *you*, if at Raleigh, with large powers," Greeley explained, "could pull North Carolina out of the Rebellion in a month, at a cost below that of a month's continuance of the War."[26]

Blair, who had also been a prewar friend of Jefferson Davis, had bigger ideas. For some time past he had been mulling his own concept for hastening the end of the bloodshed. Greeley's suggestion apparently spurred him to action, and he quickly replied to the editor explaining that he planned to approach Lincoln with a plan not simply for taking a single state out of the Confederacy but rather "to deliver our country from the course of the war." Within days the seventy-three-year-old Blair was as good as his word and appeared in Lincoln's office seeking permission to try his hand at peacemaking. Lincoln was not ready—apparently wanting to be very sure he would be negotiating from a position of strength—and told Blair to wait until after Savannah had fallen. They had not long to wait. On December 21 Federal troops marched into the city on the heels of its fleeing Confederate defenders, and the following day Sherman wired Lincoln: "I beg to present you, as a Christmas gift, the city of Savannah, with 150 heavy guns and plenty of ammunition, and also about 25,000 bales of cotton." Blair lost no time seeking Lincoln's final approval, and one week to the day after the fall of Savannah, he got his wish—or what would have to pass for it—in the form of Lincoln's permission to travel to Richmond. In negotiating there, Blair would be on his own hook, but that put little visible damp on his ardor. By December 30, Davis had received Blair's letter asking permission to visit Richmond "for certain personal objects."[27]

Meanwhile, on the Confederate side of the lines, others too had been seeking ways and means of negotiating a settlement. Even as Blair went through the intricacies of arranging passage through the opposing lines, peace sentiment in Richmond was nearing critical mass. Stephens, despite having fumbled away the chance for a separate peace in Georgia, nevertheless continued to denounce Davis in inflammatory speeches that called for immediate peace negotiations. On January 6, the Confederate Senate invited Stephens to address it in closed session, and the vice-president, who was in town for a change, readily agreed. In his speech he hammered away at all his accustomed themes. The Davis administration was wrong in practically every policy, especially conscription and the suspension of the privilege of the writ of habeas corpus. Most of all, however, Davis's policy needed to be set aside on the issue of peace, and the chance for negotiations must be offered to the North immediately. The Confederate Congress was ready to take the bit in its teeth on this issue, and on January 12, Representative Jehu Orr of Mississippi promptly introduced a set of peace resolutions that were just what Stephens would have recommended. The odds for passage looked high, and the Richmond press also began to climb on the bandwagon. President Davis found himself in a very tight spot politically.[28]

The evening before Orr introduced his resolutions, Blair, having in the meantime obtained Davis's permission to visit Richmond, arrived in the city. He had other old friends in the city besides Davis, and that evening he socialized with some of them and also talked extensively with Alexander Stephens, who earnestly pressed on him the ideas he had been preaching about a negotiated peace. The next morning, while Orr was introducing his peace resolutions in Congress, Blair made his way to Davis's office. The two held a lengthy and not unpleasant conversation, starting on the basis of a written statement Blair had gotten up, explaining his ideas for restoring peace. As his statement read and Blair elaborated in conversation, he was eager, as a native Kentuckian, to see the war ended and suggested that since the Confederacy had recently decided to enlist slaves in its army, promising them freedom in exchange, the issue of slavery no longer existed to divide North and South. Making clear that he possessed no official authority from Lincoln, he nevertheless proposed that the sections should declare an armistice and join in enforcing the Monroe Doctrine. Davis asked what he meant by that. Blair explained that they should combine their armies to drive the French puppet ruler, Archduke Maximilian, out of Mexico. According to Blair's account of the conversation, he even suggested that Davis should lead the combined forces. When Davis alluded to the great amount of bitterness that separated North and South, Blair countered that the experience of fighting together against France in Mexico would restore good feeling. Though Lincoln had not accepted official representatives of the Confederate government as such before, Blair seemed to think he now would. The aged newspaperman even said something of a "secret treaty being made."

All the while he seems tactfully to have omitted reference to whether the war in Mexico was to be waged by one nation or two. Was this a scheme for restoring the Union or for restoring peace and good harmony between the United States and a newly independent Confederate States? The military situation was by this time so lopsided that the answer to this question should have been obvious, and Blair probably considered it so. Davis took it the other way. Accordingly, the Confederate president gave Blair a letter spelling out the message he might convey to Lincoln. It read, in part, "I have no disposition to find obstacles in forms, and am willing now, as heretofore, to enter into negotiations for the restoration of peace, am ready to send a commission whenever I have reason to suppose it will be received, or to receive a commission if the United States Government shall choose to send one. That, notwithstanding the rejection of our former offers, I would, if you could promise that a commissioner, minister, or other agent would be received, appoint one immediately, and renew the effort to enter into conference with a view to secure peace to the two countries." It would have been a very reasonable letter if there had been any indication that the North was preparing to abandon the nearly completed struggle. Davis probably overestimated, among other things, both the threat Lincoln perceived from France and the difficulty the North would encounter in occupying a conquered South.[29]

Of course, Lincoln had no thoughts of recognizing the Confederacy, much less of waging a joint war with France or of making Jefferson Davis commander of the endeavor. Blair had proven a less than accurate conduit of information and may have done so again when he returned to Richmond on January 22 to tell Davis that Lincoln feared political repercussions should he enter into direct negotiations. Instead, said Blair, Lincoln wanted Grant and Lee to work out some kind of cease-fire to initiate the process. To this Davis readily agreed but, as it turned out, to no purpose. As Davis later recalled, Blair "subsequently informed me that the idea of a military convention was not favorably received at Washington."[30]

One more opening for negotiations still remained though not a very palatable one for Davis. On January 18 Lincoln had given Blair a letter stating his views on negotiations. Blair laid the letter before Davis during his second visit to Richmond. "I have constantly been, as now, and shall continue ready," Lincoln had written, "to receive any agent who he or any other influential person now resisting the national authority may informally send to me with the view of securing peace to the people of our one common country." This was not at all what Davis had in mind, but he was under considerable pressure to take steps toward peace. There was, after all, Orr's resolution, now approved by the Committee on Foreign Affairs, calling on Davis to appoint from each house of Congress three commissioners for the purpose of launching informal negotiations with the government in Washington. Though the full Congress had rejected the resolution, the vote was close. Meanwhile, throughout the Confederacy, politicians, newspapers, and others were taking up the fantasy of a joint war to enforce the Monroe Doctrine. The time lapse would have been too short for this to have been an echo of Blair's proposal; the Mexican chimera must have been more or less universally attractive to people who were grasping at straws that winter.[31]

Thus with Congress breathing down his neck, Davis made good his promise not to "find obstacles in forms." Overlooking the bit about being just an "influential person" and the invitation to negotiate only "informally," Davis prepared to send a delegation to negotiate. As Stephens later recalled, the president approached him on January 27 about the choice of commissioners and accepted Stephens's suggestion of Assistant Secretary of War (and former U.S. Supreme Court justice) John A. Campbell, Brig. Gen. (and former Georgia Supreme Court justice) Henry L. Benning, and prominent Virginian (and onetime friend of Lincoln) Thomas S. Flournoy. Stephens thought the matter was settled.[32]

Later that same afternoon, Davis brought the matter before the cabinet in one of that body's typical marathon meetings. Davis's secretary of state and alter ego, Judah P. Benjamin, opposed responding at all, on the basis that Lincoln's reference to "one common country" and Davis's to "two countries" were incompatible. Surprisingly, Davis insisted on negotiations and next took up the issue of whom to send. Secretary of the Navy Stephen Mallory suggested none other than Alexander Stephens. At first, Davis demurred, despite the fact that sending Stephens was a political stroke of genius that would put the peace faction's leader in the position of either admitting that peace was impossible or else openly accepting an agreement that provided less than independence—and for which he would thus not be empowered to treat. If Davis had intended the sending of the commission merely to discredit the peace movement, he could hardly have made a better choice. That he initially balked at the suggestion of sending Stephens is evidence that, at least at the outset, he did not view the effort as a ploy to discredit the peace movement. Apparently the Confederate president really did intend this effort to produce a settlement if one could possibly be had that met his irreducible demand for independence. In the end, he gave in and accepted Stephens. To accompany the vice-president, the cabinet agreed on Senator R. M. T. Hunter of Virginia and Campbell.

Davis met with the commissioners the following day. Not surprisingly, Stephens was adamantly opposed to going, even urging Davis to scuttle the whole project. Under Davis's urging, however, he finally relented and agreed to go. The president briefed the three commissioners orally and also gave them a letter of instruction drafted by Benjamin but significantly altered by Davis. Benjamin's original draft had carefully ignored Lincoln's reference to "one common country." Davis fixed that by inserting another reference to the "two countries." "It will never do," he explained, "to ignore the fact that there are two countries instead of but one common country." Behind the president's back, the frustrated secretary of state groused, "That is the very point that I tried to avoid. The whole thing will break down on that very point."[33]

And so it very nearly did. At ten o'clock the following morning, January 29, the commissioners went out to the Union lines under flag of truce, amid cheers from troops of both sides, who had learned or guessed the nature of their mission. There they had to wait two days while the Federals determined what to do with them. Word went up the chain of command to Lincoln, who dispatched Major Thomas T. Eckert to see if they had come pursuant to his January 18 letter to Davis by Blair. If they had not, in fact, come with power to discuss restoring peace to the "one common country," they were to be sent back. Eckert arrived on February 1 and consulted with the commissioners on board the steamer *Mary Martin*, anchored in Hampton Roads. The impasse Benjamin had foreseen became reality, as Eckert refused them passage to Washington. The commissioners appealed to Grant, who appealed to Lincoln. Once Lincoln received Grant's message, he decided to go to Hampton Roads regardless of the wording of the commissioners' letter of instruction. Before he got there, the commissioners themselves had decided to set aside their instructions, though they were unwilling to commit themselves to anything.[34]

Thus when the two parties met on the morning of February 3 aboard the president's steamer, the *River Queen*, Lincoln and Seward for the Union, Stephens, Hunter, and Campbell for the Confederacy, it was more or less without initial stipulations. It was not, however, apart from reality, as the Confederates quickly learned when Stephens asked how the war could be ended and "good feeling and harmony" restored "between the different States and Sections of the country." Lincoln replied that the only way was "for those who were resisting the laws of the Union to cease that resistance." Stephens tried to divert the discussion to the proposed Mexican adventure, but Lincoln would have none of it. The Union must be restored before North-South hostilities could cease. That was final. The Southerners then asked what terms he would grant, to which Lincoln replied that "the States would be immediately restored to their practical relations to the Union." He would not retreat from emancipation, and, as Seward revealed to the shocked Confederates, Congress had just submitted to the states a proposed constitutional amendment banning slavery.[35]

Sensing the Confederates' surprise, and probably that nothing they could do would induce the Davis government to capitulate, Lincoln put a proposal to Stephens. "Stephens, if I were in Georgia," the president began, "and entertained the sentiments I do—though, I suppose, I should not be permitted to stay there long with them; but if I resided in Georgia, with my present sentiments, I'll tell you what I would do, if I were in your place; I would go home and get the Governor of the State to call the Legislature together, and get them to recall all the State troops from the war; elect Senators and Members to Congress, and ratify this Constitutional Amendment prospectively—so as to take effect—say in five years. Such a ratification would be valid in my opinion." It was the final appeal for separate state action, but the commissioners found it unacceptable. Stephens, after all, was the man who four years earlier had called slavery and racial inequality the cornerstone of the Confederacy. The Confederacy he might be brought to give up; slavery apparently not. The meeting came to an end after more than four hours with the Confederate vice-president lamenting that it had been "entirely fruitless" and making one last unsuccessful effort to interest Lincoln in the Monroe Doctrine.[36]

Back in Richmond, Davis was as disappointed as everyone else, for he had no doubt hoped, contrary to any reasonable expectation, that Lincoln would give up the victory that was now virtually in his grasp. Yet with hopes for negotiated victory dashed, Davis now moved aggressively and skillfully to ensure that Southern disappointment did not turn into a rush to end the war on any basis less than Confederate victory. The first step was to publicize the results of the Hampton Roads conference. Stephens objected to such a step, claiming that it would rule out any possibility of Lincoln's retreating from the stand he had taken on the *River Queen*, but Davis was now not to be deterred. On February 5 the commissioners' reports were issued to the public. Four days later Davis staged a grand war rally in Richmond, urging his people to fight on to final victory. Even a deeply disgusted Stephens had to admit that Davis's speech on the occasion was "brilliant." What the North called for, the president asserted, was "an entire change of the Social Fabric throughout the South," and this would be "the most humiliating . . . degradation." Warding off that fate, he believed, called for "renewed and more desperate efforts" by the Southern people "for the preservation of themselves and their Institutions." In several days of the most energetic and skillful political activity of his life, Davis successfully prevented an immediate collapse of Confederate morale and nerved at least some portion of his people to join him in continued resistance after resistance had lost its point.[37]

Lincoln had been painfully in earnest in his desire for peace. A few days after the meeting at Hampton Roads he made good on a token of goodwill he had extended to Stephens at the conference by releasing his nephew Lt. John Stephens from a Union prisoner-of-war camp and sending him South with a note asking the Confederate vice-president in return to "select and send me that officer of the same rank imprisoned at Richmond whose physical condition most urgently requires his release." In a humorous touch, he sent a photograph of himself along with Lieutenant Stephens, quipping, "I don't think there'll be many of those down South."[38]

About that time, however, Lincoln met with another departing Confederate prisoner of war in what that prisoner, at least, believed was far more than a token of goodwill. Sometime fire-eating Virginia politician, now brigadier general Roger A. Pryor had a conversation with Lincoln before his return to Confederate lines that month. Lincoln said that in exchange for emancipation and reunion, the South might have won a general amnesty and even compensation for loss of slave property, but Davis "had made the recognition of the Confederacy a condition sine qua non" of any negotiations. Henceforth, Pryor recalled Lincoln as saying that "every drop of blood . . . shed in the further prosecution of the war" would be on Davis's head. Pryor thought Lincoln was hammering that point so fervently that he took it to mean the president "still hoped the people of the South would reverse Mr. Davis's action, and would renew the negotiations for peace." Once back in Richmond, Pryor tried, consulting Hunter and others. The answer was the same every time and always to the effect that "nothing could be done with Mr. Davis, and that the South had only to wait the imminent and inevitable catastrophe." The war would go on—for a time—and when peace came, when and however that might be, it would be the soldiers who brought it.[39]

The most striking question about the collapse of the Confederacy is not why negotiation failed but, rather, why it was never attempted in earnest, on a realistic basis, on the Confederate side. Not until the Hampton Roads conference, during the winter of 1865, did Davis dispatch a delegation with genuine intentions that it should negotiate on the subject of an end to hostilities. That he meant Stephens, Hunter, and Campbell to negotiate seriously is demonstrated by the fact that he provided them, unlike Holcombe, Clay, and Thompson, with detailed written instructions. Yet the very instructions he sent made meaningful negotiation impossible. By January 1865, it was manifestly obvious to every informed observer that the Confederacy's days were numbered and slavery's with it. The Union would be restored and slavery abolished. It was preposterous for Davis even to attempt to negotiate such matters, much less to demand them as non-negotiable conditions of any arrangement that might be made. A reasonable Confederate effort at peacemaking in early 1865 would have entailed accepting the inevitable and negotiating other valuable considerations. What Davis had to offer was an early and assured end to hostilities, saving thousands of lives and millions of dollars. What he could hope to win in exchange might have included not only the sort of delayed or gradual emancipation that Lincoln suggested as an outcome of separate state action but also *perhaps* a somewhat greater degree of state autonomy after the cessation of hostilities and even limited compensation to the former slaveholders for the loss of their erstwhile chattels. At least such items would have been reasonable topics of negotiation.[40]

Even in the summer of 1864, an especially wise and astute leader—of which history might give any number of examples—might well have decided that Confederate stock was as high as it was likely to go. Amid the Northern malaise of midsummer, such a Confederate leader might well have forced Lincoln to put the issue of emancipation on the table. Certainly a Confederate offer of peace and reunion, with both slavery and constitutional guarantees, would have made things very difficult for Lincoln indeed and might even have swung the election. Reasonable items for negotiation in such a situation (the South might not have gotten them all) might have included even the late John C. Calhoun's concurrent majority. Certainly Southern bargaining power would have been strong—*if* the South had been willing to exchange its then momentarily promising hope of independence for such concessions.

Yet Davis did not take that approach, then or at the remarkable eleventh-hour opportunity at Hampton Roads, and his fellow Confederate politicians did not force his hand. Why? Several factors may help to explain this failure.

The Confederate leaders who seemed most to favor the idea of a negotiated settlement tended to be flawed characters, who while they might enjoy considerable popularity, nevertheless would not attract sufficient support to accomplish their ends. Stephens, Brown, Holden, and others present an unusually stark and clashing mixture of good and bad characteristics, and the bad are pronounced enough to excite disgust even in modern students of the war who know that these men's assessments were correct. Their popularity with the majority of their fellow Southerners was not enhanced by the fact that some of them (Stephens and Holden, for example) had been vocal Unionists up until secession was an established fact. That and their constant harping on civil liberties issues merged into their opposition politics in such a way as to allow many to dismiss their positions as what would today be called "politics as usual."

In contrast, the individual leaders who, for whatever reasons, refused to read the handwriting on the wall were dynamic and resolute, politically skillful and personally attractive. The struggle between war veteran Zebulon Vance and newspaper scribbler William Holden in North Carolina is a prime example of such political mismatches. Davis enjoyed a like superiority over Stephens. When the Confederacy's more influential leaders chose a bitter-end resistance and refused to cut any deal, the chances of negotiated peace were slight. It may be that the very drive and steadfastness that made these men so influential also made them all but constitutionally incapable of admitting defeat.

Finally, the majority of the Southern people themselves apparently did not desire peace if peace meant Union and emancipation. While some appeared ready to abandon the struggle, more vocal and apparently larger groups were prepared to denounce any politician who flirted, ever so gingerly, with the idea of taking half a loaf. Politics has been called the art of the possible; in that sense, it may well be that a political solution to the demise of the Confederacy simply was not politically possible in the South. Union the Southerners might have accepted. Emancipation at least some of their leaders were willing to accept to save the Confederacy, if it could be done under Southern control. But emancipation administered by the North was simply too revolutionary. It could mean something approximating political and social equality, or at least so the South feared. For a large number of Southerners even as late as the beginning of 1865, no peace settlement that included such an arrangement could be considered preferable to continued resistance, however remote the chances.

Many Southerners seemed ready for peace at any price, or at least any price the North was likely to exact. This certainly seemed true of the growing multitudes of soldiers who were deserting the Confederate armies to go home and tend their often destitute families. They, at least, were voting with their feet and voting very effectively for an end to hostilities. The exact breakdown of those who favored negotiated peace as opposed to bitter-enders among the Southern population is naturally impossible to discern. Some apparently resolute citizens might have been swayed had influential leaders like Davis been pulling in the direction of peace rather than the other way. Still, the need to work public opinion carefully toward an acceptance of surrender complicated the task of those who favored that course.[41]

The combination of factors inhibiting Confederate peace negotiations proved decisive. The combatants struck no compromise deal. Southern military strength collapsed in the spring of 1865, and the fleeing Davis, pausing in Greensboro to consult his cabinet and generals, found himself surrounded by top advisers nearly all of whom told him further resistance was useless. The only prospect ahead of him was "surrender at discretion."

The North did show considerable discretion—the "charity toward all" of Lincoln's second inaugural—but no negotiated final settlement extorted from the victorious national government constitutional bulwarks for the formerly rebellious state regimes or an additional lease on life for the institution of slavery. The war had struck at the fundamental issues of slavery and freedom, anarchy and the survival of ordered self-government under law. It touched race relations and the patterns of two centuries of Southern society. Perhaps, after all, only conquest could have decided it. Perhaps it was better that way.

Notes

1. Jefferson Davis, *Rise and Fall of the Confederate Government*, 2 vols. (New York: Appleton, 1881), 2:679–83; John H. Reagan, *Memoirs*, ed. Walter F. McCaleb (New York: Neale, 1906), 199–200; Craig L. Symonds, *Joseph E. Johnston: A Civil War Biography* (New York: Norton, 1992), 354–55; William C. Davis, *Jefferson Davis: The Man and His Hour* (New York: HarperCollins, 1991), 615–17.

2. Davis, *Rise and Fall*, 2:609; Rudolph Radama von Abele, *Alexander H. Stephens: A Biography* (Westport CT: Negro Universities Press, 1946), 216–18; William C. Davis, *"A Government of Our Own": The Making of the Confederacy* (New York: Free Press, 1994), 16–17, 51–52, 71, 80, 86, 94, 129–30, 132–33, 139, 142, 205–6, 251, 286, 415–16; George C. Rable, *The Confederate Republic: A Revolution Against Politics* (Chapel Hill: University of North Carolina Press, 1994), 21–23, 26.

3. Davis, *Jefferson Davis*, 367, 445, 496, 573, 577; Rable, *Confederate Republic*, 117, 126, 166–67, 175, 207, 238, 249, 251.

4. Davis, *Rise and Fall*, 2:592; Abele, *Alexander H. Stephens*, 216–18.

5. David H. Donald, *Lincoln* (New York: Simon and Schuster, 1995), 455–56; Abele, *Alexander H. Stephens*, 216–28; Davis, *Rise and Fall*, 2:609; Edward Chase Kirkland, *The Peacemakers of 1864* (1927; rpt. New York: AMS Press, 1969), 210–12.

6. Abele, *Alexander H. Stephens*, 220.

7. Rable, *Confederate Republic*, 256–61; Davis, *Jefferson Davis*, 340–41, 347–48, 437, 445, 496; Davis, *"A Government of Our Own,"* 218, 356–58.

8. Abele, *Alexander H. Stephens*, 222–25.

9. Abele, *Alexander H. Stephens*, 225–26; Rable, *Confederate Republic*, 258–60; Kirkland, *Peacemakers of 1864*, 213–17.

10. Rable, *Confederate Republic*, 258–60; Abele, *Alexander H. Stephens*, 225–26.

11. Donald, *Lincoln*, 529–30.

12. Davis, *Jefferson Davis*, 544; Davis, *Rise and Fall*, 2:611–12; Donald, *Lincoln*, 521; Larry E. Nelson, *Bullets, Ballots, and Rhetoric: Confederate Policy for the United States Presidential Contest of 1864* (University: University of Alabama Press, 1980), 24; Kirkland, *Peacemakers of 1864*, 51–74.

13. Davis, *Rise and Fall*, 2:611–12; Donald, *Lincoln*, 521; Kirkland, *Peacemakers of 1864*, 74–77.

14. Donald, *Lincoln*, 521–23; Davis, *Rise and Fall*, 2:611–12; James M. McPherson, *Battle Cry of Freedom: The Civil War Era* (New York: Oxford University Press, 1988), 766–67; Kirkland, *Peacemakers of 1864*, 77–85.

15. Abele, *Alexander H. Stephens*, 229; Davis, *Rise and Fall*, 2:610; Donald, *Lincoln*, 523; McPherson, *Battle Cry of Freedom*, 768; Kirkland, *Peacemakers of 1864*, 85–96.

16. McPherson, *Battle Cry of Freedom*, 768–69.

17. Nelson, *Bullets, Ballots, and Rhetoric*, 28–30; Abele, *Alexander H. Stephens*, 229–30; Rable, *Confederate Republic*, 272.

18. McPherson, *Battle Cry of Freedom*, 772–76; C. Vann Woodward, ed., *Mary Chesnut's Civil War* (New York: Book-of-the-Month Club, 1994), 645.

19. Abele, *Alexander H. Stephens*, 230.

20. Rable, *Confederate Republic*, 272.

21. Brooks D. Simpson, *Let Us Have Peace: Ulysses S. Grant and the Politics of War and Reconstruction, 1861–1868* (Chapel Hill: University of North Carolina Press, 1991), 69–70; William T. Sherman, *Memoirs of General William T. Sherman*, 2 vols. (1890; reprint, Bloomington: Indiana University Press, 1957), 2:137–40.

22. Abele, *Alexander H. Stephens*, 231–32.

23. Rable, *Confederate Republic*, 274–75; Abele, *Alexander H. Stephens*, 231–32; Davis, *Jefferson Davis*, 565–68; Ulysses S. Grant, *Personal Memoirs of U. S. Grant*, 2 vols. (New York: Charles L. Webster, 1886), 2:344–47.

24. Abele, *Alexander H. Stephens*, 232.

25. William C. Harris, *William Woods Holden: Firebrand of North Carolina Politics* (Baton Rouge: Louisiana State University Press, 1987), 100–81; Rable, *Confederate Republic*, 151–53, 156, 163–65, 190–91, 201–5, 245, 265–71; Ray Shirley Franklin, "The Rhetoric of Zebulon B. Vance: Tarheel Spokesman" (Ph.D. dissertation, University of Florida, 1959), 107–8, 150–51; Edgar E. Folk and Bynum Shaw, *W. W. Holden: A Political Biography* (Winston-Salem NC: John F. Blair, 1982), 183.

26. William Ernest Smith, *The Francis Preston Blair Family in Politics*, 2 vols. (New York: Macmillan, 1933), 2:301; Charles W. Sanders Jr., "Jefferson Davis and the Hampton Roads Peace Conference: 'To secure peace to the two countries,' " *Journal of Southern History* 63 (1997): 809.

27. Donald, *Lincoln*, 556–57; Davis, *Jefferson Davis*, 589; Davis, *Rise and Fall*, 2:612–16; Kirkland, *Peacemakers of 1864*, 143–61; Smith, *Francis Preston Blair Family*, 2:302–3; McPherson, *Battle Cry of Freedom*, 821; Sanders, "Jefferson Davis and the Hampton Roads Peace Conference," 809–10; John G. Nicolay and John Hay, *Abraham Lincoln: A History*, 10 vols. (New York: Century, 1890), 10:94.

28. John B. Jones, *A Rebel War Clerk's Diary*, ed. Earl Schenck Miers (New York: Sagamore, 1958), 420, 476, 478; Alexander H. Stephens, *A Constitutional View of the Late War Between the States: Its Causes, Character, Conduct and Results*, 2 vols. (Philadelphia: National Publishing Company, 1868), 2:587; Abele, *Alexander H. Stephens*, 234; Thomas E. Schott, *Alexander H. Stephens of Georgia: A Biography* (Baton Rouge: Louisiana State University Press, 1988), 437; Kirkland, *Peacemakers of 1864*, 220; Sanders, "Jefferson Davis and the Hampton Roads Peace Conference," 808.

29. Donald, *Lincoln*, 556–57; Davis, *Jefferson Davis*, 589; Davis, *Rise and Fall*, 2:612–16; Rable, *Confederate Republic*, 281; Abele, *Alexander H. Stephens*, 235; Kirkland, *Peacemakers of 1864*, 218–27.

30. Davis, *Rise and Fall*, 2:616–17.

31. Davis, *Jefferson Davis*, 590; Davis, *Rise and Fall*, 2:616–17.

32. Stephens, *Constitutional View*, 2:593–94; Sanders, "Jefferson Davis and the Hampton Roads Peace Conference," 816.

33. Stephens, *Constitutional View*, 2:594–95; Davis, *Jefferson Davis*, 590–91; Kirkland, *Peacemakers of 1864*, 227–33.

34. Simpson, *Let Us Have Peace*, 72–74; Grant, *Personal Memoirs*, 2:420–23; Stephens, *Constitutional View*, 2:597–98; Abele, *Alexander H. Stephens*, 237–41; Mrs. Roger A. Pryor, *Reminiscences of Peace and War* (New York: Macmillan, 1905), 327–29; Kirkland, *Peacemakers of 1864*, 233–42.

35. Abele, *Alexander H. Stephens*, 240–43; Donald, *Lincoln*, 557–58.

36. Stephens, *Constitutional View*, 2:597–619; Donald, *Lincoln*, 558–64; Abele, *Alexander H. Stephens*, 241–42; Kirkland, *Peacemakers of 1864*, 242–50.

37. Sanders, "Jefferson Davis and the Hampton Roads Peace Conference," 820; Davis, *Jefferson Davis*, 592–95; Kirkland, *Peacemakers of 1864*, 251–56; Stephens, *Constitutional View*, 619–22.

38. Lincoln to Stephens, February 10, 1865, University of Georgia Library, Athens.

39. Pryor, *Reminiscences of Peace and War*, 341–42.

40. Stephens, *Constitutional View*, 617; Pryor, *Reminiscences of Peace and War*, 341–42; Kirkland, *Peacemakers of 1864*, 256. Lincoln favored compensation to slaveholders, but his cabinet was less enthusiastic about the idea.

41. On Confederate deserters and their attitudes, see Reid Mitchell, *The Vacant Chair: The Northern Soldier Leaves Home* (New York: Oxford University Press, 1993), 160, 165, and Gerry Harder Poriss and Ralph G. Poriss, *While My Country Is in Danger: The Life and Letters of Lieutenant Colonel Richard S. Thompson, Twelfth New Jersey Volunteers* (Hamilton NY: Edmonston Publishing, 1994), 109.

Mark Grimsley

Learning to Say "Enough"

Southern Generals and the Final Weeks of the Confederacy

The process by which wars end is often even less rational than the process by which they begin. The leaders of a failing cause do not coolly decide that defeat has become inevitable and they must surrender or negotiate a settlement. Often they convince themselves that the situation, though superficially grim, is far from hopeless; that with firm resolve their cause may yet prevail. Even those who despair privately often remain staunch in public, for it is hard to seem weak (even traitorous) and hard to admit that so many lives and so much treasure have gone for naught. No one wants to be the first to do it. The last months of a war thus can have a surreal quality, as the losing side continues to act as if it has a genuine chance to win.

That surreality was redolent in the Confederacy of January 1865. With the implacable Lincoln administration back in power for another four years and Union military strength still growing, it was difficult to see how the South could continue the war much longer. Yet the press remained defiant. The government insisted that it still had the will and the resources to fight on indefinitely. That, in turn, obliged the top Confederate generals to find plausible courses of action in an increasingly unyielding strategic environment. In theory, they could force the government to recognize the situation's hopelessness and openly endorse negotiation of a settlement, but within the American tradition of civil-military relations such a step was almost unthinkable. Yet the story of the Confederacy's final months is, in large part, the story of how its generals shifted from trying to fight a lost war to trying to end it. They, more than their civilian counterparts, found the courage to say "enough."

Nominally the Confederacy contained seven full generals in early 1865.[1] Of these, however, only those charged with the defense of Richmond-Petersburg

40

and the Carolinas really mattered because this region alone was vital to the Confederate government's continued survival. As long as the government remained in existence, protracted resistance remained a possibility. But if Richmond, the capital, were to fall, the government would become a fugitive. Its legitimacy, its very ability to function, might speedily wane. The continued defense of the Richmond-Petersburg sector was thus the highest priority.

Gen. Robert E. Lee's formidable Army of Northern Virginia had successfully held that sector for half a year, and after numerous failed attempts it was unlikely that the besieging Union army under Lt. Gen. U. S. Grant could break through on its own. The real peril, everyone understood, was Maj. Gen. William T. Sherman's army, then at Savannah, Georgia. If this force should manage to join Grant, Lee could not possibly hold on. Yet oddly, the Confederate government gave no single commander formal responsibility for stopping Sherman. One logical choice, Gen. John B. Hood, whose Army of Tennessee had confronted Sherman until the loss of Atlanta, was now at Tupelo, Mississippi, hundreds of miles out of position to oppose him. Another, Lt. Gen. William J. Hardee, who commanded the Department of South Carolina, Georgia, and Florida, had the jurisdictional responsibility but only a fraction of the troops required to stop Sherman. Ultimately, Gen. P. G. T. Beauregard unofficially assumed the task of organizing a defense, although as chief of the Military Division of the West his formal authority did not extend into the Carolinas.

Beauregard's first problem was to assemble enough troops in Sherman's path to defeat him. Only about nineteen thousand men were already in place. The rest would have to come from Lee's army, Lt. Gen. Edmund Kirby Smith's Trans-Mississippi Department, or the Army of Tennessee. Lee reluctantly dispatched a cavalry division under Matthew Butler and later additional horsemen under Wade Hampton, but this contribution was not nearly enough. Kirby Smith reported himself powerless to help because he could ferry no troops across a Mississippi River infested with Union gunboats. That left Hood and his Army of Tennessee.

Hood demurred. His army, he informed Beauregard, was in bad shape. Bled heavily by a four-month campaign to keep Sherman out of Atlanta and crippled by the disastrous battle of Nashville in December 1864, the troops urgently needed extended furloughs to restore their shattered morale. The Trans-Mississippi contingent in particular, Hood insisted, needed to go home for one hundred days. Beauregard passed along Hood's request to the Confederate government, which reacted sharply. "Repress, by all means, the proposition to furlough the Trans-Mississippi troops," snapped Secretary of War James Seddon; "the suggestion merely is dangerous; compliance would probably be fatal."[2] But Hood, utterly undeterred by this response, continued to insist that the troops must receive immediate furloughs.

Beauregard hurried to Tupelo and once there began to see the wisdom of Hood's proposal. A staff officer who accompanied him observed that "very little—if anything—remained of [the Army of Tennessee's] former cohesive strength. If not, in the strict sense of the word, a disorganized mob, it was no longer an army."[3] Beauregard now joined Hood in insisting to Richmond that a system of furloughs was absolutely required to prevent "disorder and desertion." Meanwhile, Hood, shaken and humiliated by the disaster at Nashville, asked to be relieved of command. President Davis replaced him with Lt. Gen. Richard Taylor.[4]

Beauregard and Taylor devised a schedule for furloughing the troops. The Trans-Mississippi soldiers, who must travel farthest, would be the first to go, then those from Tennessee, and finally those from other states. Only the Trans-Mississippi and Tennessee men actually received leave papers, however. Some troops were imperatively needed in the Carolinas to oppose Sherman's impending advance from Savannah. Beauregard therefore ordered one infantry corps under Lt. Gen. Stephen D. Lee to be transferred east by rail. Upon further reflection, he decided to send a second corps, and then a third, for a total of about fourteen thousand men. (Another three thousand went to Mobile to bolster the garrison of that city.) Thus by January 30 the furlough scheme had been abandoned, except for the fortunate Trans-Mississippi and Tennessee men. The rest, having campaigned almost nonstop since May 1864, were again on the move—not to see their families but to fight yet another battle.

The transfer carried the army through Mississippi, Alabama, and Georgia. An incomplete rail network obliged units to cross a river by ferry at one point, transfer from one railhead to another via river steamboat at another, and along still another stretch, to march across a twenty-five-mile gap of destroyed railroad created by Sherman's marauding army.[5] As if this were not awkward enough, the Southern rail system was in such disarray that troop trains made very poor time (often less than five miles an hour), and it was not unusual for the trains to halt for a day or more.[6] The result was an attenuated logistical "pipeline" in which the soldiers frequently found themselves without effective supervision and, indeed, in circumstances that made it easier to leave the pipeline rather than remain within it. In addition, these were soldiers from Mississippi, Alabama, and Georgia who were traveling through their native states and had recently seen comrades from other states given extended furloughs. The result was predictable: these men started going home, too, sometimes individually, sometimes in groups, and occasionally by entire units.[7]

Most were not deserters. They simply appropriated the same home leave as their comrades, and many eventually returned to the ranks. One officer retrieved five hundred men from his brigade; others came back singly or in small groups. By April 7, 1865, about nine thousand of the fourteen thousand originally transferred had reached the Confederate force then operating in North Carolina. But by that time, Sherman had completed his change of base to North Carolina, received twenty-five thousand reinforcements, and become unstoppable. The problem was not that the troops never arrived but that they arrived too late.[8]

Beauregard, of course, could not foresee this outcome as he grappled with his second problem, how to deploy his troops. On February 2, 1865, at a conference at Green's Cut Station, Georgia, he estimated Sherman's army at about 58,000 effectives. The Confederate force immediately available included about 14,000 of all arms under Hardee (3,000 of them South Carolina militia and reserves; 6,700 veteran cavalry under Maj. Gen. Joseph Wheeler; and 1,450 Georgia militia and reserves). Beauregard thought 10,800 effectives from the Army of Tennessee would arrive in time to resist Sherman's advance. Thus he believed he had 33,450 troops immediately or soon available to confront the enemy's 58,000: a significant numerical disadvantage but no worse than Confederate commanders routinely confronted.[9]

Ordinarily the logical plan would have been to concentrate most of this force at Branchville, South Carolina, a strategic railroad junction directly in Sherman's path. It was well known, however, that peace negotiations were imminent, and therefore Beauregard believed it was "of the highest importance to hold Charleston and Augusta, as long as it was humanly possible."[10] Thus he divided his outnumbered forces between those two points, leaving only a few small units to hinder Sherman's advance.

Within the framework of what political scientists have styled "war termination" scenarios, Beauregard's decision was quite sensible. Peace negotiations proceed from plausible estimates of the military situation and the adversaries' respective strength. A Confederacy still in possession of these two important cities would appear stronger than a Confederacy that had lost them. This was obviously the case with Charleston, the cradle of secession and a symbol of

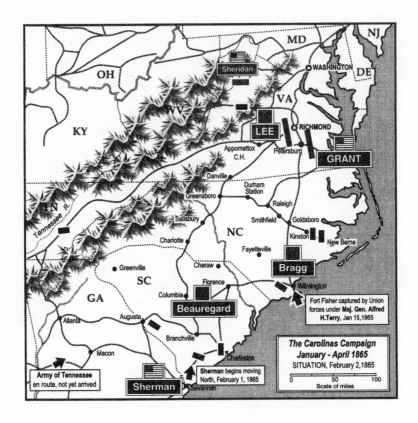

The Carolinas Campaign January - April 1865
SITUATION, February 2, 1865

Fort Fisher captured by Union forces under Maj. Gen. Alfred H.Terry, Jan 15,1865

Army of Tennessee en route, not yet arrived

Sherman begins moving North, February 1, 1865

Southern resistance. But it was no less true for Augusta because that city was the only conduit by which Confederate troops from the West could readily transfer to the eastern theater should the military contest continue. Beauregard therefore chose to shield both cities—and in so doing lost the campaign at the very outset.

Because the Hampton Roads initiative died stillborn, Beauregard's decision had no impact whatever on peace negotiations. Yet it scuttled any chance seriously to contest Sherman's advance into South Carolina. In any case, the decision came too late for a concentration at Branchville because Sherman defied the norms of Civil War campaigning by launching his offensive in the dead of winter, at a time when the rivers were high, the lowlands waterlogged, and the roads unusually muddy. By cutting sharply inland to stay on the watershed of streams and by corduroying the roads as they went, Sherman's veterans made stunning progress through the Palmetto State.

Even so, there were some Confederate troops available to slow the Federals and good natural barriers for them to defend. Beauregard had particular hopes for the Salkehatchie River, which was crossable at only a few key points and whose marshes created a mile-wide water barrier. Maj. Gen. Lafayette McLaws held the Salkehatchie line with some three thousand men and several pieces of artillery—enough to impede Sherman's men if not to stop them altogether, since any attackers would have to cross narrow causeway-bridges or else wade through waist-deep water. Yet on February 2–3, a Union division managed to pierce the position with surprising ease. McLaws's troops failed to burn any of the sixteen small bridges leading to the main span, nor did they inflict serious losses. Poor morale as well as numerical weakness was to blame for this fiasco.

With Sherman now firmly lodged in South Carolina, Beauregard urged that all available troops be assembled at Columbia, the state capital. The effort failed. The few troops opposing Sherman's army—mostly Wheeler's cavalry—proved unable even to retard the Union advance. Reinforcements coming from the Army of Tennessee progressed too slowly along the Confederacy's ramshackle rail net; only a handful made it to Columbia in time to defend the capital. Worse, the garrison at Charleston, under intense political pressure to remain, did not finally abandon the city until it was too late to go to Columbia. The Confederates abandoned Columbia on February 17, after only token resistance. Sherman's troops occupied it that same day. Other Union forces marched into Charleston unopposed on February 18.

Beauregard now ordered all troops to converge on Charlotte, North Carolina, for a united defense, but by this time it was obvious that the strategic equilibrium had been overthrown. He now proposed a desperate, bizarre plan to restore it. Shifting his proposed point of concentration to Salisbury, forty miles northeast of Charlotte, on February 21 he wrote Jefferson Davis that Lee and Gen. Braxton Bragg, commanding the Department of North Carolina, should send at least twenty thousand troops to Salisbury. Beauregard could supply another fifteen thousand of his own—although, he regretted to report, most of the Army of Tennessee reinforcements were still too far distant. Nevertheless, with the thirty-five thousand men thus assembled, Beauregard wildly believed he could "crush" Sherman, concentrate with Lee and destroy Grant's army at Richmond-Petersburg, and then "march on Washington to dictate a peace."[11] Davis forwarded the plan to Lee by mail, dryly informing him by telegram that he would shortly receive a dispatch from Beauregard "of a startling character." Lee lost no time in rejecting the fantastic proposal. He promptly ordered Gen. Joseph E. Johnston to assume charge of all troops in North Carolina, effectively relieving Beauregard of command.

Lee's replacement of Beauregard was his first important action as general in chief of the Confederate armies, a post he had assumed on February 9. Even before taking command, Lee had observed affairs in the Carolinas with increasing frustration. He could not understand why Beauregard was proving so ineffectual against Sherman. At the beginning of February, Lee knew, Beauregard had estimated Sherman's strength at "not less than" 58,000—but the estimate of Federal numbers was predicated on the assumption that the Union XIX and XXIII Corps had joined Sherman at Savannah. Lee believed that such was not the case and therefore reasoned that Sherman's force must be smaller. Since Beauregard had guessed the strength of Sherman's corps at 9,000 each, deducting the two corps erroneously credited to Sherman would leave him with about 40,000 troops, against Beauregard's own reported strength of 33,450. Not unreasonably, Lee thought Beauregard could detain or defeat Sherman with such a force.

Lee was correct in his belief that the XIX and XXIII Corps had not joined Sherman, but Beauregard had in fact come close to Sherman's actual strength (just over 60,000 men). That would have been bad news for the Confederates had they known it. Far worse, Beauregard's own strength soon turned out to be much less than his estimate because he was counting heavily on the arrival of at least 15,000 reinforcements from the Army of Tennessee and the use of 1,500 state "reserve" troops from Georgia. The Georgia troops never materialized and, as we have seen, the Army of Tennessee arrived slowly and in much weaker numbers than expected. But neither of these realities would be clear to Lee for several weeks.

Even if they had, he would still have wondered why the available forces proved so impotent to stop Sherman's advance. After all, Sherman was moving in the dead of winter, through a hostile country, with no line of communications. To keep his army supplied he had to live off the land, which in turn required him to spread his army over a wide swath of territory so as to secure sufficient food and forage and to maintain a steady advance. If he concentrated or halted his army for even a few days, his men would begin to starve in the field. Sherman would then have no choice but to abandon the campaign.

Sherman's army was thus inherently vulnerable. Lt. Gen. Wade Hampton, a veteran of Lee's army and closely acquainted with Lee's style of warfare, tersely expressed one option to Beauregard on February 18: "As General

Sherman marches in so extended a manner it occurs to me that we might concentrate on one of his corps and destroy it. . . . With a few thousand more men we can cripple Sherman greatly."[12] Indeed, this strategy was obvious to everyone—Beauregard, Lee, Davis, and Sherman himself, to say nothing of numerous newspaper editors. The problem was that Beauregard's initial dispositions made it impossible to concentrate effectively. On February 16, Beauregard informed Lee that he possessed twenty thousand infantry and artillery, "more or less demoralized," occupying a circumference of 240 miles from Augusta to Charleston, with Sherman occupying the center of the arc at Columbia.[13] This made the prospect of the needed concentration distinctly unpromising.

But there was a second alternative: if Sherman depended on supplies from the countryside, they should be destroyed before he could reach them. On February 20, Gen. Samuel Cooper, the Confederate adjutant general, ordered Beauregard and several other commanders in the Carolinas to remove or destroy all supplies in Sherman's path.[14] Five days later Lee repeated these instructions to Beauregard, adding, "If you can deprive enemy of subsistence [I] think he cannot advance."[15] He gave the same counsel to Johnston, writing, "[Sherman's] progress can be embarrassed and retarded by removing or destroying all kinds of supplies on his route, and I hope you spare no effort to accomplish this object."[16]

Unfortunately for the Confederates, neither of these instructions were implemented consistently or systematically. Few Confederate soldiers could muster the ruthlessness to carry out a "scorched earth" policy. The reluctance began at the very top, with Joe Johnston. "I don't know how we can 'remove or destroy all kinds of supplies on the enemy's route,' " he wrote in response to Lee's directive. "We are compelled to leave in the houses of the inhabitants the food necessary for their subsistence, but the U.S. officers feel no such obligation."[17]

Johnston wrote those words on March 1, barely one month after Sherman's advance from Savannah had begun. In that period of time the Union army had traveled almost the entire length of South Carolina. Worse, on February 22 the port of Wilmington, North Carolina, had fallen, opening a path for an additional Union force of some twenty-five thousand under Maj. Gen. John Schofield to begin moving inland as well. At about this time, Lee wrote his wife that Grant would move against him soon, adding, "Sherman & Schofield are both advancing & seem to have everything their own way, but trusting in a Merciful God, who does not always give battle to the strong, I pray we may not be overwhelmed." Still, he concluded by inquiring what his wife, who lived in Richmond, would do if it became necessary for his army to abandon the Richmond-Petersburg line.[18]

It is impossible to know what Lee thought of the Confederacy's military prospects when 1865 began. That he considered the situation serious cannot be doubted; whether he believed it hopeless is harder to discern. Like any other general, Lee was capable of asking his superiors for more troops and supplies and predicting disaster if these were not forthcoming—though Lee was always circumspect enough to say that he did not see how disaster could be avoided rather than to predict it outright. If these pronouncements are taken at face value, as some historians have done, then Lee had considered the Confederate cause lost for nearly a year.[19] At other times, however, Lee was more sanguine—or at least more combative. For example, in a telegram to Beauregard notifying him that Johnston was taking command, Lee concluded by saying, "Together, I feel confident that you will beat back Sherman."[20]

It seems apparent, however, that by that date Lee believed the Confederate cause was hopeless. Shortly after the failure of the Hampton Roads conference, he had visited Virginia senator R. M. T. Hunter one evening and, by Hunter's account, talked with him nearly all night. "He said if I thought there was a chance for any peace that would secure better terms than were likely to be given after a surrender at discretion, he thought it my duty to make the effort." Hunter told Lee that he had earlier tried to exert his influence in this direction but had gotten nowhere. Lee, unimpressed, told Hunter to try again. If Hunter believed the Confederate cause was lost, he considered it Hunter's duty to offer a peace resolution in the Senate. If he himself were to publicly recommend negotiations, Lee continued, "it would be almost equivalent to surrender." Hunter concurred but riposted that if Lee truly thought the chance for success desperate he should say so to the president. "To this," Hunter wrote, "he made no reply."[21]

Throughout their long conversation, Hunter recalled, Lee "never said to me he thought the chances were over; but the tone and tenor of his remarks made that impression on my mind."[22] Apparently Lee was making the best effort he could to promote negotiations for peace without compromising his perceived obligation as a soldier to remain subordinate to civilian authority. Plainly he did not believe he could speak publicly on this issue. The best he could do was to go to the appropriate civilian official and urge *him* to press for negotiations. Even then, as Hunter makes clear, Lee carefully avoided saying outright that the military situation was hopeless.

In all likelihood, the Virginia senator was not the only official whom Lee approached. Hunter reported that Secretary of War John C. Breckinridge visited him soon afterward and "repeated Lee's advice in so nearly the same words that I almost began to suspect them of concert of action."[23] Of course, the most obvious official to approach would have been Jefferson Davis, but the evidence suggests that Lee was reluctant even to broach the subject of a negotiated peace to him. His letter to Davis, informing the president that he had placed Johnston in charge of stopping Sherman, brimmed with cautious but soldierly optimism. Even so, Lee also prepared Davis for the possibility that, should Johnston be forced north of the Roanoke River—the last significant military obstacle south of Petersburg—Lee would unite his own army with Johnston "in a blow against Sherman before the latter can join Genl Grant." In that event, he would have to abandon the Richmond-Petersburg line, "for which contingency every preparation should be made."[24]

In late February, after the failure of the Hampton Roads conference, Union corps commander Maj. Gen. E. O. C. Ord essayed a peace feeler of his own. Using a flimsy pretext to meet with Lee's senior subordinate, Lt. Gen. James Longstreet, Ord took the opportunity to suggest that since the civilian authorities had been unable to initiate negotiations, the military men ought to do it themselves. He urged a suspension of hostilities so that Lee and Grant could discuss the possibility of peace. Curiously, he also suggested that Mrs. Longstreet and Mrs. Grant, who had been good friends before the war, should get together as well. Longstreet took the proposal to Lee. After consultation, Lee, Longstreet, President Davis, and Secretary of War Breckinridge agreed to pursue the opening, and Longstreet summoned his wife to Richmond. Neither the generals nor the wives met, however. When Lee wrote Grant to request an interview, Grant declined, saying that he had authority to treat only on purely military matters.[25]

At about this time, Lee may have confided in one of his corps commanders, Lt. Gen. John B. Gordon. Gordon claims as much in his memoirs, but Gordon is known to have prevaricated on other matters and thus is not the best witness. If what he says is true, however—and there is nothing save Gordon's reputation that makes it unlikely—then his account provides one of the best windows into Lee's thought during this crucial period.

According to Gordon, Lee began by asking the corps commander to read a stack of reports about the Army of Northern Virginia's shockingly desperate condition. He then analyzed the military situation, starting with the fact that he had about 50,000 troops, of whom 35,000 were fit for duty, compared with Grant's estimated 150,000 immediately on hand. He believed (erroneously) that a 30,000-man Union army was coming up from Knoxville, Tennessee, and (correctly) that 20,000 more would shortly arrive from the Shenandoah Valley. Against these troops, Lee said, "I can oppose scarcely a vidette." Finally, Sherman was en route through the Carolinas and Lee had recently learned from Johnston that only 13,000–15,000 troops were available to stop him.

Lee then asked Gordon "to state frankly what I thought under those conditions it was best to do." Gordon saw only three courses, which he outlined in order of preference: "First, make terms with the enemy, the best we can get. Second, if that is not practicable, the best thing we can do is to retreat—abandon Richmond and Petersburg, unite by rapid marches with General Johnston in North Carolina, and strike Sherman before Grant can join him; or, lastly, we must fight, and fight without delay."

Lee agreed. But he went on to say that he had not told Davis or Congress his views regarding negotiations because "he was a soldier, and that it was his province to obey the orders of the Government, and to advise or counsel with the civil authorities only upon questions directly affecting his army and its defence of the capital and the country." He also doubted whether Davis would consent to a retreat from Richmond, and he did not think he could get his army safely away.

Gordon had the strong impression that Lee wanted peace. "Without an explicit expression to that effect, the entire trend of his words led me to the conclusion that he thought immediate steps should be taken to secure peace." Gordon then suggested it was appropriate for Lee to speak to Davis on the subject, that the Southern people "are looking to you for deliverance more than to President Davis or the Congress, or both combined," and that the Confederacy would likely obtain better terms while the army was still organized than if it weren't. Lee agreed and left almost immediately for the capital. A few hours later he returned, summoned Gordon, and told him flatly that nothing could be done. "The Congress did not seem to appreciate the situation," Gordon recalled Lee as saying, and Davis was "very pertinacious in opinion and purpose."[26]

The only option left to Lee was to fight: either to defeat Grant's army outright or to put the enemy off guard while Lee abandoned the Richmond-Petersburg position and went to join Johnston's army in North Carolina. Since the first objective was out of the question, Lee began preparing for the second. He apparently pursued no other attempts at peace.

Lee's ability to fight depended on keeping Sherman at bay. His order to Johnston reflected as much: "Concentrate all available forces and drive back Sherman."[27] Johnston was anything but pleased to receive the assignment. In his memoirs, Johnston claimed that he took the assignment in full awareness of the fact that "we could have no other object, in continuing the war, than to obtain fair terms of peace; for the Southern cause must have appeared hopeless then, to all intelligent and dispassionate Southern men."[28] Certainly his mood was deeply pessimistic. His initial response to Lee's order was to declare flatly that it was "too late to expect me to concentrate troops capable of driving back Sherman."[29] His misgivings deepened when he rode the short twenty miles between Lincolnton and Charlotte to confer with Beauregard, who agreed to remain and assist Johnston in any way he could. There he received detailed information about the troops available to him. These consisted mainly of twelve thousand men under Hardee, who had abandoned Charleston on February 16 and were now at Cheraw, South Carolina, not far from the North Carolina border. He also controlled six thousand cavalry under Wade Hampton. Finally, scattered through the Carolina up-country were the remnants of the Army of Tennessee, estimated at about fifty-six hundred men. All in all, Johnston had perhaps twenty-five thousand troops.[30]

What could be done with so meager a force? For several days, Johnston considered the situation hopeless. On February 25 he informed Lee that his conference with Beauregard had simply confirmed his belief that it was too late to stop Sherman. Not only was the Union army much larger than his own—Johnston estimated it at forty thousand, which actually fell far short of its real strength of sixty thousand—but it was also interposed between the various bodies of Confederate infantry, complicating the already difficult job of bringing the outnumbered Rebel forces together. The only ray of sunlight was the possibility that if Bragg's troops could be combined with his own, "the progress of Sherman's army might be stopped, otherwise it may unite with that of Schofield." The likely place for such a linkup of Confederate forces was Fayetteville, North Carolina.[31]

Johnston's mood brightened a bit on March 1, when he received the formal order for his assignment and, with it, Lee's detailed letter of instruction. After reading it, Johnston telegraphed Lee that "the general views you express strengthen my hopes greatly."[32] The letter clearly showed that the general in chief possessed a realistic grasp of the strategic environment, thereby obviating Johnston's initial suspicions that Lee underestimated the seriousness of the situation in the Carolinas. It authorized Johnston to direct the movements of Bragg's troops should his operations bring them within reach, as seemed almost certain to happen within a few days. Finally, it discussed combining Johnston's and Lee's armies to strike Sherman if the Federal commander reached the Roanoke River along the North Carolina–Virginia border.[33]

Johnston seized on this last point to suggest a modified version of Lee's proposal. Although Lee regarded it as a plan of last resort that would entail the abandonment of the Richmond-Petersburg sector, Johnston recast it as a way to retrieve the situation by defeating Sherman and Grant successively. "Would it be possible," he inquired, "to hold Richmond itself with half your army, while the other half joined us near Roanoke to crush Sherman? We might then turn upon Grant."[34] For the next two weeks, Johnston and Lee conducted a halting dialogue concerning this course of action, with an average of four days elapsing between the dispatch of each letter by one man and its receipt by the other. In the meantime Johnston struggled to concentrate his forces, which as of March 6 formally included the six thousand men of Bragg's Department of North Carolina.

By then Johnston had gone to Fayetteville, his preferred point for the Confederate concentration. He left Beauregard at Charlotte as his second in command with orders to facilitate the rail transfer of the Army of Tennessee. In the meantime he sent a division to reinforce Bragg, who was contesting the advance of Schofield's column from Wilmington. Buttressed by this addition, Bragg was able to check the lead elements of Schofield's force at Kinston, North Carolina, on March 8, although he was too weak to capitalize on the victory and fell back to Goldsboro, a strategic railroad junction in the eastern part of the state. Bereft of decision, the battle of Kinston was nevertheless a rare military success for the Confederates and a much needed tonic to the army's morale. But Sherman continued to plow forward remorselessly. It soon became obvious that Sherman would reach Fayetteville before the Confederates could concentrate. Moving on to Raleigh, Johnston pondered what to do next.

He had still heard nothing from Lee, but in a second letter to the general in chief Johnston expressed deep skepticism about the prospect of defeating Sherman on his own and instead pursued the the idea of combining with Lee somewhere along the Roanoke. The latest reports, he wrote, suggested that Sherman had already reached Fayetteville, that Schofield's force was also advancing, and that it appeared to be Sherman's intention to unite both forces near Kinston or Goldsboro. But it was also possible that Sherman might march

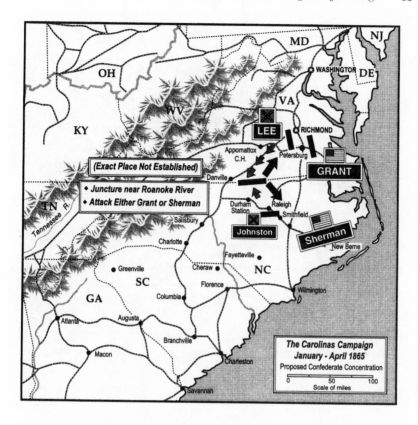

The Carolinas Campaign
January - April 1865
Proposed Confederate Concentration

directly for Raleigh. Whatever the case, Johnston doubted that his army was in shape to accomplish much on its own.

"In a battle with Sherman on equal ground the chances would be decidedly against us," Johnston informed Lee. Hardee's command consisted mainly of garrison troops, unused to field service, and few of its senior leaders seemed competent. It had lost about a thousand men when the governor of South Carolina recalled the state militia; it was losing still more to desertion. The Army of Tennessee was badly in need of reorganization and had lost many of its best leaders in the disastrous autumn campaign. Bragg's force was in better shape, but the recent fight at Kinston had cost it about five hundred men. The only unequivocal good news concerned the Confederate cavalry, which was more numerous than Sherman's and better commanded. Even so, Johnston's total force numbered fewer than thirty thousand, whereas reports placed Sherman's army at forty-five thousand.

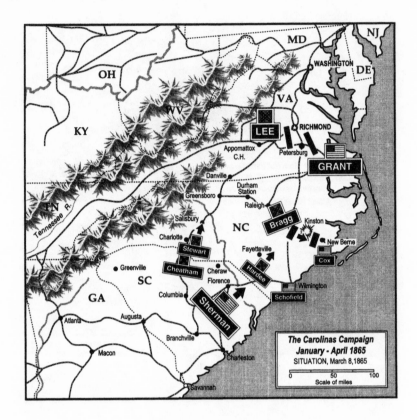

The Carolinas Campaign
January - April 1865
SITUATION, March 8, 1865

Under such circumstances, Johnston continued, he would not try to give battle against Sherman's united army unless Lee's situation absolutely required it, though he would fall upon a portion of Sherman's force if he found it divided. But in any event, should Sherman and Schofield combine forces, "their march into Virginia cannot be prevented by me." Since Lee had already indicated that he would meet Johnston at the Roanoke River in that event, Johnston suggested, why not "hold one of the inner lines at Richmond with one part of your army, and meet Sherman with the other, returning to Richmond after fighting?" Johnston closed by asking Lee to tell him as much as he thought prudent of the effect on Lee's army should the Federal army interdict the railroad at Raleigh.[35]

On March 15, Sherman's army reached Fayetteville. Since the town was accessible to Union steamboats by the Cape Fear River, the arrival restored its communications with the North. Sherman took advantage of this to resupply his army and divest himself of thousands of runaway slaves that had joined it during the trek through South Carolina. He then lingered at Fayetteville for two days in order to destroy the town's war resources and reorganize his force for the next leg of its journey.

Johnston now made plans for the operation that Confederates had fruitlessly been trying to mount for weeks: an offensive against one portion of Sherman's army. The question was where to strike, and that depended on Sherman's next move. Johnston strongly suspected that after leaving Fayetteville, Sherman would head east toward a rendezvous with Schofield, but the chance remained that the Union commander might press on directly toward Raleigh. Unable to risk that possibility, Johnston ordered his own forces to concentrate at Smithfield, halfway between Raleigh and Goldsboro, so as to move to defend either objective. He left Hardee's infantry and Hampton's cavalry to watch Sherman and gauge his destination once he began to move.

Hardee took up a position near Averasboro, where the main road north from Fayetteville diverged, one fork leading to Raleigh, the other to Goldsboro. On March 15–16 he got into a sharp battle with Sherman's XX Corps. Hardee withdrew after several hours' fighting but remained near enough to confirm that when it resumed its advance, the Union force took the eastern fork, which made it all but certain that Goldsboro was Sherman's destination. The Union army was marching toward Goldsboro in two wings: the Left (the XIV and XX Corps) under Maj. Gen. Henry Slocum; and the Right (the XVI and XVII Corps) under Maj. Gen. Oliver O. Howard.

In the meantime, on March 16 Johnston finally received a response from Lee concerning his earlier proposal. It was terse and disappointing. Lee merely stated that he could not hold his position at all if the railroad to Raleigh were interrupted and intimated that it was vital for the supply of his army. If Johnston were to withdraw as far as the Roanoke River, "both armies would certainly starve." If there was to be any chance of hanging on to Richmond, Lee said in effect, Johnston would have to stop Sherman on his own. "You must judge what the probabilities will be of arresting Sherman by battle," Lee counseled. "If there is a reasonable probability I would recommend it. A bold and unexpected attack might relieve us."[36] Johnston's response was soldierly: "I will do my utmost to fulfill your wishes."[37]

Johnston's objective was the Left Wing—in particular the lead XIV Corps under Maj. Gen. Jefferson C. Davis. In theory, if he could destroy the XIV Corps, he might then be poised to wreck the rest of the Left Wing, and if that were done it was possible that Sherman might retreat to Fayetteville or

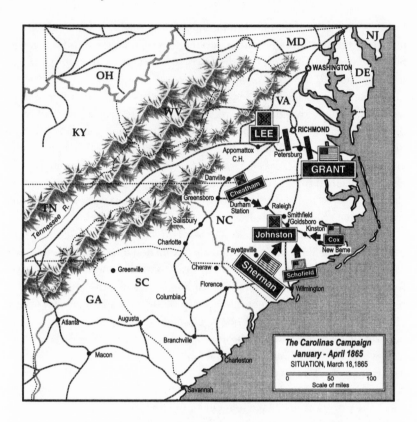

The Carolinas Campaign
January - April 1865
SITUATION, March 18, 1865

Wilmington, which would buy time for the Confederacy. Concentrating every available man near Bentonville, just north of the Goldsboro Road, Johnston created a gigantic ambush. He placed a blocking force under Bragg to bar the highway and deployed the rest of his army almost at right angles, in the fields and woodlands north of the road. As soon as the Federals ran into Bragg, Johnston's main force—about eleven thousand men—would strike the Northerners' left flank.

The battle of Bentonville began on March 19, and its first hours went well for the Confederates. The lead Union division was surprised, flanked, and put to flight. But the Confederates simply did not have the manpower to sustain their early advantage long enough to gain a major success. By afternoon enough Federal reinforcements arrived to halt the Rebel assault, and from then on Johnston's men were firmly on the defensive. By the following day, most of Sherman's army had appeared on the battlefield.

Intriguingly, Johnston stood his ground, notwithstanding the fact that his army was now heavily outnumbered and surrounded on three sides by Sherman's forces, with a rain-swollen creek to its back and only a single rickety bridge by which to retreat. In doing so he ran a very long risk. Indeed, on March 21 he nearly lost his entire army when an enterprising Union division briefly pierced his line and penetrated almost as far as the crucial bridge before being repulsed. Why did Johnston take so great a chance?[38]

Afterward the Virginian claimed that he did so solely to carry off his wounded but that "very bad roads, and the want of comfortable means of transportation, compelled us to devote two days to the operation."[39] That explanation seems insufficient, however, particularly when it is recognized that defeated armies on both sides routinely left their wounded to the enemy and that in this instance, Johnston had every reason to believe that Sherman's well-supplied medical corps could care for his wounded better than his own. The real answer is probably bound up in Johnston's reasons for attacking Sherman in the first place.

It is hard to believe that Johnston expected to win the fight at Bentonville. Since assuming command he had been convinced that he lacked the manpower to stop Sherman on his own. Like Beauregard, he believed that the sole chance for success lay in a combined attack by his forces and Lee's army. But Lee ruled out that option by insisting that the Richmond-Petersburg sector must be held at least until Sherman neared the Roanoke River. That left Johnston with only two alternatives: he could husband his army and wait to join Lee on the Roanoke, or he could attack Sherman with the force immediately at hand.

Johnston probably had three reasons for offering battle at Bentonville. The first was to comply with Lee's expressed wish—it was never a direct order—for him to attack Sherman if the chance arose. Yet Johnston's desire to be a loyal subordinate would not have altered his perception of the military realities. Lee wanted him to attack if a favorable opportunity presented itself. At Bentonville it had, but in Johnston's mind it was less a chance to defeat Sherman than to comply with Lee's request without risking complete disaster to his own forces. Having made a good faith effort to do things Lee's way, Johnston was then in a position to say to Lee, as he did in reporting the outcome of the battle, "I respectfully suggest that it is no longer a question whether you leave [your] present position; you have only to decide where to meet Sherman."[40]

A second reason, perhaps, was the perception that if Johnston could hurt Sherman he could demonstrate that the Confederate army was still dangerous and might in that way improve his government's bargaining position when and if peace negotiations resumed. We have no direct evidence of this, but it is a plausible extrapolation from Johnston's belief that the Confederacy's only sensible object in continuing the war was to obtain fair terms for peace. If that were the case, the Confederate government's military forces constituted its principal negotiating leverage. The more formidable those forces could be made to appear, the greater the leverage.

But a third reason also animated Johnston to a significant degree. Put simply, it was that if he did not use the army he possessed, he might very well lose it—not to the enemy but to demoralization and desertion. It was already well known that hundreds if not thousands of men from the Army of Tennessee had taken unauthorized leaves while passing through the lower South and that Hardee's troops had a serious desertion problem. Johnston seems to have believed that the steady succession of military reverses was causing the men to lose heart.

Whatever the specific reason, however, the general problem was a sense that the situation was hopeless and that the Confederate forces were helpless. Under such circumstances, it made little sense to husband his force in the expectation that over time it would grow stronger. On the contrary, if he did not do something to counter the incipient defeatism, his force would surely dwindle. Thus the morale factor was critical. Johnston's decision to fight at Bentonville and, especially, his decision to remain on the battlefield for almost forty-eight hours after he had lost his opportunity to hurt Sherman, make the most sense in light of this consideration.[41]

Bentonville was thus not intended as a "last stand in the Carolinas," but rather as a means to preserve the army for its next round of maneuvers, especially the impending fight along the Roanoke River. The successful initial attack on Sherman's Left Wing marked the first time in months that the Confederate soldiers had seen the backs of their enemies and felt a sense of their own power and prowess. That was a valuable tonic; Johnston risked the possibility of total disaster so that his troops might carry it from the battlefield. A precipitate retreat with wounded comrades left abandoned would have felt psychologically like a defeat. A stout defense and a departure in its own good time made the battle seem a success. Certainly Johnston believed it did. In his memoirs, the general readily conceded that Bentonville had done nothing to stop or even significantly delay Sherman's linkup with Schofield. "One important object was gained, however—that of restoring the confidence of our troops, who had either lost it in the defeat at Wilmington, or in those of

Tennessee. All were greatly elated by the event."[42] Johnston claimed much the same in his after-action report to Lee. "The moral effect of these operations has been very beneficial," he wrote on March 27. "The spirit of the army is greatly improved and is now excellent. I am told by persons of high standing that a similar effect is felt in the country."[43]

Johnston's last sentence highlights an additional concern that was much on the minds of Confederate leaders during this period. At the beginning of the war, one Southern politician expressed a common sentiment when he opined that no country of the South's geographical expanse had ever been conquered—"if true to itself"—in the history of the world. The qualifier had once seemed cause for reassurance, but in early 1865 it gave reason for alarm. On every side, the Confederate leadership saw indications that civilian morale was crumbling. The implications for the military struggle were serious and immediate. Without the civilians' willingness to shoulder the burden of war, the Confederate army would have trouble supplying itself. The people would thwart conscription and no new volunteers would come forward. Worst of all, the families and friends of soldiers in the ranks would dissolve the opprobrium normally attached to desertion, would shelter soldiers who left the army, and would even encourage them to do so.[44]

Lee summarized a common view among the Confederate senior leadership. On February 24, he complained to North Carolina Governor Zebulon Vance that "the state of despondency" prevalent among the people was having a bad effect on the troops. "Desertions are very frequent and there is good reason to believe that they are occasioned to a considerable extent by letters written to the soldiers by their friends at home. . . . It has been discovered that despondent persons represent to their friends in the army that the cause is hopeless, and that they had better provide for themselves." Lee urged Vance to encourage "influential citizens" to exhort the population and cheer their spirits, and he was specific about what they might say:

> If they would explain to the people that the cause is not hopeless; that the situation, though critical, is critical to the enemy as well as ourselves; that he has drawn his troops from every other quarter to accomplish his designs against Richmond, and that his defeat now would result in leaving nearly our whole territory open to us; that this great result can be accomplished if all will work diligently and zealously; and that his successes are far less valuable in fact than in appearance, I think our sorely tried people would be induced to make one more effort to bear

their sufferings a little longer, and regain some of the spirit that marked the first two years of the war. If they will, I feel confident that, with the blessing of God, what seems to be the greatest danger will prove to be the means of deliverance and safety.[45]

On March 28 Johnston wrote seven Southern governors to inform them that many stragglers "from the troops of your State belonging to this army are about their homes. I ask your aid in bringing them back to the ranks."[46]

After Bentonville Johnston withdrew his army to Smithfield, where he could monitor Sherman's army, shield the district around Raleigh from which Lee's army drew its supplies, and maintain a clear line of retreat to Greensboro, where the railroad from Raleigh intercepted the Danville railroad down which Lee's army must come once it was forced to abandon the Richmond-Petersburg line. Sherman made no attempt to pursue. Instead, he clung to his original union with Schofield at Goldsboro. Once there, the combined Union army—now almost one hundred thousand strong—threw up encampments. From prisoners seized by his cavalry, Johnston learned that the Federals did not expect to resume their march very soon but planned to linger at Goldsboro to rest and refit.

Johnston was grateful for the breather. He felt safe enough to send part of his cavalry, under Maj. Gen. Joseph Wheeler, to western North Carolina to block a Union mounted raid from Knoxville. He used the time to implement a much needed reorganization of his infantry, which contained too many undersized units and far more officers—especially general officers—than required by a force its size. During this time the strength of Johnston's army continued to grow, modestly but significantly. Two days after Bentonville it numbered about 26,275; by April 3 it was up to 29,929, a figure that reflected both additions from the Army of Tennessee and, just as important, reduced attrition through desertion.[47]

By streamlining the army's organization, Johnston hoped to enable it more efficiently to carry out its next campaign—the planned linkup with Lee's army, followed by an attack on either Grant or Sherman. Although the forces at his disposal, added to the fifty to sixty thousand troops that Lee might bring with him from Virginia, would not outnumber either Federal army, a combined strength of eighty to ninety thousand men offered a realistic prospect for a military success that might at least restore the strategic equilibrium. Johnston had done his part to lay the groundwork for such a stroke. The rest was up to Lee.

After March 25, however, Johnston received no further news from the Confederate general in chief. After several days the lack of information must surely have become troubling. Then, on April 5, Johnston saw press dispatches stating that the Davis administration had evacuated Richmond three days previously. From this news Johnston inferred that Lee was about to abandon the defense of the capital to unite with him. The newspapers did not report that Lee's army had in fact been attacked and forced from Richmond by Grant. This would have been disturbing news because although it would not rule out the possiblity of a linkup on the Roanoke, it would have meant that Lee was retreating in haste, with no head start on the enemy, and that in all likelihood the enemy was in aggressive pursuit. Johnston, however, knew none of this.

Nor was he enlightened when he inquired of Lee to Secretary of War John C. Breckinridge, whom he guessed had gone to Danville after leaving Richmond. Breckinridge was not there but Davis was, and in his absence the president responded. There had been no recent news of Lee, Davis wrote, but at last report he was nearing Amelia Court House, Virginia, a village about halfway between Petersburg and Danville. There were rumors of hard fighting but no official intelligence. Davis therefore advised, "Your knowledge of General Lee's plans will enable you to infer future movements and his wishes with regard to your forces."[48] This was little help, however, because Johnston knew of Lee's intentions only in general terms. Lee would head for the Roanoke River if he could, but Johnston had no idea when or where he planned to cross. In the short run, the best Johnston could do was to recall Wheeler's cavalry and hold his force in readiness to move when Lee summoned him or when Sherman resumed his march, which, given the news from Virginia, Johnston expected Sherman to do any day.

On April 8 Johnston received two updates, one from an aide to President Davis, the other from Breckinridge. The first was upbeat. Although there was still no official word from Lee, "all private accounts [are] cheering and represent the army in good condition and spirits. Little straggling." The second was much more sober. Breckinridge reported that he had left Lee's army the previous day at Farmville. He did not think Lee was hard-pressed by the enemy, for he had heard little firing, but even so, "Straggling has been great and the situation is not favorable." Nor, despite his recent contact with Lee, could Breckinridge offer any specifics about the general in chief's intentions. "He will still try to move around toward North Carolina," the secretary of war reported, but "he did not know what route circumstances would permit him to take."[49]

Two days later, having heard correctly that Sherman was about to move, Johnston put his army on the road to Raleigh. The march was made in good order and without incident, but shortly after midnight on April 11, Johnston received a shocking telegram from Davis, who had just reached Greensboro: "A scout reports that General Lee surrendered the remnant of his army near to Appomattox Court-House yesterday [April 9]. No official intelligence of the event, but there is little room for doubt as to result." Later that day, in response to a query from Johnston, Davis replied that yes, it would be well for Johnston to go to Greensboro, where they could confer in person.[50] Beauregard would be present as well.

Lee's surrender, of course, completely transformed the strategic situation. There was now no possibility whatever of even checking, much less defeating, Grant or Sherman, and as Johnston rode by train to Greensboro he supposed that when he arrived the subject of the discussion would focus on how best to negotiate a surrender. Beauregard, coming up from Charlotte, thought the same. Instead both men discovered that Davis intended to fight on; for him the only issue was how best to continue resistance.

Beauregard arrived first and gave Davis a detailed rundown of the latest military developments and the balance of forces, not just in North Carolina but throughout the Confederacy. It consisted of a long litany of powerful Union field armies poised to go wherever they might wish and confronted either by inadequate Confederate forces or no forces at all. Davis listened attentively but at the end of the briefing was "undismayed." He believed the war could be still be won if the Confederacy exploited all its "latent resources." If worst came to worst, the Confederate government could cross the Mississippi River with whatever troops might make the retreat, unite with Kirby Smith's army—whose strength he estimated at sixty thousand, almost double the reality—and continue the war indefinitely. These visionary hopes astonished Beauregard.[51] Davis continued in the same upbeat vein when Johnston arrived on April 12. He expressed confidence that by gathering conscripts and deserters the Confederacy could soon create a field army large enough to sustain the war. Johnston and Beauregard objected that it was unlikely that the government could enforce conscription and that deserters who had left the army when the situation was less bleak would not likely return now. Davis refused to hear of it and merely adjourned the meeting until Secretary of War Breckinridge could join the discussion next day.

Johnston and Beauregard now faced a decision. Having conveyed the military situation to their president they could now, like dutiful subordinates,

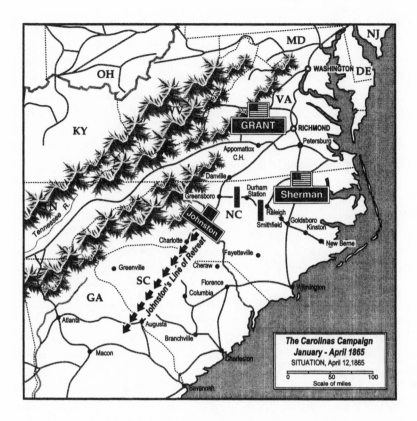

The Carolinas Campaign
January - April 1865
SITUATION, April 12,1865

await whatever orders Davis might choose to give, or they could actively lobby to urge the Confederate government to capitulate. They chose the second course. That afternoon Breckinridge arrived from Danville, bringing with him confirmation of Lee's surrender at Appomattox. Hearing this news, the two generals met, reviewed the military situation, and agreed that "the Southern Confederacy was overthrown." Then they went to Breckinridge and told him as much. "The only power left in the President's hands," Johnston declared, "was that of terminating the war," a power he should exercise without delay. He told Breckinridge that he was ready to tell Davis this to his face. Breckinridge promised to give him the opportunity at the next cabinet meeting.

That evening Secretary of the Navy Stephen Mallory came to Johnston, saying that he was anxious to see negotiations begun to end the war and that he believed Johnston was the man to suggest such a course to the president.

Johnston demurred. This was the first time he had heard a high government official endorse the idea of a negotiated peace, and although willing to advocate such a course himself, he thought it would be better coming from one of Davis's "constitutional advisers." Mallory evidently agreed to do so, but as events transpired it was Johnston who actually first broached the subject.

True to his word, Breckinridge arranged to have Johnston and Beauregard join Davis and his cabinet after they had conferred privately for a time. As Beauregard had already done, Johnston reviewed the military situation and the balance of forces, but he did not stop there. The people, he continued, "are tired of the war, feel themselves whipped, and will not fight." The country was overrun, its military resources greatly diminished, while those of its enemy, already immense, were capable of enlargement. "My men are daily deserting in large numbers," Johnston went on, "and are stealing my artillery teams to aid their escapes to their homes. Since Lee's surrender they regard the war as at an end. If I march out of North Carolina her people will all leave my ranks."[52] With no prospect of recruiting for his ranks and every prospect of losing the men who yet remained with the colors, he concluded that "under such circumstances it would be the greatest of human crimes to continue the war."[53] Johnston thus did what no American commander has ever done, before or since: he exercised the full weight of his military position to tell his government how to conclude a war.

It is possible that even without Johnston's outburst, the cabinet would have broached the subject on its own. Certainly once Davis asked those present what they thought of Johnston's words, he discovered that with one exception, every member of his cabinet agreed with Johnston, as for that matter did Beauregard.[54] Whatever the case, faced with such an array of opinion contrary to his own, Davis had little choice but to explore the possibility of a negotiated settlement. The assemblage rapidly agreed on a list of acceptable terms; the next step was to see if the Federal government would be willing to discuss them. Presently it was decided that the proper way to proceed would be to ask Sherman for a truce, "the object being to permit the civil authorities to enter into the needful arrangements to terminate the existing war."[55] Although Davis composed the wording of the request, it went out over Johnston's signature, and to Johnston went the task of sending it to Sherman.

Sherman's army had reached Raleigh by the time he received the letter at midnight on April 13. He responded at once, telling Johnston that he would suspend the further advance of his forces and stood ready to offer Johnston's men the same terms that Grant had given Lee (though neither Johnston nor the Confederate government as yet knew the details of those terms). The rival commanders met on April 17 near Durham Station, about equidistant between the lines of the two armies, to discuss the matter.

The meeting began under a heavy cloud, for Sherman had just received a telegram from Secretary of War Edwin M. Stanton stating that Lincoln had been assassinated. Further, Stanton's dispatch suggested that the Confederate government might well have orchestrated the murder. Sherman considered this highly plausible, though he doubted that Johnston or any other Confederate general was involved. Still, his first order of business upon meeting Johnston was to tell him of the assassination. Sherman noted that the news made Johnston literally start to sweat.

Sherman began the main discussion with a military surrender in mind and rejected out of hand the notion embodied in Johnston's letter of suspending hostilities so that the "civil authorities" could negotiate a settlement. Since the Federal government did not concede the legal existence of the Confederacy, he said, it followed that it recognized no Confederate "civil authorities." Sherman could therefore only repeat his offer to grant Johnston the same terms that Lee had received at Appomattox.

That might have ended the discussion right there, for Johnston correctly pointed out that the "relative positions" of the armies in North Carolina were different from those of the armies in Virginia. Lee had been surrounded; Johnston had a clear line of retreat available to him. If Sherman could accept only a military capitulation, and Johnston had no authority to capitulate, there was nothing to talk about. But Johnston adroitly proposed a third course. Harkening back to the example of European generals—he specifically mentioned Napoleon's parley with the Archduke Charles—he suggested that he and Sherman might arrange a permanent peace.

For reasons that remain cloudy after more than a century, Sherman leaped at the suggestion. Apparently he believed the political objectives of the Federal government were clear enough that he could outline a peace settlement without instructions from Washington; moreover, he later claimed that at a recent meeting between himself, Grant, and Lincoln he had acquired a detailed grasp of the president's thinking. It is also possible that he mistrusted the ability of Lincoln's successor, Andrew Johnson, to create a workable agreement, particularly in the midst of the charged environment that doubtless prevailed in Washington in the wake of Lincoln's murder.

Johnston was equally willing to speak on behalf of his government. And so for much of the afternoon the two generals essentially negotiated a peace settlement, rapidly agreeing on everything save amnesty for Jefferson Davis and the Confederate cabinet. This Johnston felt obliged to press for, but it was the one point on which Sherman was unsure of his government's stance, and it remained the principal sticking point between them when they decided to adjourn for the day.

That evening two things happened. When Johnston returned to Greensboro to report on the negotiations in progress, he discovered that President Davis had already departed for Charlotte with most of his entourage. He was, however, able to consult with Secretary of War Breckinridge and Postmaster General John H. Reagan. In response to Johnston's news, Reagan placed the Confederate government's terms in writing, and at Beauregard's suggestion, it was agreed that Breckinridge would accompany Johnston when his meeting with Sherman resumed.

The two commanders met at 2 P.M. the next day. At first Sherman bridled at permitting a Confederate civil official to join the meeting, but he agreed once Johnston pointed out that Breckinridge was also a Confederate major general; thus the military complexion of the conference would not be compromised. Ostensibly he also spurned Reagan's proposed terms, but his own terms closely resembled Reagan's, and Johnston noticed that he kept Reagan's draft close at hand while he composed them. The resulting agreement was, all things considered, amazingly liberal. It called for a cease-fire, the disbandment of the Confederate army and the collection of its weapons at Southern state arsenals, recognition of the existing state governments in the South, the reestablishment of Federal courts in the region, and full amnesty for Southern citizens who had assisted the Confederate war effort. Essentially, it restored the status quo antebellum.

The two commanders now sought formal approval of their handiwork from their respective governments. Sherman dispatched the document to Washington, while Breckinridge personally carried it to Davis and the Confederate cabinet in Charlotte. Johnston awaited the verdict with his army at Hillsboro. Several days passed while the Davis government deliberated. Davis had each cabinet officer prepare a written analysis of both the military situation and the proffered terms.

These analyses are intriguing for the way they illuminate how the Davis cabinet understood the Confederacy's predicament. They examined first, the current military situation and balance of forces, then the possibility of acquiring additional resources to continue the struggle. All regarded the situation as hopeless if unredressed. Most, however, declared or implied that the South contained the "latent resources" of which Davis continued to speak but went on to say in effect that the Southern population had lost the will to tap them. John H. Reagan was direct on this point: "Much as we have been exhausted in men and resources, I am of opinion that if our people could be induced to continue the struggle with the spirit that animated them during the first years of the war our independence might yet be within our reach; but I see no reason to hope for that now."[56] All concluded that under the circumstances, Sherman's proposed terms were acceptable, even lenient. As Judah Benjamin expressed it, they "imply no dishonor, impose no degradation, [and] exact only what the victor always requires, the relinquishment by his foe of the object for which the struggle was commenced."[57] Davis concurred. He wired Johnston to accept the terms if the U.S. government gave Sherman authority to follow through with the arrangement.[58]

Johnston had barely received Davis's go-ahead when a curt dispatch arrived from Sherman, stating that his government had disapproved the arrangement and instructed him to limit his negotiations only to securing the military surrender of Johnston's "immediate command" on the same terms that Grant had extended to Lee. A second dispatch warned that he would resume hostile operations in forty-eight hours.[59] Johnston promptly relayed the news to Davis. "Have you instructions?" he inquired, then offered his own unvarnished recommendation: "We had better disband this small force to prevent devastation to the country."[60]

Davis did not see it that way. Johnston had a clear line of retreat available toward Charlotte and thence into South Carolina, the Confederate government had done what it could to place supplies along the route, and if Johnston could not elude Sherman by a conventional march south, he could at least send his cavalry away, along with as many infantry as he could mount on horses and some light artillery, disband the remaining infantry and artillery, and establish a point where at least some of the disbanded soldiers could rendezvous and continue the struggle.[61] He instructed Breckinridge to convey this course of action to Johnston.

Knowing Johnston's conviction that it would be a "crime" to continue the war, Breckinridge broached the matter gingerly:

> Does not your suggestion about disbanding refer to the infantry and most of the artillery? If it be necessary to disband these they might still save their small-arms and find their way to some appointed rendezvous. Can you not bring off the cavalry and all of the men you can mount

from transportation and other animals, with some light field pieces? Such a force could march away from Sherman and be strong enough to encounter anything between us and the Southwest. If this course be possible, carry it out and telegraph your intended route.[62]

But although delicate in tone, the order was unmistakable enough in intent. Plainly the Confederate government had adopted a policy of continuing the war by making its way to the Trans-Appalachian Confederacy—"the Southwest"—to rally the still significant military forces beyond the mountains. Johnston's instructions were essentially to ensure the implementation of this plan by protecting the government while in transit. Was the proposed course of action militarily feasible? Surely it was. One suspects that Robert E. Lee would have carried it out.

Johnston, however, refused. In a brief, biting response, he telegraphed Breckinridge the next morning: "We have to save the people, spare the blood of the army, and save the high civil functionaries. Your plan, I think, can only do the last." He was willing to give a cavalry escort to Davis—"who ought to move without the loss of a moment"—but otherwise he thought the proposal "impracticable" and asserted that his commanders agreed. Soon afterward he fired off a second wire: "I have proposed to General Sherman military negotiations in regard to this army."[63] He surrendered his army the following day, April 26, 1865.

With that act, Gen. Joseph E. Johnston ordained the final fate of the Confederacy. The surrender in North Carolina transformed the hitherto orderly retreat of the Davis government into the "flight into oblivion" of memory. The cabinet soon scattered; Davis himself was caught by Union cavalry in southern Georgia on May 10. Whether the Confederate president could have carried on the struggle, perhaps beyond the Mississippi, and whether the pursuing Union armies would indeed have devastated the land, as Lee, Johnston, and others feared, will forever remain moot because a military commander facing a clear-cut military decision stepped beyond the traditional, almost sacred boundaries of American civil-military relations and refused to fight a lost war any longer.

The Carolinas campaign says much about the reasons for Confederate defeat. To begin with, it underscores the bankruptcy of the beloved Lost Cause notion that the South was beaten down by sheer weight of numbers. Certainly the North possessed significant military and economic advantages, but this had been a fact of life since the beginning of the struggle. Moreover, as Lee pointed out in his letter to Governor Zebulon Vance, the Federal army actually controlled little more of the South than it had done the previous year, when the Confederate position had still seemed viable. If the military situation in early 1865 was critical, most high-ranking civil and military officials agreed that it could yet be retrieved if the South could mobilize its remaining war resources, particularly its manpower.

One need not resort to speculation based on census figures, as the *Richmond Whig* did, to get a handle on the extent of the military manpower still available. The Confederate surrender figures speak eloquently. Almost alone among the South's armies, Lee's Army of Northern Virginia surrendered fewer men at Appomattox than its effective strength in preceding weeks. The returns for late February 1865 showed almost 58,000 men in Lee's command. After the Confederate chieftain faced Grant in the parlor of the McLean house, Grant's officers signed the paroles of 27,000 men. Elsewhere the ratio was reversed. Although Johnston's army numbered fewer than 20,000 effectives on the eve of the surrender, many Confederate soldiers who had left the army clarified their legal position by accepting Federal parole, so that almost 37,000 Confederates were paroled at Greensboro. And since Johnston's military jurisdiction also included South Carolina, Georgia, and Florida, an eventual 52,543 men surrendered to Federal authorities in those states, making a total of 89,270.[64]

Substantial numbers also surrendered beyond the mountains. Most remaining Confederate forces east of the Mississippi—some 42,000 men—capitulated at Citronnelle, Alabama, on May 8. By the close of that month almost all troops west of the Mississippi had surrendered as well. Here the ratio of effective strength to strength surrendered mirrored that of the Army of Northern Virginia, albeit for different reasons. In March 1865 the Trans-Mississippi Department probably had 30,000 men in the ranks. But the number paroled in this last major capitulation numbered just 17,686; many soldiers had simply walked away from the army by the time the department formally surrendered.

The official total for all Confederate forces thus surrendered came to 174,223.[65] The impressive total tells much about the manpower resources that the Confederacy still theoretically possessed in 1865. Although far short of the Union army, a field force that size would have been quite capable of protracted resistance well into the summer, particularly when one recognizes that the bulk of the Union army was now composed of men with limited combat experience. Most of the volunteers of 1861 were dead, disabled, or back in civilian life. The enlistments of the second great wave of Federal volunteers—also hard hit by casualties—would start expiring in August 1865. Thus the claims of Davis, other civilian officials, and, in their sanguine moments, even Beauregard, Lee, and Johnston, that the Confederate cause could yet be retrieved are not entirely to be dismissed.

But how to create the conditions for continued resistance? The perspective of the Confederate leadership on this critical issue is fascinating. Plainly they understood—as Richard E. Beringer, Herman Hattaway, Archer Jones, and William N. Still Jr. have reminded us—that the commitment of the Southern population was flagging. But they also grasped James M. McPherson's point about the crucial role played by "contingency" in undermining that commitment, specifically the sickening impact of Union military victories.[66] They believed that if contingency could operate against them, it could also work in their favor. A significant military success might revive Southern morale and bring thousands of wayward Confederate soldiers back into the ranks, along with fresh conscripts and volunteers.

We need not concur with this perspective to accept it as the basis on which the Confederate high command planned its strategy for 1865. Given its assumptions, the critical tasks were two: first, the maintenance of the military equilibrium in the Carolinas and Virginia theaters; second, the achievement of a signal victory over Union forces—not a decisive victory that would overthrow the enemy's advantage but one that would galvanize Southern morale and thereby create the conditions in which a protracted resistance was once again possible. The only practical way to achieve this victory was to bring additional troops into the critical theater, concentrate them to arrest Sherman's progress when he resumed his march from Savannah, and ultimately exploit an opportunity to defeat part of his army and force the rest to abandon its campaign. This was the task the Confederate government set for itself. One may fairly ask how well it managed the resources at hand to bring about this hoped-for restoration of morale.

The short answer is, Not well at all. The Richmond authorities neither named an overall commander to oppose Sherman nor began shifting troops into the Carolinas theater until the eve of the campaign. At that point they essentially ratified Beauregard's adoption of the role of ad hoc generalissimo and began funneling the Army of Tennessee toward the Carolinas by rail, but even then they chose to divert three thousand men from that army to join the defense of Mobile, Alabama, a port that had been closed to Confederate blockade runners since August 1864.

Although twenty-one thousand men began the trek to the Carolinas, barely four thousand were on hand at the battle of Bentonville nearly six weeks later. Why? A substantial desertion rate bore most of the blame, but the reasons for the desertions are more complicated than the usual picture of Johnny Rebs abandoning the cause and going home. Morale in the Army of Tennessee was teetering on the brink, principally because of the hard, almost continuous campaigning it had been asked to endure since May 1864. Under such circumstances, Hood and ultimately Beauregard came to believe that furloughs for the men were critical to the restoration of the army's effectiveness, but the implementation of furloughs proved disastrous. By granting leaves to the Trans-Mississippi and Tennessee troops and almost simultaneously embarking the others on yet another campaign, Hood and Beauregard got the worst of both worlds. Not only did they lose the manpower thus furloughed, they also set the stage for the "French leaves" taken by thousands of other soldiers who justifiably felt unfairly treated. But the perception of unfairness formed only one of the reasons for these unauthorized absences. Some men undoubtedly had lost faith in the cause; others were simply homesick or tired of getting shot at. A good many, seeing or hearing of the damage done by Sherman's army in its trek through Georgia and South Carolina, left out of concern for their families.

Whatever their motives, the botched rail transfer rendered this mass exodus almost ludicrously easy. With the army moving by dribs and drabs, in fits and starts, it was frequently easier to get away from the army than to follow it on its journey. At this distance, it is hard to tell how much of the problem owed to the deterioration of the Southern transportation infrastructure and how much owed to mismanagement, but the limited evidence suggests that both factors operated in abundance. In September 1863 the Confederacy successfully transported twelve thousand troops a distance of 775 miles in two weeks; in 1865 it proved unable to perform an equivalent task in two months.[67]

Interestingly, however, hundreds of the men who left the army also returned five or ten or fifteen days after reaching their homes or simply after having some time away. Their example suggests a median body of soldiers who were neither totally alienated nor die-hards but whose sense of duty wavered and revived in much the same fashion as the Confederate authorities hoped was characteristic of most of the one hundred thousand men believed to be away without leave.

Even more serious than the failure to infuse the Carolinas theater with the reinforcements earmarked for it was the failure effectively to concentrate the troops already there. From the eve of the campaign until its end, the Confederate high command plainly understood that it must gather all its available forces into a compact whole if it expected to delay Sherman, much less stop him. Yet week after frustrating week went by and the troops in the Carolinas remained scattered. As Wade Hampton complained after the war, "It would scarcely have been possible to disperse a force more effectively than was done in our case."[68]

Most of the blame for this state of affairs can be traced to the Confederate deployments at the campaign's outset. By defending both Augusta and Charleston, Beauregard essentially offered Sherman a relatively clear path to Columbia. Once embarked in that direction, Sherman rapidly interposed himself between the divided Rebel forces; their inability to unite enabled him to continue his forward progress and so prolong their division. The prowess shown by Sherman's army in the Carolinas campaign cannot be gainsaid. Its ability to overcome swollen rivers and mud-clogged roads fully deserves Joe Johnston's famous comment that, when he heard of its hardihood, "he made up his mind that there had been no such army since the days of Julius Caesar."[69] But it is fair to observe that the dearth of significant Confederate resistance was a critical factor in Sherman's triumphant, desolating advance.

Sherman's rapid march through South Carolina, coupled with the arrival of Schofield's powerful supporting force at Wilmington, transformed the Confederacy's strategic position from merely serious to desperate. In no Confederate general was this situation more clearly reflected than in Beauregard, whose reaction mirrored that of a cancer patient when the fatal diagnosis, abstractly understood, asserts itself in flesh and pain and becomes a shattering reality. The imperative need to concentrate against Sherman now combined with fantasies of total redemption; the result was his February 21 proposal to summon Lee's army from the Petersburg trenches, pulverize Sherman, defeat Grant, and dictate peace in the White House.

Beauregard's proposal, however, merely offered in extreme form a course of action that both Johnston and (more reluctantly) Lee came to see as the only militarily sound option that remained. Their difference on this question was mostly one of timing. Johnston thought the sooner he and Lee joined forces, the better would be their chance of staving off defeat. Lee, following the preferences of the Davis government as well as his own, thought it better to protract resistance in the Richmond-Petersburg sector as long as possible. One gathers that the problem in his mind was not simply the difficulty of making a clean getaway from Grant but rather that the blow to morale following the loss of Richmond would overwhelm whatever benefit accrued from a check to Sherman. In this Lee was probably right. Whatever slim chance the Confederacy had to retrieve the situation depended on the ability of the troops in the Carolinas to stop Sherman on their own.

It was, of course, Johnston who finally managed to achieve the long frustrated concentration of Confederate forces and land the long deferred blow upon Sherman's army. Even the closest students of this offensive, launched so late in the campaign, with so few troops, concede that it had no chance of success. Yet the ambush at Bentonville went well enough to provoke the question, If the Confederates were able to assault one of Sherman's wings with such fury and effect with fewer than twenty thousand troops and at a time when Sherman was barely a day removed from his junction with Schofield, what would have been the result if it had been made with twice that strength, not in late March but in mid-February, and not in eastern North Carolina but in central South Carolina? Like any other counterfactual question, there can be no conclusive answer. But its conditions correspond to what a better-conducted Confederate campaign could have achieved, and it is at least reasonable to suppose that such an attack could have halted Sherman or led him to advance with far more caution.

A signal victory was thus within the Confederacy's reach, even in the winter of 1865. Would it have served to revive flagging Southern morale? Probably, but whether enough to place the Confederacy once more on the road to independence is far less likely. Even then, the stronger Yankee battalions might have done in fact what they did in myth—bludgeon the gallant Southern people into submission. But surely "contingency" continued to operate even after the reelection of Lincoln and the battle of Nashville. The Confederacy had a real chance to prolong the war as late as February 1865.

Would that have made a difference? One outcome of such a scenario might have been not Confederate victory but heightened control over the conditions for the eventual restoration of the Union. Significant elements within the South were already at work to promote a negotiated settlement. Several efforts in that direction had already been made. The principal impediment was Jefferson Davis, whose advantageous official position, political gifts, and sheer stubborn determination made him a formidable obstacle indeed.

Even so, Davis's cabinet eventually turned against him, albeit only after the Confederacy had lost most of its negotiating leverage. Perhaps a protracted though losing defense would have given the peace proponents time enough to organize, break Davis's viselike grip on the Confederacy's helm, and use the South's evident military strength to gain reunion on terms that would have assured "home rule" and control over the implementation of emancipation. After all, Lincoln had publicly stated that reunion and emancipation were his only preconditions for peace; all other terms were negotiable. Andrew Johnson did in fact permit a "self-reconstruction" almost as lenient as any Confederate could wish, while the North discovered after a few years of postwar agitation and political violence that it was quite willing to restore to Southern whites both home rule and economic control over the lives of the former slaves. A negotiated peace is not at all difficult to imagine.

More likely, however, a Confederate military success in 1865 would have strengthened Davis's hand, not weakened it. The proven ability to protract the war would have confirmed Davis's view of the struggle as winnable and simply produced a replay of the spring of 1865 in the summer, autumn, or winter. Here the role played by the military commanders takes on new significance. Consider the moment when Davis's cabinet finally turned against him and insisted that he open negotiations with Sherman. The catalyst was not John C. Breckinridge, John H. Reagan, Stephen R. Mallory, or any other cabinet official. It was Joe Johnston. By ignoring the American officer corps' traditional subordination to civilian authority, Johnston played the crucial role in compelling the Confederate government to sue for peace, just as days later his unilateral decision to surrender rendered that government a mere gaggle of fleeing fugitives. He did so, as he informed the governors of several Southern states afterward, "to spare the blood of the gallant little army committed to me, to prevent further sufferings of our people by the devastation and ruin inevitable from the marches of invading armies, and to avoid the crime of waging hopeless war."[70]

One cannot help comparing Johnston's conduct with that of Lee and wondering what each would have done in the other's position. By February 1865, Lee clearly thought that the Confederacy must seek peace, but his sense of propriety and due subordination obliged him only to seek out high government officials to whom he could outline the darkening military situation as clearly as possible. He invariably stopped short of drawing the obvious political conclusion. And once ejected from the Richmond-Petersburg lines, he did nothing to "spare the blood" of his own "gallant little army" but rather conducted a fighting retreat until thoroughly cornered, at which point he surrendered. Even in his last official dispatch to Jefferson Davis, written on April 20, Lee balked at telling the president to make peace. The closest he could come was to "recommend" measures "for the suspension of hostilities and the restoration of peace," and this only after reaffirming that "it is for Your Excellency to decide . . . what is proper to be done."[71] Given Lee's attitude, it is difficult to imagine that he would have disobeyed Davis's order to retreat to the southwest after the failure of the Sherman cartel. Whatever his misgivings, he would have accepted the president's authority like the dutiful subordinate he was and thereby led the South to some other, probably more bloody and destructive, outcome.

What Johnston would have done in Lee's place, especially with his prestige and authority, poses an equally fascinating question. Almost certainly he would have flatly refused to fight on once Grant broke through the Richmond-Petersburg lines. But it is quite possible that, like Lee, he would earlier have pursued efforts to persuade Confederate authorities to accept a negotiated peace, bluntly rather than with Lee's tender circumspection. The result might have had far-reaching and disquieting consequences, not just for Reconstruction but for the future of American civil-military relations. Perhaps that is one small reason why Lee's surrender at Appomattox is so well known while Johnston's surrender at Durham Station is largely forgotten. It is more comfortable to recall the dutiful subordinate than the general who defied his government and refused any longer to fight a lost war.

Notes

1. In order of seniority, these generals were Samuel Cooper, R. E. Lee, Joseph E. Johnston, P. G. T. Beauregard, Braxton Bragg, Edmund Kirby Smith, and John Bell Hood. An eighth full general, Albert Sidney Johnston, had perished at Shiloh in April 1862.

2. J. A. Seddon to Beauregard, January 8, 1865, *War of the Rebellion: A Compilation of the Official Records of the Union and Confederate Armies,* 128 vols. (Washington DC: U.S. Government Printing Office, 1880–1901), Ser. I, 45; pt. 2, 770. Cited hereafter as OR. Unless noted, all citations are to Ser. I.

3. Alfred T. Roman, *The Military Operations of General Beauregard in the War Between the States,* 2 vols. (1884; rpt. New York: Da Capo, 1994), 2:331–32.

4. In addition to commanding the Army of Tennessee, Taylor continued to head the Department of Alabama, Mississippi, and Eastern Louisiana.

5. Robert C. Black, *The Railroads of the Confederacy* (Chapel Hill: University of North Carolina Press, 1952), 272–73. In addition, at Columbus, Georgia, the gauge

of the railroad changed from 4 feet 8½ inches to 5 feet, necessitating a complete change of cars. The route described here corresponds with the initial route taken by the transferred troops; eventually almost all traffic went via Mobile, Alabama.

6. For detailed descriptions of the rail transfer and its glacial pace, see, e.g., Walter A. Clark, *Under the Stars and Bars: Or Memories of Four Years of Service with the Oglothorpes of Georgia* (1900; rpt. Jonesboro GA: Freedom Hill Press, 1987), 182–87; Wirt Armistead Cate, ed., *Two Soldiers: The Campaign Diaries of Thomas J. Key, C.S.A. and Robert J. Campbell, U.S.A.* (Chapel Hill: University of North Carolina Press, 1938), 182–86; Lilla Mills Hawes, ed., "The Memoirs of Charles H. Olmstead, Part XI," *Georgia Historical Quarterly* 45 (June 1961): 149–53.

7. See C. L. Stevenson to J. M. Otey, with Beauregard's endorsement, OR, 47: pt. 2, 1285–86.

8. Hawes, ed., "Memoirs of Charles H. Olmstead," 153.

9. "Notes of conference had on the 2d day of February, A.D. 1865," February 3, 1865, OR, 47: pt. 2, 1084.

10. OR, 47: pt. 2, 1085.

11. Beauregard to Davis, February 21, 1865, OR, 47: pt. 2, 1238.

12. Wade Hampton to Beauregard, February 18, 1865, OR, 47: pt. 2, 1218–19.

13. Beauregard to Lee, February 16, 1865, OR, 47: pt. 1, 1048.

14. Cooper to Beauregard, February 20, 1865, OR, 47: pt. 2, 1228.

15. Lee to Beauregard, February 25, 1865, OR, 47: pt. 2, 1272.

16. Lee to Johnston, February 23, 1865, OR, 47: pt. 2, 1257.

17. Johnston to Lee, March 1, 1865, OR, 47: pt. 2, 1297.

18. Lee to his wife, February 21, 1865, in Clifford Dowdey and Louis H. Manarin, eds., *The Wartime Papers of R. E. Lee* (New York: Bramhall House, 1961), 907.

19. Alan T. Nolan, *Lee Considered: General Robert E. Lee and Civil War History* (Chapel Hill: University of North Carolina Press, 1991), 112–33.

20. Lee to Beauregard, February 22, 1865, OR, 47: pt. 2, 1248.

21. R. M. T. Hunter, "Peace Commission—Hon. R. M. T. Hunter's Reply to President Davis' Letter," *Southern Historical Society Papers*, 3 (1877): 308.

22. Hunter, "Peace Commission," 309.

23. Hunter, "Peace Commission," 309.

24. Lee to Davis, February 23, 1865, in Dowdey and Manarin, eds., *Wartime Papers*, 909.

25. For the Ord-Longstreet exchange, see James Longstreet, *From Manassas to Appomattox* (Philadelphia: Lippincott, 1896); Jeffry D. Wert, *General James Longstreet: The Confederacy's Most Controversial Soldier* (New York: Simon and Schuster, 1993), 397–98.

26. John B. Gordon, *Reminiscences of the Civil War* (New York: Charles Scribner's Sons, 1905), 385–93.

27. Lee to Johnston, February 22, 1865, OR, 47: pt. 3 1247. See also Special Orders No. 3, February 22, 1865, OR, 47: pt. 3, 1248.

28. Joseph E. Johnston, *Narrative of Military Operations During the Civil War* (1874; rpt. New York: Da Capo, 1990), 372. Johnston is also said to have told Sherman during the surrender talks that he had known since Lincoln's reelection that the Southern cause was "hopeless—that they must succumb, sooner or later." See James S. Robinson to "Friend Hunt," April 20, 1865, James S. Robinson Papers, Ohio Historical Society, Columbus.

29. Johnston to Lee, February 22, 1865, OR, 47: pt. 2, 1247.

30. Johnston to Lee, February 25, 1865, OR, 47: pt. 2, 1271.

31. Johnston to Lee, February 25, 1865, OR, 47: pt. 2, 1271.

32. Johnston to Lee, March 1, 1865, OR, 47: pt. 2, 1297.

33. Lee to Johnston, February 23, 1865, OR, 47: pt. 2, 1257.

34. Johnston to Lee, March 1, 1865, OR, 47: pt. 2, 1298. The *Official Records* also contain a "Sketch of Plan of Operations for the Spring Campaign of 1865," dated March 1, 1865, in which Beauregard urged Johnston to concentrate all Confederate forces at Fayetteville, supplement them with nine thousand reinforcements from Lee's army, "destroy" Sherman's army, then unite with Lee, "attack Grant with superior numbers," and defeat him. See OR, 47: pt. 2, 1298–99. Curiously, Alfred T. Roman does not mention this memorandum in his biography of Beauregard.

35. Johnston to Lee, March 11, 1865, OR, 47: pt. 2, 1372–73. For the sake of clarity, I have altered the order in which Johnston presented his points.

36. Lee to Johnston, March 11, 1865, OR, 47: pt. 2, 1372.

37. Johnston to Lee, March 16, 1865, OR, 47: pt. 2, 1398.

38. The battle of Bentonville is detailed in two excellent studies: Mark L. Bradley, *Last Stand in the Carolinas: The Battle of Bentonville* (Campbell CA: Savas Woodbury, 1996); and Nathaniel Cheairs Hughes Jr., *The Battle of Bentonville: The Final Battle Between Sherman and Johnston* (Chapel Hill: University of North Carolina Press, 1996). See also John G. Barrett, *Sherman's March Through the Carolinas* (Chapel Hill: University of North Carolina Press, 1956), 159–85.

39. Johnston, *Narrative*, 389. See also Johnston to Lee, March 21, 1865, OR, 47: pt. 2, 1055.

40. Johnston to Lee, OR, 47: pt. 2, 1453–54.

41. Evidence is sketchy concerning Johnston's precise rationale for attacking Sherman at Bentonville. Historians have been left to speculate based on the general trend of Johnston's thought during this period and on what is known of his personality.

Hughes, *Battle of Bentonville*, 222–23, offers three reasons for Johnston's decision to attack at Bentonville. First, the situation offered an opportunity, "however slim, to wrest the initiative from Sherman and wound his army." Second, Johnston "longed for an occasion to confound his critics," especially Davis, who derided him as too cautious and defensive. Third, he believed it would improve his army's morale by demonstrating that "a calculated offensive thrust, though limited in resources and objectives, could yield important results." Bradley, *Last Stand in the Carolinas*, 143, offers a somewhat different rationale. He suggests that Johnston attacked at Bentonville because it was his only opportunity to strike Sherman before Sherman united with Schofield; because he believed "that a stunning blow to Sherman's army might give the South greater leverage at the bargaining table"; and because, having recently learned that Lee, not Davis, had been the prime mover in restoring him to command, Johnston "was determined to do all in his power to aid his long-time friend and comrade."

42. Johnston, *Narrative*, 389.

43. Johnston to Lee, March 27, 1865, OR, 47: pt. 1, 1057.

44. For comments on the state of civilian morale during this period, see, e.g., J. G. Martin to "Major," March 31, 1865, OR, 47: pt. 3, 730–31.

45. Lee to Vance, February 24, 1865, OR, 47: pt. 2, 1270–71.

46. Johnston to the governors of Virginia, North Carolina, South Carolina, Georgia, Alabama, and Mississipi, March 28, 1865, OR, 47: pt. 3, 707.

47. This figure includes the temporarily absent cavalry.

48. Johnston, *Narrative*, 395; Davis to Johnston, April 5, 1865, OR, 47: pt. 3, 755.

49. John Taylor Wood to Johnston, April 8, 1865, OR, 47: pt. 3, 767–68; Breckinridge to Johnston, April 8, 1865, OR, 47: pt. 3, 767.

50. Davis to Johnston, April 10, 1865, OR, 47: pt. 3, 777.

51. Roman, *Military Operations of General Beauregard*, 2; 390–92.

52. Stephen R. Mallory, "Last Days of the Confederate Government," *McClure's*, December 1900, 240–42.

53. Johnston, *Narrative*, 398–99.

54. The exception was Secretary of State Judah P. Benjamin. One cabinet member, Secretary of the Treasury George A. Trenholm, was absent because of illness.

55. Johnston to Sherman, April 14 [13], 1865, OR, 47: pt. 3, 207.

56. Reagan to Jefferson Davis, April 22, 1865, OR, 47: pt. 3, 824. For similar statements, see Judah P. Benjamin to Jefferson Davis, April 22, 1865, OR, 47: pt. 3, 821–22; George Davis to Jefferson Davis, April 22, 1865, OR, 47: pt. 3, 828; Stephen R. Mallory to Jefferson Davis, April 22, 1865, OR, 47: pt. 3, 833.

57. Benjamin to Davis, April 22, 1865, OR, 47: pt. 3, 822.

58. Davis to Johnston, April 24, 1865, OR, 47: pt. 3, 834.

59. Sherman to Johnston, April 24, 1865, OR, 47: pt. 3, 293; Sherman to Johnston, April 24, 1865, OR, 47: pt. 3, 294.

60. Johnston to Davis, April 24, 1865, OR, 47: pt. 3, 835.

61. Jefferson Davis, *The Rise and Fall of the Confederate Government*, 2 vols. (1881; rpt. New York: T. Yoseloff, 1958), 2:689.

62. Breckinridge to Johnston, April 24, 1865, OR, 47: pt. 3, 835.

63. Johnston to Breckinridge, April 25, 1865, OR, 47: pt. 3, 836.

64. William T. Sherman, *Memoirs of William T. Sherman*, 2 vols. in 1 (1875; rpt. Bloomington: Indiana University Press, 1957), 2; 699.

65. Thomas L. Leonard, *Numbers and Losses in the Civil War in America, 1861–1865* (1900; rpt. Bloomington: Indiana University Press, 1957), 7.

66. Richard E. Beringer, Herman Hattaway, Archer Jones, and William N. Still Jr., *Why the South Lost the Civil War* (Athens: University of Georgia Press, 1986); James M. McPherson, "American Victory, American Defeat," in *Why the Confederacy Lost*, ed. Gabor S. Boritt (New York: Oxford University Press, 1992), 4.

67. Roger Pickenpaugh, *Rescue by Rail: Troop Transfer and the Civil War in the West, 1863* (Lincoln: University of Nebraska Press, 1998), 27–44.

68. Wade Hampton, "The Battle of Bentonville," in Clarence C. Buel and Robert U. Johnson, eds., *Battles and Leaders of the Civil War*, 4 vols. (New York: Century, 1887–88), 4:701.

69. Jacob D. Cox, *The March to the Sea—Franklin and Nashville* (New York: Charles Scribner's Sons, 1882), 168n.

70. Johnston to the Governors of South Carolina, Georgia, and Florida, April 30, 1865, OR, 47: pt. 3, 855.

71. Lee to Davis, April 20, 1865, in Dowdey and Manarin, eds., *Wartime Papers*, 939.

Brooks D. Simpson

Facilitating Defeat

The Union High Command and the Collapse of the Confederacy

Abraham Lincoln's reelection on November 8, 1864, meant that the United States would not let up in its relentless efforts to conquer the Confederacy and reunite the American republic. There would be no need to implement the dire plans foreshadowed by the president's private memorandum of August 23, 1864, in which he proposed that in the event of an "exceedingly probable" electoral defeat the outgoing administration should cooperate with its successor so "as to save the Union" through an all-out desperate military effort before the installation of the new regime on March 4, 1865, for he believed that the incoming chief executive "will have secured his election on such ground that he can not possibly save it afterwards." Freed of the pressures imposed by the political calendar and the need to produce quick results on the battlefield to convince the folks at home that ultimate victory was on the horizon, Lincoln and his generals could now move deliberately to crush the rebellion systematically.[1]

Even as the voters settled the question of who would prosecute the war in the future, new ones arose. For the way Lincoln and his civil and military subordinates went about destroying the Confederacy was as important as actually doing so. The Civil War was no traditional nineteenth-century conflict between two rival nation-states, to be concluded with a peace treaty that outlined shifts in boundaries or the trading of territory. For the Union to claim victory, the Confederacy had to be completely extinguished and the South reincorporated into the United States. Yet the war to preserve the Union had also transformed it, most notably in making emancipation a war aim. Even as he despaired of reelection during the summer of 1864, Lincoln rejected proposals to renounce abolition. Mindful of the advice proffered by advocates of this approach, who argued that by reaffirming reunion as the sole goal of the administration the president might defuse Democratic efforts to play the race card in decrying the sacrifice of whites' lives for blacks' freedom, Lincoln nevertheless remarked that to make such an announcement "would be worse than losing the presidential contest— it would be ignominiously surrendering it in advance." How the task of emancipation would be completed remained an open question, although Lincoln believed that a constitutional amendment abolishing the peculiar institution achieved that goal through legitimate channels.[2]

From Washington the president continued to press for the restoration of loyal civil governments across the South; he remained committed to his efforts aimed at "moulding society for durability in the Union" throughout the South by eradicating slavery by any available means. Lifting the blockade from ports under Union occupation, he hoped to smooth the way to reunion by placating the impoverished. And yet some of the very reasons that impelled him to move forward before November 1864 were now absent. He no longer had to worry about hurrying along the process of emancipation and reconstruction in case he failed of reelection. Although he remained committed to using the erection of new civil governments and the restoration of trade as ways to weaken the Confederacy, he did not need to worry about tipping the military balance before the election. Abolition by constitutional amendment would obviate questions about the continued viability of the Emancipation Proclamation after the termination of hostilities and would hasten the process in the loyal border states, especially Kentucky and Delaware, where efforts to spark state-initiated emancipation had failed.[3]

In his annual message in December 1864 Lincoln renewed his attempts to woo Southern whites back to the Union. Declaring that he firmly believed that "no attempt at negotiation with the insurgent leader could result in any good" because of Jefferson Davis's firm commitment to Confederate independence, Lincoln remarked: "What is true, however, of him who leads the insurgent cause, is not necessarily true of those who follow." Ending the war remained a simple matter for these people: "They can, at any moment, have peace simply by laying down their arms and submitting to the national authority under the Constitution. After so much, the government could not, if it would, maintain war against them. . . . If questions should remain, we would adjust them by the peaceful means of legislation, conference, courts and votes, operating only in constitutional and lawful channels." It was a carefully worded offer, and Lincoln further hedged it by pointing out that Congress would be a partner in the process and that following the end of war his own powers would contract; furthermore, "I retract nothing heretofore said as to slavery." Rather, he concluded, "I mean simply to say that the war will cease on the part of the government, whenever it shall have ceased on the part of those who began it."[4]

Lincoln did what he could to hasten that process. Although he could not risk entering into talks that might indicate that he recognized the legitimacy of the Davis government, he could undertake more covert or indirect efforts. First was the curious proposal broached by the veteran political insider Francis P. Blair Sr. Prodded by Horace Greeley, whose previous efforts at amateur diplomacy had succeeded only in embarrassing Lincoln (and demonstrating again the dangerous combination of egotism and gullibility that possessed the mercurial newspaper editor), Blair secured from Lincoln a pass to visit Richmond. There, meeting with Davis, Blair outlined a plan whereby the two warring sides would declare an armistice followed by the formation of a joint military force that would reclaim Mexico from the French-supported regime of Maximilian. The scheme, reminiscent of Secretary of State William H. Seward's April 1861 suggestion that the best way to prevent war from breaking out was to pick a fight with a European power, nevertheless appeared to Davis to offer an opportunity to open negotiations "with a view to secure peace to the two countries." Armed with a letter containing this phrase, Blair returned to Washington and on January 18 shared it with Lincoln.[5]

Lincoln, who had no use for Blair's Mexico plot, quickly rejected the premise of Davis's letter; perhaps Davis knew that he would. Intrigued by Blair's account of growing Confederate demoralization, however, Lincoln sought to salvage something from the contact. Blair returned to Richmond armed with a note from Lincoln announcing that he was prepared to commence conversing with the insurgents "with the view of securing peace to the people of our one common country." Even if Davis did not accept the offer, Lincoln doubtless hoped that the talkative Blair would share the contents of the missive with other leading Confederates, thus opening the door to a resolution of the conflict short of unconditional surrender. Blair, struggling to keep his plan alive, suggested that perhaps Grant and Lee might meet to construct a military convention.[6]

The Confederate president had reason to believe that Lincoln was sincerely interested in negotiations, for within days of his first encounter with Blair, a second visitor from Washington arrived at Richmond. James W. Singleton was a Democratic congressman from Illinois who identified with the peace wing of his party. On January 5 Lincoln had signed a pass for Singleton to go south, supposedly on matters of business; however, Singleton had also chatted with Greeley about the prospects of a negotiated peace. Arriving in Richmond on January 13, Singleton spent several weeks talking with various Confederate leaders, including Davis and Robert E. Lee, before returning to Washington. Like Blair, Singleton was impressed with the eagerness of the Confederates to bring an end to the war; more ominous was their refusal to give up slavery except on their terms, which included possible compensation as well as a liberal policy on reconciliation.[7]

Lincoln met with Blair on January 28 and with Singleton on February 1. By the latter date the situation had become more complicated. First, a delegation of three Confederate representatives, headed by Vice-President Alexander H. Stephens, had appeared under a flag of truce seeking a meeting with the president—presumably in accordance with his message to Blair that he would be willing to meet with representatives appointed by Davis. Instead of going to Grant's headquarters to meet the commissioners, Lincoln sent Major Thomas Eckert of the War Department with instructions to find out whether the Confederates were willing to discuss peace on the basis of reunion. The next day, January 31, Seward, at Lincoln's behest, left for Fort Monroe, where he would await word on what to do next. That same day the House of Representatives narrowly approved the Thirteenth Amendment, calling for the abolition of slavery; it had been passed by the Senate the previous April. Lincoln had long worked to secure that result, and he hastened to send it out to the states for ratification. To a gathering outside the White House on the evening of February 1, he called the amendment "a King's cure for all the evils. It winds the whole thing up. . . . It was the fitting if not indispensable adjunct to the consummation of the great game we are playing."[8]

At first it seemed that the Confederate commissioners would be thwarted in their effort to confer with Lincoln directly. Eckert, following instructions that required on the commissioners to agree to the basis of negotiations outlined in Lincoln's January 18 letter to Blair, told them that any other talks would be fruitless. When the Rebel trio failed to meet that precondition, only the intervention of Ulysses S. Grant prevented the enterprise from collapsing. After chatting with Stephens and his associates, Robert M. T. Hunter and former Supreme Court justice John A. Campbell, Grant informed Secretary of War Edwin M. Stanton that Stephens and Hunter appeared to want to reach an agreement based on the principles of peace and reunion and that for the mission to be aborted "will have a bad influence." It was a skilled move by the general in chief to circumvent Eckert, who insisted on his authority in the matter; Grant knew Lincoln would see the dispatch. In the meantime Grant also convinced the commissioners to send Eckert a new letter that did much to obviate the latter's objections to a meeting. The new missive said that they were willing to base their negotiations on Lincoln's January 18 letter "or upon any other terms, or conditions that he may hereafter propose not inconsistent with the essential principles of self government and popular rights upon which our institutions are founded." The general trumped the major, for the president decided to meet with the commissioners, although he did not see their revised letter until he had arrived at Hampton Roads on the evening of February 2.[9]

The meeting that followed was not worth the trouble involved in setting it up, largely because the commissioners were not in a position to agree to the end of the Confederacy's quest for independence. Perhaps Lincoln knew as much and used the conference to let the commissioners know just how far he was willing to go to secure that result in an effort to loosen Davis's control over Confederate policy. If that was the case, the plan backfired, for Davis chose to interpret the collapse of negotiations as a sign that Lincoln was bent on waging war to the bitter end to subjugate the Confederacy and destroy slavery. That interpretation distorted Lincoln's position. Although he never abandoned emancipation as an ultimate goal, he appeared flexible about the means to achieve it; once more he raised the prospect of compensation for slave owners. Beyond that he could not go, nor did he need to. Throughout the war he had sought to make reunion and emancipation acts of voluntary compliance by white Southerners seeking redemption in a return to the Union, but he remained perfectly willing to achieve the same ends through coercion. Nevertheless, his interest in efforts to secure that result through discussions rattled some of his supporters. Secretary of the Navy Gideon Welles, who frowned at anything that smacked of Seward's involvement, noted that Lincoln, despite possessing "much shrewdness and much good sense, has often strange and incomprehensible whims; takes sometimes singular and unaccountable freaks."[10]

The intervention of Ulysses S. Grant in the negotiations leading up to the Hampton Roads conference suggested the degree to which civil and military policy were becoming intertwined as the Union high command sought to bring the war to a successful conclusion. Grant himself was willing to become directly involved in efforts to subvert the Confederacy that went beyond the battlefield proper. Weeks after the election he had met with Alabama Unionist J. J. Giers to discuss ways to undermine Confederate rule; however, Giers's contacts with Confederate officers proved unproductive. Grant also instructed General Lew Wallace to investigate the possibility of reaching an accord with Confederate authorities in Texas in ways that transcended mere military capitulation. In light of what was to follow, Wallace's draft agreement proved intriguing. It promised to grant surrendered Confederates "a full release from and against actions, prosecutions, liabilities, and legal proceedings of every kind," adding that civil and military officials who took an oath of allegiance would "be regarded as citizens of that Government, invested as such with all the rights, privileges, and immunities now enjoyed." But Wallace's mission also came to naught.[11]

Grant's interest in these initiatives did not mean a slackening in his commitment to win the war on the battlefield. If anything, Lincoln's reelection proved profoundly liberating to the general. It removed the pressure to achieve victory and avoid defeat simply because of the effect such events might have on the president's political fortunes. That pressure was greatest in August, when stalemate prevailed everywhere. Acknowledging that victory against Lee had slipped through his hands several times, Grant nevertheless told a friend that he looked to the future with confidence: "We will peg away, however, and end this matter, if our people at home will be but true to themselves. If they would but reflect, everything looks favorable." Just over two weeks later he learned of the fall of Atlanta. Ironically, that triumph introduced new challenges, for soon Grant sensed that the administration did not want to risk the advantage thus gained. Philip H. Sheridan's triumphs in the Shenandoah Valley later that month came as a pleasant surprise. As Grant later recounted, "I had reason to believe that the administration was a little afraid to have a decisive battle fought . . . for fear it might go against us and have a bad effect on the November elections." Although he continued to place pressure on Lee's lines covering Richmond and Petersburg, Grant no longer risked much to strike a major blow, contenting himself with incremental gains and minimizing setbacks. Sheridan's victory at Cedar Creek in October completed the process of persuading wavering voters that ultimate victory was certain; Grant made sure that William T. Sherman did not commence his march toward Savannah until after the November returns were in.[12]

With the election concluded, Grant looked forward to mounting new offensives against the Confederacy. Chief among them was Sherman's drive through Georgia, to be followed by operations along the North Carolina coast.

Grant chose to pin Lee and the Army of Northern Virginia in their trenches to prevent the massing of Confederate forces to check either operation. Had it not been for John Bell Hood's invasion of Tennessee, the Union general in chief might have had a reasonably successful holiday season. Instead, he wondered whether George H. Thomas would punish the invaders or let them slip past; it did not help that telegrams from Washington were openly critical of Thomas (even comparing him to George McClellan) and yet questioned the wisdom of relieving the Rock of Chickamauga. While Grant awaited word of Sherman's appearance outside Savannah and was scrambling to mount an amphibious assault on Fort Fisher, North Carolina, reports from Nashville that Thomas kept postponing the offensive proved too much. Not fully aware of the condition of both armies and the horrendous weather in Middle Tennessee that December, Grant was on the point of displacing Thomas when he heard of the tremendous victory at Nashville. Coming on the heels of reports of Sherman's reappearance, Thomas's triumph brought the campaigns of 1864 to an end, leaving Grant to ponder how to defeat the Confederacy in 1865.[13]

At least Grant was able to make decisions largely on his own terms. Lincoln's reelection freed the general in chief from the need to consider the political impact of removing generals who owed their positions largely to their political influence. Such considerations had hampered him severely in constructing a command team in 1864; the performance of several political appointees had devastating military consequences. Yet Grant had bowed to his civil superior's needs in most cases, gaining his point only when Nathaniel P. Banks's and Franz Sigel's military liabilities became so manifest that the political costs of removing them faded away. Once reelected, Lincoln proved far more willing to honor Grant's requests. When Banks lobbied for his reinstatement in Louisiana, Lincoln responded that though he still held the Massachusetts Republican in esteem, he could not comply with the request, for "he whom I must hold responsible for military results, is not agreed." Instead, Banks returned to Louisiana as a presidential envoy to assist in the process of reconstruction.[14]

Even more gratifying was the fall of Benjamin F. Butler. Grant had long looked for ways to shelve the Massachusetts general but was thwarted when it became apparent that the political costs of dealing directly with Butler were too high. Those considerations no longer obtained after November 1864. The next month, after an army-navy expedition under the command of Butler and David D. Porter failed to establish even a foothold opposite Fort Fisher,

Lincoln wired Grant seeking an explanation; the general, terming the foray "a gross and culpable failure," assured the president: "Who is to blame I hope will be known." The obvious candidate was Butler. On January 4, 1865, Grant requested his removal; the next day he pressed Lincoln on the matter. Two days later General Orders No. 1, Series of 1865, from the War Department announced that Butler was displaced "by direction of the President." Lincoln's support of Butler's dismissal extended to his refusal to allow the Massachusetts general to publish his report without Grant's permission. Fort Fisher soon fell to a new expedition.[15]

Meanwhile, the president pressed his generals to continue the pressure. When news came of Thomas's initial triumph at Nashville, Lincoln, who had expressed uneasiness at Thomas's deliberateness even as he wavered on whether to replace him, sounded a note of urgency as he congratulated the general: "You have made a magnificent beginning. A grand consummation is within your reach. Do not let it slip." In thanking Sherman for the general's Christmas gift of Savannah, Lincoln asked, "But what next?" When Sherman informed Henry W. Halleck that he would "make a good ready" before penetrating the Carolinas, the president betrayed even more impatience when he wired Stanton, who was conferring with Sherman in early January, that "*time,* now that the enemy is wavering, is more important than ever before. Being on the down-hill, & and some what confused, keeping him going."[16]

Lincoln was not alone in expressing impatience with the pace of military operations at the beginning of 1865. Aside from Butler, the foremost victim of such sentiments was George H. Thomas. Any reprieve Thomas gained as a result of his victory at Nashville was short-lived. He shattered Hood's Army of the Tennessee but did not destroy it; he pledged to resume operations in the spring. Chief of staff Halleck, not known for his quickness in the field, wired Grant: "This seems to me entirely wrong. In our present financial condition we cannot afford this delay." Another general might mimic Sherman's recent march and move into Alabama, but Halleck thought Thomas "entirely too slow to live on the country." John M. Schofield requested that he and his command be transferred east, away from Thomas and toward what Schofield believed to be the theater of decision, Virginia.[17]

Grant, his skepticism about Thomas's qualifications for conducting offensive operations undiminished by Nashville, moved quickly. He ordered Schofield east; ultimately that general joined Sherman in North Carolina. Believing that Thomas was "too ponderous in his preparations and equipments" to strike southward, he began to strip units away from Thomas's command with orders to undertake the very operations he doubted Thomas could conduct.[18]

Even as he urged other generals to move, Grant was content with the status quo in Virginia. Occasionally he tried to exploit opportunities to improve his position or even to strike unexpectedly at Richmond itself, but on the whole he thought it best to pin Lee in place while other armies did the work—especially after Schofield's command took Wilmington, North Carolina, and began to advance on Goldsboro, where it would link up with Sherman's men as they made their way northward through the Carolinas. He prodded Sheridan to sever the Virginia Central rail line and the James River Canal, although inclement weather delayed the movement. In February, he moved closer to snapping Lee's remaining lifelines by stretching westward across Hatcher's Run south of Petersburg, thereby tightening his chokehold on the enemy.[19]

Grant squeezed the foe in other ways as well. At last he prevailed in his long-running argument with Lincoln and members of his cabinet that trade with citizens in the Confederate states should be curtailed and in most cases suspended.[20] And yet in one case he backed off. Among the changed circumstances in the aftermath of Lincoln's reelection, perhaps none was so welcome as the resumption of prisoner exchanges with the Confederacy. The exchange system had collapsed in late 1863 because of the failure of Confederate prisoners (and their government) to observe paroles, most notably those issued to the surrendered garrison at Vicksburg. When Union soldiers captured some of these unexchanged Confederates at Chattanooga, Stanton decided that something had to be done. Making matters worse, the Confederacy refused to exchange captured black Union soldiers. Stories that Confederate soldiers murdered black captives carried more impact after Nathan Bedford Forrest's men stormed Fort Pillow on April 12, 1864, and killed black soldiers who were attempting to surrender. During the summer of 1864 Grant pointed out that the refusal to exchange prisoners, however harsh it might seem, drained the Confederacy of much needed manpower; exchanged Confederates would return to the ranks to kill more Yankees, complicating calculations based on the supposed humanity of exchanges. Had Confederate authorities agreed to exchange black soldiers, however, the exchanges would have resumed; and in January 1865 Confederate authorities agreed that it was best to exchange "all" prisoners, regardless of color. Had Grant's manpower argument been used to *initiate* the no-exchange policy (as opposed to a description of its consequences), it would have been just as valid in 1865 as it was in 1864—but the shift in Confederate policy opened the way for the resumption of exchanges. Grant worked to minimize the impact of the resumption on Confederate manpower sources by directing that Rebel prisoners who hailed from states under Union control or who were disabled be given priority.[21]

In short, even as Abraham Lincoln waved the olive branch during the abortive attempts at a negotiated peace in the first five weeks of 1865, Grant continued to wield a sword. Soon came news from South Carolina that Sherman and his men were proving skilled with the torch as well. Two weeks after the Hampton Roads conference, fires raged in the streets of Columbia, the capital of the Palmetto State. Much would be written on who or what was responsible for the conflagration, but Sherman did not regret the terror white South Carolinians felt as his army blazed a trail across the state. Nor did his superiors flinch from the result. Hard war and a lenient peace were two sides of the same policy to crush the Confederacy, targeting will as well as resources. "Everything looks like dissolution in the South," Grant reported the last week in February. Orders went out to press matters forward, including the destruction of crops, railroads, and factories. Before long the roads would be dry and the campaign in Virginia could begin in earnest.[22]

Through February 1865 Lincoln and his commanders had pursued parallel paths in the effort to achieve final victory. Even as he contemplated a negotiated settlement, the president urged his generals to press forward. In turn, Grant, despite his blatant if well-intentioned intervention in the events leading to the Hampton Roads conference, continued to profess the credo of the simple soldier, telling Seward: "I do not profess to be a judge of the best civil policy to pursue to restore peace and the integrity of the Union, my duty being to apply force to accomplish this end." During the next two months, however, the delineation between civil and military policy, hitherto subject to occasional blurring, became problematic with the realization that the collapse of the Confederacy would come on the field of battle.[23]

The first sign that traditional lines of responsibility were giving way came at the end of February. During a meeting over problems arising from the exchange of prisoners, Edward O. C. Ord and his Confederate counterpart, James Longstreet, began discussing ways to bring the war to an end. Ord suggested that Longstreet take up the matter with Lee; Longstreet replied that Davis "was the great obstacle to peace," for Lee "considered the cause of the South hopeless." This, Ord concluded, meant that peace was too important to be entrusted to the political leaders of both sides. The men who did the fighting could best bring an end to it—although Ord also thought it might help if Julia Dent Grant and Louise Longstreet, whose friendship dated back to their days together in St. Louis, could come together to discuss old times.[24]

Ord related the results of the discussions to Grant, who expressed interest in what arrangements Ord and Longstreet might make—although he dismissed the notion of using his wife as a diplomatic envoy, explaining to Julia: "The men have fought this war and the men will finish it." But Ord went too far in assuring Longstreet that Grant was empowered to negotiate a peace settlement. Perhaps Jefferson Davis might entrust Lee with that responsibility, but Grant, reaffirming his previous comments, knew that it was up to Lincoln to appoint him as the president's representative. Thus when, on March 2, the Union commander received a letter from Lee that expressed the Confederate general's interest in "the possibility of arriving at a satisfactory adjustment of the present unhappy difficulties by means of a military convention" so as to leave "nothing untried which may put an end to the calamities of war," Grant forwarded it to Stanton and requested instructions.[25]

Stanton shared the dispatch with Lincoln. Although, according to later reports, the president was intrigued by Lee's proposal, ultimately he was persuaded by the war minister's reminder that such questions should remain in Lincoln's hands. Off went a reply, composed by Lincoln but signed by the secretary, informing the general that the president "wishes you to have no conference with Gen Lee unless it be for the capitulation of Lee's army, or on some solely minor and purely military matters"; Grant was "not to decide, discuss, or confer upon any political question" but should continue to "press to the utmost, your military advantages." Another telegram singled out Ord for reprimand. The curt tone of these telegrams offended Grant, who immediately reminded Stanton: "It was because I had no right to meet Gen. Lee on the subject proposed by him that I referred the matter for instructions."[26]

For the moment, it seemed, Grant had to rest content with waging war. Unaware of who had drafted the reply signed by Stanton, he did not associate the president with the rebuke. Meanwhile, he sought to keep Lee pinned so that Sherman and Sheridan could continue their operations without fear that they might run into the Army of Northern Virginia. He remained convinced that once the roads were dry, Lee and Joseph E. Johnston, recently restored to field command in North Carolina, would unite their forces and seek to take on the Union field armies in turn. With the spring campaign imminent, it might not be a bad idea to touch base once more with the president on what to do—especially if Stanton did not accompany Lincoln on a visit to headquarters.[27]

Grant's request coincided with Lincoln's growing concern with the course of military operations. "He has been apprehensive that the military men are not very solicitous to close hostilities,—fears our generals will exact severe terms," reported Gideon Welles. Such contradictory sentiments suggested that the president was indeed out of touch with his commanders, especially in the wake of his refusal to allow Grant to confer with Lee. Moreover, although the president desired a quick end to the conflict, he feared the price in blood. A visit to Grant's headquarters at City Point might clear matters up, especially when Sherman chose the same time to pay a visit to his trusted comrade.[28]

The three men met aboard the president's steamer, the *River Queen*, on March 27 and 28. Accounts of the conversations left by Sherman and David D. Porter have been the subject of scholarly controversy, and yet it is clear that although the president conveyed his desire for lenient treatment of the defeated Confederates, he did not dictate specific terms. Rather, the generals gained the impression that the once clear demarcation between civil and military authority would erode to some degree when it came to framing those terms of surrender. Whatever concern Lincoln had about possible procrastination on the part of his generals dissipated as he watched Grant go to work to bring Robert E. Lee and his army to bay; they ended altogether on April 3 when he walked the streets of Petersburg. The following day he entered Richmond.

Hindsight imbues the Appomattox campaign with the sense that the demise of the Army of Northern Virginia was a foregone conclusion. It is too easy to overlook the strength of Confederate forces at the end of March or that army's ability to elude its longtime antagonist. Lee himself viewed his situation as serious but not hopeless. Unable to draw Grant into peace negotiations at a time when the military situation gave him some leverage, Lee now waited for the right moment to spring loose from Petersburg and Richmond and regain the ability to conduct mobile operations, either by joining up with Johnston's command in North Carolina or by seeking refuge in the Blue Ridge Mountains. To be sure, these military options were divorced from the political objective of securing Confederate independence—or at least the establishment of an independent Confederacy that in any way resembled the republic its founders had envisioned in 1861—but success on the battlefield might create the conditions for a negotiated peace, a reasonable supposition in light of that winter's attempts at such a settlement. Moreover, the abandonment of the Confederate capital and the displacement of the Davis administration rendered it unlikely that Lee would be able to consult any more with his superiors in timely fashion (unless Davis chose to accompany Lee's army).

Grant knew that Lee would move when spring came and the roads dried out. He was worried about how to deprive his foe from seizing and retaining the initiative. "I was afraid, every morning, that I would awake from my sleep to hear that Lee had gone, and that nothing was left but a picket line," he later remarked. "I knew he could move much more lightly and rapidly than I, and that, if he got the start, he would leave me behind so that we would have the same army to fight again farther south—and the war might be prolonged another year."[29] If so, Grant might have to fight the one last bloody battle Lincoln so regretted; it might also complicate the problems of making peace, especially if Grant had to track down Lee's forces in the Blue Ridge.

For Grant to succeed, he had to retain the initiative and plan a campaign of encirclement—either by trapping Lee in Richmond and Petersburg or by forcing him out into the open, blocking his path to join Johnston, pursuing him, and closing off the possibility of his escape. Simply to smash Lee was not enough. Should remnants of the Confederate army take to the hills to continue fighting, the result would be a nasty, uncontrolled war, the guerrilla conflict Grant so dreaded and detested, which would generate bitterness and shatter chances for a lenient peace based on the principles of reconciliation and reunion. With these thoughts in mind, the Union commander mapped out a military campaign to achieve an objective as much political as it was military— the elimination (not merely the defeat) of the Army of Northern Virginia.

Grant's plan took shape in mid-March. He urged Phil Sheridan to bring his horsemen from their position east of Richmond to below Petersburg to cut communication and transportation links between Lee and Johnston; having cleaned out the areas north of Richmond to deprive Lee of the chance to draw resources from there, he now prepared to cut off Lee's remaining lifelines to the south. Sheridan was to sweep across Lee's right, severing the Southside Railroad, then continue westward to Burkesville to tear up more track; he would let Sheridan decide whether the cavalry would then link up with Grant or Sherman, who had just occupied Goldsboro, North Carolina. "When this movement commences I shall move out by my left with all the force I can, holding present intrenched lines," he told Sherman. "I shall start with no distinct view further than holding Lee's forces from following Sheridan. But I shall be along myself and will take advantage of anything that turns up."[30]

It was a most revealing statement. Although Grant was setting forth the basic premises of the campaign, he knew that the fluid nature of battlefield conditions precluded following any set-piece plan; in suggesting that he would be present, he revealed that this time he would not entrust the operation to the Army of the Potomac's generals. Several days later he offered Gen. George G. Meade a more detailed plan and set March 29 as the day to commence the campaign. Should Lee respond to the movement by coming out to meet the attacking columns, Grant would order an all-out attack against the Confederate fortifications, reasoning that Lee would have to pare down his garrison "to the merest skeleton" to form an attack force. "I would have it particularly enjoined upon Corps Commanders that in case of an attack from the enemy those not attacked are not to wait for orders from the commanding officer of the Army to which they belong, but that they will move promptly and notify the commander of their action. I would also enjoin the same action on the part of Division commanders when other parts of their Corps are engaged. In like manner I would urge the importance of following up a repulse of the enemy." He wanted to force his subordinates to exercise initiative in conformity with his expectations by explicitly laying out those expectations—a sign that he did not expect them to exercise initiative.[31]

On March 25, the day after Grant issued this directive, Lee attacked Fort Stedman, just east of Petersburg. He hoped to force Grant to contract his lines to prevent a strike at the main Federal supply depot at City Point, thus leaving the way open for the Confederates to make their way to join Johnston in North Carolina. The attack's initial success proved temporary, and by the end of the morning it was apparent that the operation had failed miserably. But that it took place at all alerted Grant to Lee's preparation to move. During the next several days, as he met with Lincoln and Sherman, he kept a watchful eye on matters at the front. The arrival of Sheridan and his horsemen provided the mobile strike force he needed to turn Lee's right. "I feel now like ending the matter," he informed his chief cavalryman.[32]

Grant worked to ensure that nothing would go wrong this time. When the deployment of Meade's line left Sheridan without the services of the VI Corps, which had served under him in the Shenandoah Valley, Grant, well aware of and sharing Sheridan's reservations about V Corps commander Gouverneur K. Warren, authorized Sheridan to relieve Warren should he be displeased with Warren's performance. Because there had previously been

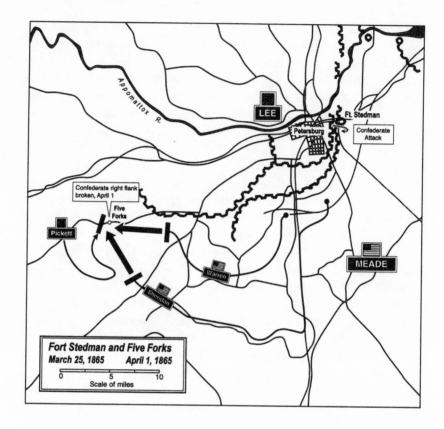

Fort Stedman and Five Forks
March 25, 1865   April 1, 1865

friction between the two men, it was only a matter of time before Warren found himself a casualty of Sheridan's wrath even as the Yankees smashed Lee's flank at Five Forks on April 1. The removal itself, however hasty and unjustified, sent a signal to the rest of the army: generals would pay with their commands if they erred. Had Warren invested half the energy in exercising command before his removal that he did in seeking vindication afterward, he never would have suffered such humiliation.[33]

Grant followed up news of Sheridan's triumph with orders for a grand assault against the Confederate fortifications covering Petersburg. He reasoned that the Rebel trenches were so thinly held that they would readily give way. This did not happen, and one may wonder whether it would have been better had Grant chosen to hold Petersburg's defenders in place while sending more men around the Confederate right in an effort to bag the whole army. Grant, however, had the satisfaction of riding into Petersburg on the morning of April 3. There he encountered an ecstatic Lincoln, who reminded his general of his preference for lenient terms. That the president did not say more suggests that he had come to trust Grant to render those wishes in a surrender document.[34]

For the next six days Grant urged his men westward, reminding his subordinates that it was essential to get in front of Lee and corner the Confederates. First he headed for Burkesville, a rail junction some forty miles due west of Petersburg. Possession of that crossroads would thwart any attempt by Lee to join Johnston in North Carolina. By the time Sheridan's horsemen had secured it on April 4, Grant learned that Lee, looking to move further west, had ordered rations to be sent to him at Farmville, less than fifteen miles west of Burkeville. The next day, upon receiving a dispatch from Sheridan that claimed that Meade's orders suggested following Lee instead of cutting him off, Grant rode forward to confer with both generals at Jetersville, just northeast of Burkeville. That Meade was ill made little difference to Sheridan, whose impatience with the commander of the Army of the Potomac was now legendary; Grant once more concurred with his cavalryman, and Meade issued new orders.[35]

At this point Grant decided to take charge of the pursuit. For over a year he had allowed Meade to exercise command of his army, despite advice that two heads were not better than one. But by now he was well acquainted with the officers and men of the Army of the Potomac; Meade's usefulness had declined, and his poor health offered an excuse. Grant reorganized the men under his command into strike forces, ordering Horatio Wright to shift his VI Corps from the army's right all the way across to its left so it could work alongside Sheridan; the V Corps, now under the command of Charles Griffin, was placed on the army's right. Grant would oversee the operations of the Army of the James.[36]

These moves soon paid off. On April 6 Union forces smashed into the retreating Confederates at Sailor's Creek, just east of Farmville; at the same time Sheridan and Wright reached Farmville. The next day, Grant arrived at Farmville, then opened a correspondence with Lee in anticipation of the surrender of the Army of Northern Virginia. Stalling for time, Lee first inquired as to the terms Grant was willing to offer, then remarked that he would consider a proposal for "the restoration of peace," all the while insisting that he was prepared to continue the struggle. That pretense melted away on the morning of April 9, when Lee's advance forces discovered Union infantry astride the road to Appomattox Station; the rations awaiting Lee there had already been captured by Sheridan.[37]

That afternoon, in the parlor of Wilmer McLean's house, Lee surrendered the Army of Northern Virginia to Grant. The terms Grant composed, however, were no mere military accord. Much would be made of the Union commander's generosity in allowing Confederate officers to retain their side arms and in allowing both officers and men to take their farm animals home to assist in spring planting. But these acts, however magnanimous, paled beside Grant's assurance that as long as the paroled Confederates obeyed the law, they would not be disturbed by United States authorities. In short, Confederate military personnel, including Lee himself, would not face trial on the charge of having committed treason or in engaging in an insurrection against the United States. Grant was fully aware of the implications of the offer; he knew that he had taken an important step toward the establishment of a lasting peace settlement, holding out the promise of lenient treatment in exchange for absolute submission. That afternoon, he ordered an end to the noisy celebration of his men, observing: "The war is over. The Rebels are our countrymen again."[38]

Abraham Lincoln had kept a close eye on Grant's movements following the fall of Richmond and Petersburg. Seeing a telegram from Sheridan to Grant, in which the cavalryman, fresh from Sailor's Creek, concluded, "If the thing is pressed I think that Lee will surrender," Lincoln wired Grant: "Let the *thing* be pressed." Reading Grant's terms, the president, pleased with the general's negotiating ability, endorsed them. Moreover, the surrender agreement helped Lincoln escape the consequences of a rather dubious exercise in presidential diplomacy. No sooner had he entered Richmond on April 4 than he encountered John A. Campbell, one of the Confederate commissioners from the Hampton Roads conference. Together the two men formulated a scheme for the members of the Virginia legislature to meet, not in formal legislative session but as like-minded individuals who would take Virginia out of the Confederacy. To facilitate that process, Lincoln pledged to use his pardoning power liberally.[39]

This was a stupid idea, for it would entangle the president in many sensitive questions. The members of the Virginia legislature could secure the removal of Virginia's soldiers from the Confederate army only if they acted in session—meaning that Lincoln, who had already recognized a group of Virginia Unionists as the legitimate government of the state, would now

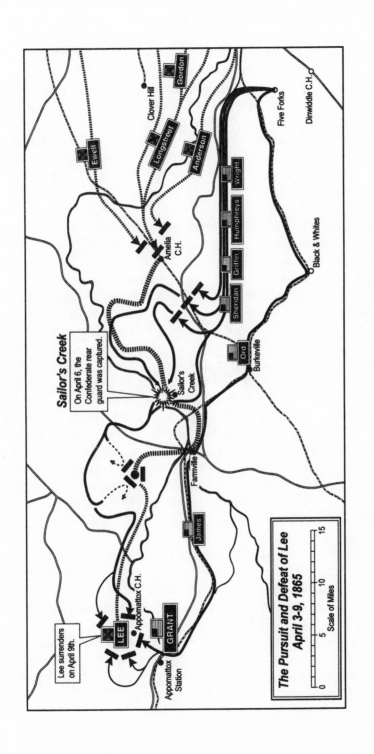

The Pursuit and Defeat of Lee
April 3-9, 1865

Sailor's Creek

On April 6, the Confederate rear guard was captured.

Lee surrenders on April 9th.

Clover Hill

Gordon

Ewell

Longstreet

Anderson

Five Forks

Dinwiddie C.H.

Wright

Humphreys

Griffin

Sheridan

Amelia C.H.

Black & Whites

Ord

Burkeville

Sailor's Creek

Farmville

James

Appomattox C.H.

LEE

GRANT

Appomattox Station

Scale of Miles

0   5   10   15

be recognizing a Confederate state legislature. There simply was no way around this problem for only as members of a state legislature did the Virginia representatives exercise power legitimately. Moreover, the proposal implied that Lincoln actually thought that Lee might escape and that Grant would be unable to catch him. In light of the president's earlier skepticism about the ability of his generals to conduct such sensitive negotiations, this bungling, ill-conceived initiative suggests that perhaps he could do no better.[40]

In the end, of course, it was Grant and not Lincoln who succeeded in devising a way to remove Virginians from the Confederate army. The general believed that the Appomattox terms, embodying Lincoln's notion of a lenient peace, would facilitate the end of the war. He held on to that hope even after Lincoln fell victim to an assassin's bullet, yet he also knew that while he might have stepped over the line separating civil and military policy making, he had not trampled it. He realized as much on April 21, when he saw the proposed agreement of surrender between William T. Sherman and Joseph E. Johnston signed three days earlier.[41]

Sherman's agreement was all the more astonishing because he had assured Grant that he would offer Johnston the same terms Grant had given Lee, taking care "not to complicate any points of civil policy."[42] Sherman, however, even more than Grant, feared that if he could not secure the surrender of Confederate armies in the field, they might disintegrate into bands of guerrillas committed to carry on the conflict indefinitely. That possibility, plus the news of Lincoln's death (which Sherman believed might result in a backlash against the Confederates), led the general to draw upon Confederate proposals to frame a document that far exceded the legitimate exercise of military authority, including the restoration of civil rule, the recognition of legitimate governments, and the restoration of full civil and political rights to all white Southerners—leaving unclear the fate of slavery. Even Sherman recognized that he was exceeding the bounds of his proper authority, for he sent the agreement to Washington for approval. Instead, it was roundly rejected, and some critics even suggested that Sherman was either crazy or a traitor—sparking heated exchanges among Sherman, Stanton, and others. Grant hurried down to North Carolina, informed Sherman that the authorities had rejected his proposals, and made sure that Sherman and Johnston signed virtually the same agreement he had offered Lee at Appomattox.[43]

Clearly Sherman had exceeded the terms a military commander was permitted to include in a surrender agreement; though he later insisted that he was acting in accordance with Lincoln's wishes, Lincoln had not authorized him to act to realize those wishes. Grant had a far better understanding of what the president would allow his generals to do. Lincoln was willing to allow such men as Horace Greeley, Francis P. Blair Sr., and James Singleton to serve as go-betweens, but he dared not trust his generals to do the same— although in the end they and not the various civil contacts brought the war to a close. The reason was simple: Lincoln could not compel Jefferson Davis or his representatives to drop their claims that they represented an independent nation. At best, his proposals might erode support for the Confederacy, but only if they were well-publicized; however, he failed to go beyond the formal documentation to make public a formal peace proposal. Davis would not accede to his precondition of a cessation of hostilities and submission to United States authority, for that would deprive the Confederates of most of their bargaining leverage. Lincoln would not negotiate until Davis accepted those prerequisites. It was left to Grant and Sherman to achieve those prerequisites; in securing the capitulation of enemy forces, they obviated the need for further negotiations.

And yet it is worth pondering the costs as well as the benefits of a conflict brought to a close by the capitulation of armies in the field rather than through civil negotiations. It seems improbable that such negotiations could have taken place as long as Jefferson Davis was president of the Confederacy, at least until after the surrender of Lee and his army. But the conduct of Union military operations from November 1864 through the spring of 1865, though successful in eroding popular support for the Confederacy as well as the ability of Confederate armies to wage war, may have complicated the process of reconciliation Lincoln so devoutly desired. This was especially true of Sherman's marches. As he later remarked, he sought "to whip the rebels, to humble their pride, to follow them to their inmost recesses, to make them fear and dread us." In waving the sword so vigorously, did Sherman allow the olive branch to wither? It is very doubtful, however, whether negotiation before surrender was a viable alternative. Sherman clearly knew how to calibrate his policy in response to circumstances, for in sparing Savannah and in ordering his men to restrain themselves as they entered North Carolina, he hoped to foster submission through acquiescence. "I am satisfied that with a little judicious handling and by a little respect being paid to their prejudices, we can create a schism in Jeff Davis's dominions," he remarked. Grant was aware of the need to prevent unnecessary destruction. Though he had been eager to launch several blows at the Confederate heartland in the early months of 1865, delays in commencing the campaigns rendered them of questionable utility. "They were all eminently successful," he later observed, "but without any good result. Indeed much valuable property was destroyed and many lives lost at a time when we would have liked to spare them."[44]

Civil and military concerns were intrinsically interwoven during the six months between Lincoln's reelection and the end of major military operations in April 1865. At the close of the war Sherman noted "how intermingled have become civil matters with the military, and how almost impossible it has become for an officer in authority to act a purely military part." Grant's own activities during the Appomattox campaign revealed as much. "There was no let up," recalled staff officer Adam Badeau, but just "fighting and marching, and Grant negotiating and fighting all at once." It was left to the generals to do what the president and his representatives could not accomplish—to bring an end to the war through securing the surrender of enemy armies. Just as military events had secured Lincoln's reelection and led to thoughts of eventual peace, so too did military events result in the end of the war itself in the wake of failed efforts at securing that end through negotiation.[45]

Notes

1. Lincoln, memorandum, August 23, 1864, in Roy A. Basler et al., eds., *The Collected Works of Abraham Lincoln*, 8 vols. (New Brunswick NJ: Rutgers University Press, 1953), 7:514.

2. John Nicolay and John Hay, *Abraham Lincoln: A History*, 10 vols. (New York: Century, 1890), 9:221.

3. Lincoln to Stephen A. Hurlbut, November 14, 1864, in Basler et al., eds., *Collected Works*, 8:106; Lincoln to Edward R. S. Canby, December 12, 1864, in Basler et al., eds., *Collected Works*, 8:163–64; Proclamation, November 19, 1864, in Basler et al., eds., *Collected Works*, 8:115; Fourth Annual Message, December 6, 1864, in Basler et al., eds., *Collected Works*, 8:140, 148–49.

4. Fourth Annual Message, December 4, 1864, in Basler et al., eds., *Collected Works*, 8:151–52.

5. James G. Randall and Richard N. Current, *Lincoln the President: Last Full Measure* (New York: Dodd, Mead, 1955), 4:324–25.

6. Lincoln to Blair, January 18, 1865, in Basler et al., eds., *Collected Works*, 8:220–21; Randall and Current, *Lincoln the President*, 329.

7. Randall and Current, *Lincoln the President*, 330–31.

8. Lincoln to Seward, January 31, 1865, in Basler et al., eds., *Collected Works*, 8:250–51; "Resolution Submitting the Thirteenth Amendment to the States," in Basler et al., eds., *Collected Works*, 8:253; "Response to a Serenade," February 1, 1865, in Basler et al., eds., *Collected Works*, 8:254–55.

9. The relevant exchanges are contained in Lincoln's February 10, 1865, response to an inquiry concerning these negotiations; see Basler et al., eds., *Collected Works*, 8:274–85.

10. Howard K. Beale and Alan W. Brownsword, eds., *The Diary of Gideon Welles*, 2 vols. (New York: Norton, 1960), 2:231–32 (January 30, 1865).

11. Brooks D. Simpson, *Let Us Have Peace: Ulysses S. Grant and the Politics of War and Reconstruction, 1861–1868* (Chapel Hill: University of North Carolina Press, 1991), 70–71.

12. Grant to Daniel Ammen, August 18, 1864, in John Y. Simon et al., eds., *The Papers of Ulysses S. Grant*, 22 vols. (Carbondale: Southern Illinois University Press, 1967–), 12:35–36; Ulysses S. Grant, *Personal Memoirs of U. S. Grant*, 2 vols. (New York: Charles Webster, 1885–86), 2:332.

13. Edwin M. Stanton to Grant, December 2, 7, 1864, and Henry W. Halleck to Grant, December 8, 1864, in Simon et al., eds., *Papers of Grant*, 13:50, 79, 84.

14. Lincoln to Banks, December 2, 1864, in Basler et al., eds., *Collected Works*, 8:131.

15. Lincoln to Grant, December 28, 1864, and Grant to Lincoln, December 28, 1864, in Basler et al., eds., *Collected Works*, 8:187; Grant to Stanton, January 4, 1865, in Simon et al., eds., *Papers of Grant*, 13:223; Grant to Lincoln, January 5, 1865, in Simon et al., eds., *Papers of Grant*, 13:223; General Orders No. 1, War Department, January 7, 1865, in Simon et al., eds., *Papers of Grant*, 13:223; Lincoln to Butler, January 10, 1865, in Basler et al., eds., *Collected Works*, 8:207.

16. Lincoln to Thomas, December 16, 1865, in Basler et al., eds., *Collected Works*, 8:169; Lincoln to Sherman, December 26, 1864, in Basler et al., eds., *Collected Works*, 8:181–82; Sherman to Halleck, December 31, 1864, in Basler et al., eds., *Collected Works*, 8:201; Lincoln to Stanton, January 5, 1865, in Basler et al., eds., *Collected Works*, 8:201.

17. Halleck to Grant, December 30, 1864, in Simon et al., eds., *Papers of Grant*, 13:188; Schofield to Grant, December 27, 1864, in Simon et al., eds., *Papers of Grant*, 13:188–89.

18. Grant to Halleck, January 18, 1865, in Simon et al., eds., *Papers of Grant*, 13:273.

19. Grant to Ord, February 2, 1865, in Simon et al., eds., *Papers of Grant*, 13:353–54; Grant to Stanton, February 4, 1865, in Simon et al., eds., *Papers of Grant*, 13:362;

Grant to Meade, February 4, 1865, in Simon et al., eds., *Papers of Grant*, 13:365; Grant to Sheridan, February 8, 1865, in Simon et al., eds., *Papers of Grant*, 13:394.

20. Grant to Canby, February 13, 1865, in Simon et al., eds., *Papers of Grant*, 13:418.

21. James M. McPherson, *Battle Cry of Freedom: The Civil War Era* (New York: Oxford University Press, 1988), 799–800; Grant to Stanton, February 2, 1865, in Simon et al., eds., *Papers of Grant*, 13:352.

22. Grant to Elihu B. Washburne, February 23, 1865, in Simon et al., eds., *Papers of Grant*, 14:31; Grant to Canby, February 27, 1865, in Simon et al., eds., *Papers of Grant*, 14:62.

23. Grant to Seward, February 19, 1865, in Simon et al., eds., *Papers of Grant*, 14:443.

24. Grant to Ord, [February 27, 1865], and annotation, in Simon et al., eds., *Papers of Grant*, 14:63–64; Simpson, *Let Us Have Peace*, 75–76.

25. Simpson, *Let Us Have Peace*, 76. The possible result of such a conference became clear the following month, for on April 10, 1865, when Grant and Lee met for the second time at Appomattox Court House, Lee reportedly remarked, "If General Grant had agreed to the interview he had asked for some time ago they would certainly have agreed on terms of peace then, as he was prepared to treat for the surrender of all the Confederate armies." See Charles A. Dana to Stanton, April 12, 1865, in *War of the Rebellion: A Compilation of the Official Records of the Union and Confederate Armies*, 128 vols. (Washington DC: U.S. Government Printing Office, 1880–1901), Ser. I, 46: pt. 3, 716–17; see also Sylvanus Cadwallader, *Three Years with Grant* (1955; rpt. Lincoln: University of Nebraska Press, 1997), 334.

26. Grant to Stanton, March 2, 4, 1865, and Stanton to Grant, March 3, 1865 (two telegrams), in Simon et al., eds., *Papers of Grant*, 14:90–91, 100. John Y. Simon has argued rather unconvincingly that "Lincoln rather than Grant pushed toward the goal of unconditional surrender" in these negotiations. As Grant himself never framed terms looking to either a conditional or an unconditional surrender of the entire Confederacy, one is at a loss to understand the source of Simon's assertion, which appears to ignore Lincoln's activities concerning peace negotiations between November 1864 and April 1865 or his concerns about the harsh terms he feared Grant and Sherman might demand; the comment is little more than a gratuitous slap at Grant. See Simon, "Lincoln, Grant, and Unconditional Surrender," in *Lincoln's Generals*, ed. Gabor S. Boritt (New York: Oxford University Press, 1994), 193.

27. Grant to Meade, March 3, 1865, in Simon et al., eds., *Papers of Grant*, 14:95; Grant to Sheridan, March 21, 1865, in Simon et al., eds., *Papers of Grant*, 14:196.

28. Beale and Brownsword, eds., *Diary of Welles*, 2:264 (March 23, 1865).

29. Grant, *Personal Memoirs*, 2:424–25.

30. Grant to Sheridan, March 21, 1865, in Simon et al., eds., *Papers of Grant*, 14:195–96; Grant to Sherman, March 22, 1865, in Simon et al., eds., *Papers of Grant*, 14:202–3.

31. Grant to Meade, March 24, 1865, in Simon et al., eds., *Papers of Grant*, 14:211–14.

32. Grant to Sheridan, March 29, 1865, in Simon et al., eds., *Papers of Grant*, 14:253.

33. Bruce Catton, *Grant Takes Command* (Boston: Little, Brown, 1969), chaps. 22 and 23, offer the best brief overview of the Appomattox campaign from Grant's perspective.

34. Simpson, *Let Us Have Peace*, 79.

35. Grant, *Personal Memoirs*, 2:466–69.

36. Grant, *Personal Memoirs*, 2:473.

37. Grant, *Personal Memoirs*, 2:625–27.

38. Simpson, *Let Us Have Peace*, 84–85. Often overlooked in the attention lavished on the events of April 9 is the encounter between Grant and Lee the following day. Lee remarked that had the two men been able to confer the preceding March, they might have brought the war to a close. Seizing upon Lee's expressions of hope for peace, Grant urged him to "use his influence with the people of the South—an influence which was supreme—to bring the war to an end." Lee demurred and did not immediately adopt Grant's suggestion to confer with Jefferson Davis, although eventually he did write his civil superior to press for an abandonment of further resistance. See Simpson, *Let Us Have Peace*, 86–88.

39. David Herbert Donald, *Lincoln* (New York: Simon and Schuster, 1995), 576–80.

40. Randall and Current, *Lincoln the President*, 4:353–59.

41. Simon et al., eds., *Papers of Grant*, 14:358.

42. Sherman to Grant, April 15, 1865, in Brooks D. Simpson and Jean V. Berlin, eds., *Sherman's Civil War: Selected Correspondence of William T. Sherman, 1860–1865* (Chapel Hill: University of North Carolina, 1999), 862.

43. John F. Marszalek, *Sherman: A Soldier's Passion for Order* (New York: Free Press, 1993), 340–49.

44. William T. Sherman, *Memoirs of William T. Sherman*, 2 vols. (New York: D. Appleton, 1875), 2:249; Sherman to Stanton, January 19, 1865, in Simpson and Berlin, eds., *Sherman's Civil War*, 801; Grant, *Personal Memoirs*, 2:518.

45. Simpson, *Let Us Have Peace*, 254–55.

William B. Feis

Jefferson Davis and the "Guerrilla Option"

A Reexamination

Civil War historians have often reflected on the critical events and decisions of the war that, had they been different, might have resulted in a Confederate victory and ultimately Southern independence. Generations of Southerners have also reveled in this postwar counterfactual debate. As William Faulkner described so eloquently in his novel *Intruder in the Dust*, at some point in his life every Southern boy has daydreamed about that fateful July afternoon in 1863, just before Maj. Gen. George E. Pickett's division crossed that deadly field at Gettysburg, and thought *"This time. Maybe this time. . . ."* Standing at the "absolute edge of no return," wrote Faulkner, the Confederacy chose not to "turn back . . . and make home" but to "sail irrevocably on and either find land or plunge over the world's roaring rim."[1] Aside from this famous episode during the Confederacy's short and violent existence, scholars have identified other crucial crossroads at which the South could have chosen a different path and perhaps altered the war's outcome. One of the more tantalizing of these was the Confederates' refusal to resort to a large-scale guerrilla or partisan war as their armies crumbled in 1865.[2]

Instead of surrendering, what if Confederate leaders had dispersed the armies and instructed the officers and men to "take to the hills" and continue fighting as guerrillas? The so-called guerrilla option, the argument runs, was a plausible strategy by which to exhaust the Union armies, undermine Northern support for the war, and eventually realize the dream of Southern independence. Every field, farm, road, and village would become a battleground in a large-scale unconventional war designed to erode the North's determination to subdue the recalcitrant Rebels. And with thousands of men still under arms across the entire Confederacy, the South possessed the capability to prolong the war indefinitely. As one scholar has observed, had the Confederacy opted for guerrilla warfare on a grand scale in April 1865, "the South could have been made virtually indigestible." More to the point, the authors of one study concluded that the refusal to pursue the guerrilla option may have cost the South its independence.[3]

Several historians contend that Confederate president Jefferson Davis was the foremost advocate of this option and that he actually proposed its adoption shortly after the fall of Richmond, when he proclaimed on April 4 that the war had entered "a new phase."[4] Some have argued that Davis even issued a direct order to Gen. Joseph E. Johnston to disperse his men into partisan bands rather than surrender to Union forces.[5] On the contrary, this essay will demonstrate that Jefferson Davis neither embraced nor advocated the guerrilla option as a means to revive the Confederacy near war's end. The Confederate president seemingly adhered to the Clausewitzian dictum—that the "political object is the goal, war is the means of reaching it, and means can never be considered in isolation from their purpose"—when he concluded that extensive guerrilla warfare was *not* an appropriate military strategy with which to achieve the political goal of Southern independence.[6] This essay will argue that instead of advocating the costly and prolonged guerrilla war that some historians believe he endorsed, Davis searched for a conventional solution to the South's plight in that desperate spring of 1865.

On the night of April 2, 1865, Robert E. Lee's Army of Northern Virginia abandoned Richmond and Petersburg and marched into the dark Virginia countryside. Moving toward Danville, Virginia, Lee hoped to join Joseph E. Johnston's Army of Tennessee still facing William T. Sherman's troops in North Carolina. The dogged pursuit of Ulysses S. Grant's troops soon dashed that hope. As Lee's army staggered toward Appomattox Court House, where he would surrender his army on April 9, Jefferson Davis and the remnants of the Confederate government arrived in Danville to coordinate the junction of the two armies. With these united forces, Davis hoped to defeat Sherman and then, using interior lines, turn and smash Grant. While in the new Confederate capital at Danville, Davis also tried to check the deterioration of Southern morale as a result of Richmond's fall with a dose of his own unquenchable determination.[7]

On April 4 the Confederate president issued a proclamation that exuded an unwavering faith in ultimate victory. In his address he urged all "patriots" to remain steadfast in their support of the cause despite the loss of the Confederate capital, the symbol of Southern defiance for four years. Davis placed the evacuation in a more positive light by emphasizing that, until now, Lee had been forced to "forgo more than one opportunity for promising enterprises" because of his obligation to defend the city. Now freed from that burden, the Army of Northern Virginia could once again fight the war on its own terms. In addition, the president believed that the Federals had staked everything on Richmond's fall and that its capture "would be the signal for our submission to their rule." He admonished his countrymen to deny the enemy that satisfaction and to reveal through sheer determination and perseverance the depths of the North's self-deception.

Davis then issued what would become one of his more famous—and perhaps most misinterpreted—declarations:

> We have now entered upon a new phase of a struggle, the memory of which is to endure for all ages, and to shed ever increasing lustre upon our country. Relieved from the necessity of guarding cities and particular points, important but not vital to our defence with our army free to move from point to point, and strike in detail the detachments and garrisons of the enemy; operating in the interior of our own country, where supplies are more accessible, and where the foe will be far removed from his own base, and cut off from all succor in case of reverse, nothing is now needed to render our triumph certain, but the exhibition of our own unquenchable resolve. Let us but will it, and we are free.

Davis also promised never to relinquish "one foot of soil" in any of the Confederate states. In particular, he vowed to defend Virginia, even though the Federals already occupied much of the state and the Confederate government had been forced to flee toward North Carolina. Cognizant of his precarious hold on Virginia and seeking to brace the South for the worst, Davis qualified his pledge to hold the Old Dominion: "If by stress of numbers, we should ever be compelled to a temporary withdrawal from her limits, or those of any other border State, again and again will we return, until the baffled and exhausted enemy shall abandon in despair his endless and impossible task of making slaves of a people resolved to be free."[8]

Historians have consistently viewed the above passages as Davis's endorsement of the guerrilla option. Emory Thomas declared that the address "exhorted Southerners to take to the hills and resist as long as necessary to secure independence."[9] He also stated bluntly that the " 'new phase' of which the President spoke was a guerrilla phase." More recently, William C. Davis wrote that in the speech Davis "was announcing a policy of partisan warfare on a grand scale."[10] In an extreme example of the "Vietnamization" of the Civil War, Robert L. Kerby argued that by April 4 the Confederate leader had finally realized that "independence demanded revolution" and judged his proclamation worthy of Mao Tse-tung and Ho Chi Minh. He went on to contend that the South could have prevailed if it had embraced a guerrilla war in 1861 and waged a modern-day "war of national liberation" against the North.[11] Scholars like Thomas and Kerby have portrayed Davis as so unwilling to conscience defeat that he wholeheartedly endorsed this desperate and radical step. Their conclusions, however, rest more on conjecture than solid evidence. In fact, Davis's correspondence and actions during the flight of the Confederate government from April 2 to May 10, not to mention the "new phase" declaration itself, reveal that the Confederacy's chief executive never embraced the guerrilla option and instead proposed something quite different and far less extreme.

Nowhere in the April 4 proclamation did Davis specifically request that Southerners "take to the hills" and fight as partisans. If indeed he wanted to inspire the people to rise en masse as guerrillas, and if he thought this was a viable way to achieve independence, why did the normally blunt president fail to urge this solution upon his people in more explicit language? Moreover, if he had settled upon the guerrilla option, what prevented him from publicly warning the North that, unless it ceased hostilities, more misery and death would be inflicted upon its soldiers at the hands of millions of Southern civilians? Instead, in the address Davis spoke primarily of continuing a conventional defense, not about organizing or inciting partisan activity, a strange omission if indeed that was his purpose. He stressed that the Army of Northern Virginia could now maneuver and fight, a statement designed to stir memories of the glory days when Lee and Thomas J. "Stonewall" Jackson consistently prevailed over numerically superior enemy forces through boldness and initiative. Even in the dark hours after Richmond's fall, Davis and many other Southerners still believed that Lee and his magnificent army would succeed against the odds. Thus when Davis stated that should "we" be driven from Virginia by the weight of Union numbers, "we" would return to regain the Old Dominion, he was not referring to guerrilla bands but to the Army of Northern Virginia that on April 4 was, *as far as he knew*, still marching toward Danville to continue the fight.

Sharing the feelings of many Southern citizens, Davis had always looked to the noble soldiers in the national armies to achieve Southern independence, not to unsavory and unreliable "bushwhackers." Shocked by the violence unleashed by and against civilians in "Bleeding Kansas" in the late 1850s, Davis had concluded early on, as Grady McWhiney observed, "that wars should be fought only between organized armies."[12] Composed of troops from all the Southern states, the Confederate armies—especially the Army of Northern Virginia—represented the soul of the would-be nation as well as symbolized its power and legitimacy. Gary W. Gallagher has argued compellingly that white Southerners saw Lee and his army as the embodiment of the Confederacy and as the "preeminent symbol of the Confederate struggle for independence and liberty."[13] Davis would have agreed. To him the very fate of the nation rested on "the complete blending of military strength of all the states into one united body, to be used anywhere and everywhere as the exigencies of the contest may require for the good of the *whole*."[14] Even after issuing his alleged "guerrilla manifesto" on April 4, Davis continued to stress the importance of maintaining united and organized forces. On April 18, for example, he rejected a request from members of a Virginia infantry battalion serving in North Carolina to be sent home to protect their families. "Our necessities exclude the idea of disbanding any portion of the force which remains to us," he explained, because organized armies remained "our best hope of recovering from the reverses and disasters."[15]

Davis also warned that sending regiments home "would reduce the Confederate power to the force which each State might raise for its own protection."[16] Already he had battled with peace factions in North Carolina and Georgia who had attempted to "secede" from the Confederacy and negotiate separately with the North and had witnessed an effort by South Carolina's governor to mount a defensive alliance with the militias of three other states. These proposals posed a direct challenge to Davis's authority and to the power and legitimacy of the central government because they involved, among other things, the breakup of the armies—the last remaining vestige of Confederate solidarity and nationalism. Given his adamant objections to these schemes and his earlier statements regarding the primacy of collective defense, Davis was not about to cede control of the war effort to the individual states whose priorities may have shifted away from Confederate independence toward more local, self-serving ends. Davis seemed determined to prevent what Assistant Secretary of War John A. Campbell predicted would occur once the Confederates abandoned Richmond and Virginia. The moment the South lost these important points, wrote Campbell, "The war will cease to be a national one."[17]

That Davis balked at abdicating the central government's war powers to the states made it even more unlikely that he would have reverted to a messy and uncontrollable partisan war strategy, or what one scholar has termed "self-organized warfare." Scattering the armies into guerrilla bands would disperse Confederate military strength even more than the plan to create state armies. Because of the lack of adequate communications in the Confederacy, a guerrilla war would also pose insurmountable command and control problems for the government. Already Davis's power and influence extended only as far as the lines held by Confederate forces.[18] Moreover, who would supervise the numerous bands of civilian irregulars that would inevitably spring up after the collapse of organized resistance? Without centralized direction to ensure that everyone focused on the same goals, the guerrilla units—whether composed of civilians or former soldiers—might tend toward more parochial agendas and adopt methods of achieving them injurious to the cause of independence. This tendency toward provincialism had already taken hold by 1865 as more of the South fell under Union control. "As the Confederacy shrank," observed George Rable, the "citizens' sense of the cause more than ever narrowed to their own states and communities."[19] A staunch Confederate nationalist who had battled such localistic impulses throughout his presidency, Davis realized that only by maintaining a national army aimed at a common goal could the South achieve independence. An observation by Don Higginbotham with regard to George Washington's Continental army and its vital role in the success of the American Revolution is also applicable to the Confederacy's situation in 1865. Higginbotham wrote: "A martial approach that stressed guerrilla methods would inevitably tilt the Revolution in the wrong direction—toward localism and provincialism, with each colony-state devising its own ways of striking at the enemy. Thus, among other things, Washington's army—appropriately called the Continental Army—was a nationalizing factor in American life."[20]

Likewise, the Confederate armies, composed of troops from all over the South, were a nationalizing influence and the most tangible evidence of Southern unity, legitimacy, and resolve. Throughout the war, the would-be nation had, as Lt. Gen. William J. Hardee observed, "staked our all on the success of our arms."[21] As a result, the Confederacy's chances for independence and recognition from abroad rose or fell on the battlefield. By April 1865, little had changed. The Confederate armies still remained the last, best hope for success.[22] And since the main forces east of the Mississippi, not to mention those out west, had not yet succumbed when Davis proclaimed that the war had entered a "new phase," the president was calling for renewed confidence in the armies and for increased sacrifices to sustain them, not for the commencement of large-scale guerrilla operations.

Like Davis, Lee had also recognized that achieving Southern independence depended on the armies, especially his Army of Northern Virginia, and not on guerrillas.[23] Eleven days after surrendering to Grant, Lee told Davis: "I see no prospect by that means [i.e., guerrilla warfare] of achieving a separate independence."[24] Essentially, Lee failed to see how partisans, who had not been a decisive factor in the war thus far, could succeed where his army, whose soldiers had carried the hopes of the Confederacy on their bayonets for four years, had failed. That Lee rejected the guerrilla option before capitulating to Grant and urged the Confederate president to follow suit should be no surprise given his feelings about this mode of warfare. In 1864, the lifelong professional soldier had expressed grave concerns about the efficacy of the organized partisan units established as part of the regular army by an act of the Confederate Congress in April 1862.[25] "The system gives license to many deserters & marauders who assume to belong to these authorized companies & commit depredations on friend & foe alike," he complained to Davis. According to Lee, moreover, the organized partisan units also hurt conscription and discouraged volunteers from joining the army because the lax discipline and lure of booty appealed to many potential soldiers.[26]

Many Confederate officers and much of official Richmond concurred with Lee's assessment. Brig. Gen. Henry Heth saw these bands as mere "thieves and murderers" who "do as they please—go where they please." Cavalryman Thomas Rosser complained that the partisan rangers "never fight; can't be made to fight" and that "[most] have engaged in this business for the sake of gain." Secretary of War James A. Seddon also lobbied Davis to discontinue the creation of official partisan units because they had "come to be regarded as more formidable and destructive to our own people than to the enemy."[27] In fact, when guerrilla leader William Clarke Quantrill swaggered into his office seeking a regular commission and touting the efficacy of his "no quarter" brand of warfare epitomized by his recent activities in Kansas, Seddon recoiled at the thought of endorsing this "barbarism" and denied his request for a colonelcy in the Confederate army.

Fed by reports of guerrilla depredations, the widespread resentment toward partisans in both military and government circles reflected a common view that guerrilla warfare was a reprehensible and dishonorable mode of fighting.[28] Reflecting the feelings of many Confederate officers, Col. Walter H. Taylor, Lee's adjutant, despaired at the thought of becoming "a guerrilla & an outlaw" should the Army of Northern Virginia be defeated.[29] When asked whether he supported the adoption of the guerrilla option after the collapse of organized resistance, Hardee not only bristled at the thought but promised to "fight to put an end to it" if such a conflict ensued. In May 1865, Lt. Gen. Richard Taylor, in command of Confederate forces in Alabama and Mississippi, implored his soldiers to maintain their organization and to allow "no false pride, no petty ambition, [and] no improper motives" to interfere with their soldierly bearing and devotion to duty. "We have but one course to take, and that is to manfully and honorably meet our responsibilities as soldiers and citizens," he proclaimed. In an observation that foretold the success of the postwar "Lost Cause" proponents in elevating the South's rebellion to a nobler plane, Taylor claimed that if Confederates pursued such a dignified course, "even our enemies will respect our manliness and consistency and do justice to our motives."[30] Perhaps the advice given by a Virginian while trying to convince his son not to become a guerrilla at war's end reflected the prevailing sentiments of many Southerners. "Nothing," he warned, "can justify a gentleman becoming an outlaw."[31]

Worse yet, Davis had also received complaints about regular units that sometimes gravitated toward guerrilla tactics and, in so doing, eroded support for the Southern cause in their area of operations. In late 1862 Col. C. Franklin complained that pillaging, burning, and other lawless acts committed by Confederate cavalry under J. O. Shelby and John S. Marmaduke, who he claimed acted more like "old jayhawking captains" than regular officers, had become commonplace during raids into Missouri. As a result, observed Franklin, the Confederate uniform now represented "all the dread and terror which used to attach to the Lincoln blue." During these operations men, women, and children became "objects of prey" regardless of whether they were friend or foe. The indiscriminate terrorism and banditry, he continued, only alienated Missourians from the Confederacy and accounted for the lack of new recruits coming from the state. Franklin probably echoed the sentiments of many Confederates when he wrote: "I do not wish to belong to a mob or an army which, by its conduct, cannot be distinguished from one."[32]

The degenerate behavior displayed by both government-sanctioned partisan and regular units, the rise of banditry in vital areas such as Middle Tennessee, and the nasty internecine struggle raging in Missouri all foreshadowed the ugly consequences should the South rely on guerrillas as the main instrument of Confederate military policy in 1865.[33] As Michael Fellman has observed, during the war the Confederate government "could not control the guerrillas, could not curtail their war on civilians (even within the Confederacy), could not conscript them into the regular army, and could not persuade them to follow orders."[34] Susceptible to the lure of riches gained through pillaging, easily sidetracked by parochial agendas and opportunistic plundering, and operating free of any supervision from a constituted authority, guerrillas tasked with continuing the war in 1865 might well behave the same or worse than their predecessors. Who would prevent criminals like Quantrill, "Bloody Bill" Anderson, and others of that stripe from terrorizing and alienating the Southern population for personal gain or vengeance? But the behavior of these irregular warriors came as no surprise to Davis. "Revolutions develop the high qualities of the good and the great," he observed, "but they cannot change the nature of the vicious and the selfish."[35] Given this sentiment, as well as the prevailing mood in official Richmond and within the officer corps, it is unlikely that Davis viewed a guerrilla strategy as the appropriate remedy for the Confederacy's woes.

Davis and Southern elites had other reasons for rejecting the guerrilla option. According to George M. Fredrickson, Southern elites eschewed such warfare because it would have "turn[ed] the social order on its head." Upperclass Southerners, including Davis and many Confederate military and civilian officials, feared that resorting to guerrilla warfare, which required strong local leadership, would mean giving positions of power and authority to whites from the lowest ranks of Southern society whose values "involved more primitive and less refined conceptions of honor and manhood than the gentry customarily espoused." The status and dominance so long enjoyed by the Southern upper crust, Fredrickson concluded, "would have been put at risk if bushwhacking had become the order of the day."[36] In other words, Davis and other Southern elites had more to lose by pursuing the guerrilla option than by fighting conventionally and, if necessary, surrendering with honor. The latter alternative had a better chance of preserving their dominant position in the postwar Southern social order than did an unpredictable and uncontrollable partisan war. In March 1865, John A. Campbell touched upon this theme. "The South may succumb," he observed, "but it is not necessary that she should be destroyed." Furthermore, he continued, "I do not regard reconstruction as involving destruction unless our people should forget the incidents of their heroic struggle and become debased and degraded."[37]

Those who believe Jefferson Davis proposed that the South resort to guerrilla warfare in 1865 often cite historical examples that he may have used for inspiration. One of the most frequently mentioned precedents was the Spanish resistance to Napoleon after 1808.[38] So successful were the Spanish *guerrilleros* in frustrating the French during the Peninsular War that the emperor referred to the conflict as his "Spanish ulcer."[39] Many West Point–trained officers in the Civil War may have become acquainted with this campaign from studying Baron Antoine Henri Jomini's interpretation of Napoleonic warfare. In his classic *The Art of War*, Jomini described these national or "intestine" wars like the one mounted by the Spanish as "the most formidable of all" because a united people in arms posed such insurmountable obstacles that an invading army would "inevitably yield after time." In the abstract, the type of war Jomini described, which offered the weaker side a potent method of resistance, appeared to be the perfect solution to the South's deteriorating military situation in 1865.[40]

The argument that the Spanish example, as seen through Jomini, would have been a natural model for Davis to emulate rests more on interpretation than hard evidence. First, it ignores the fact that even the success of the Spanish *guerrilleros* depended heavily on the intervention and aid of a conventional force (i.e., the British army). Second, as Grady McWhiney has argued, the Confederate president may not have been familiar with Jomini's works. During Davis's West Point cadetship *The Art of War* had not yet been translated into English or become part of the academy's curriculum. And although Davis may have studied Jomini's writings after graduation, no evidence suggests that he did.[41] Even if he was familiar with the *The Art of War* and the discussion of the partisan war in Spain, why should we assume that Davis came away from his study with a *positive* opinion of the Spanish insurrection? Instead of recognizing the possibilities offered by the guerrilla option, Davis could just as easily have adopted Jomini's pronounced abhorrence of this brand of warfare, which the theorist described as an endless procession of "reprisals, murder, pillage, and incendiarism throughout the country."[42] Moreover, given Davis's conventional military leanings as a West Point graduate and former secretary of war, his desire to maintain the Confederacy's dignified standing and respectability in the eyes of the world, and a realization that the elite-dominated Southern society might not survive such a conflict, the Spanish example would have been an inappropriate precedent for the Confederate republic to follow. Even William T. Sherman recognized that Davis would likely eschew guerrilla warfare because it was "derogatory to the high pretenses of his cause."[43]

The views expressed by both soldiers and civilians toward guerrillas and guerrilla warfare suggest rather that Davis and other Southerners would have applauded Jomini's preference for "the good old times" when armies "courteously invited each other to fire first" over the ugliness of a partisan

war in which "priests, women and children . . . plotted the murder of isolated soldiers."[44] The president and his constituents took great pride in the
civilized comportment of their armies, symbolized by their exemplary conduct
during the invasions of Maryland and Pennsylvania, and capitalized on every
opportunity to use the contrasting "barbaric" behavior of Yankees rampaging
across the South as a propaganda bludgeon against the North. Even as the
Confederacy's prospects dimmed, Davis proclaimed that "our people have
fought so as to command the admiration of mankind."[45] For the Confederate
president to have embraced a strategy that depended on uncontrollable and
unsavory partisans—capable of committing even worse depredations and
inflicting more harm upon the South than the North ever did—would have
gone against the South's treasured self-image as a civilized nation worthy of
respect from its peers. "All Confederates would have found such warfare
distasteful," observed the authors of *How the North Won*. "Such a further
struggle for independence would have been no less an admission of defeat
for a nation which had commenced the war with all the trappings and status
of sovereignty."[46]

The American Revolution probably offered a more fitting precedent for
Davis and the South to embrace when their world turned upside down in
1865. Southerners were intimately familiar with that hard-won struggle for
the rights they believed were now threatened by Yankee tyranny. In fact, Confederate political tracts, newspaper editorials, speeches, and correspondence
teemed with comparisons between the revolutions of 1776 and 1861. Davis
often invoked the patriotic images and ideals of those bygone days, particularly
after Confederate arms suffered reverses on the battlefield, to boost morale
and to show the powerful connection between the two sacred struggles. The
Revolutionary forefathers had also stared defeat in the face, he proclaimed,
but they had prevailed despite the overwhelming odds against them. "To
show ourselves worthy of the inheritance bequeathed to us by the patriots
of the Revolution," Davis asserted in 1862, "we must emulate that heroic
devotion which made reverse to them the crucible in which their patriotism
was refined." The example of the American Revolution would permeate
Davis's perspective even as the Confederacy disintegrated around him.[47]

The War of American Independence seemed to offer other inspirational
examples to Southerners as well. Aside from Washington's campaigns, the
feats of such patriot partisans as Francis Marion, Thomas Sumter, Andrew
Pickens, and Richard Henry Lee seemed to provide ample evidence of the
effectiveness of guerrilla warfare in expelling invaders, particularly since these

famous guerrilla leaders operated—of all places—in the South. Coupled with the more recent exploits of Confederate partisan units, in particular Mosby's Rangers, and the capacity for resistance still available by 1865, the guerrilla option—in theory—appeared to be a potent weapon of salvation. Yet to have embraced partisan warfare in 1865 on a much larger scale than heretofore seen in American history assumes that Davis and other Southerners learned from the Revolution that, after the defeat of conventional forces, guerrilla warfare *alone* could be decisive. On the contrary, most people in the nineteenth century understood that Washington's Continental army, not partisans, had defeated the British and achieved American independence. Moreover, as one scholar has pointed out, in the nineteenth century "guerrilla warfare was quite rightly regarded as only a minor technique that could not carry the day and that was best used to back up a regular army."[48] Neither the Revolutionary experience nor the minor contributions of Confederate partisans had demonstrated anything different to Southern leaders.[49]

Besides drawing inspiration from the tenacity and willpower of the patriots in the Revolution, Davis perhaps absorbed more concrete lessons, and ones that had little to do with guerrillas, from George Washington's military campaigns against the more powerful British. In fact, the basic military strategy outlined in the Confederate president's April 4 proclamation resembles that implemented by Washington to turn the tide after a series of disasters that nearly destroyed his army in 1776. In his address, the Confederate president first put the loss of Richmond in a more positive light by portraying it as an opportunity to let the army do what it did best—maneuver and fight. Perhaps drawing encouragement from the fact that Washington eventually defeated the British *despite* having lost Philadelphia—his nation's capital—in 1777, Davis emphasized the bitter disappointment the enemy would experience when they discovered that the loss of fixed points—even politically and symbolically significant ones—meant little to the South. He had expounded on this theme in a message to Congress the previous November. "There are no vital points on the preservation of which the continued existence of the Confederacy depends," he proclaimed, and "no military success of the enemy which can accomplish its destruction." Not even the capture of Richmond or Atlanta or any key Southern city could "save the enemy from the constant and exhaustive drain of blood and treasure which must continue."[50]

Significantly, Davis did not include Southern military forces on his list of nonvital elements that the South could afford to lose. He realized, just as Washington did after the loss of New York in 1776, that upon the armies hung the fate of the cause. Cities and geographical regions were expendable; as long as organized forces remained in the field, the cause of independence remained alive.[51] Washington's observation that "the fate of unborn millions" depended on "the Courage and Conduct" of the army would not have been lost on the Confederate president. Although specifically addressing the Continental army's role in the Revolution, Don Higginbotham's prescient observation also pertains to the situation as Davis saw it in 1865. For the Continental army to exist, Higginbotham contended, "was almost a guarantee that Britain could not prevail." Throughout the war one of Davis's primary assumptions had been that as long as the Confederacy fielded an army, victory would inevitably elude the North.[52]

To implement this "persisting" strategy, Davis proposed a return to the approach used by Washington in the dark days of the Revolution. After losing New York and suffering a string of defeats in New Jersey in 1776, the American general realized that he could neither engage the British army in open battle nor pursue a static "War of Posts" and still hope to prevail. Seeking to preserve his army but understanding the need for offensive action and victories to buttress American morale and stimulate recruiting, Washington adopted a conservative yet opportunistic approach. Marshaling his smaller force, Washington retreated into the interior of the country and awaited opportunities to strike enemy outposts and small detachments. Russell Weigley described this approach as a "strategy of erosion" whereby Washington would "wear away the resolution of the British by gradual, persistent action against the periphery of their armies." Besides sapping the British will to prosecute the war, Washington hoped to buoy patriot spirits and engender more support for the army, both of which had reached low ebb following the recent disasters.[53] Through this strategy he hoped to "effect something of importance, or at least give such a turn to our Affairs as to make them assume a more pleasing aspect than they now have." His patience reaped significant benefits when he attacked and defeated small enemy detachments at Trenton and Princeton. These twin victories raised American morale, revived patriot recruiting efforts, chipped away at British will, and helped keep the Revolution alive.[54]

Similar to Washington's strategy, Davis allotted the preservation of the Confederate armies the highest priority. Moreover, he believed the Confederacy would have its own Trentons and Princetons, which would in turn raise morale and spur thousands of able-bodied soldiers currently absent from their regiments to return to the front. "The show of resistance," he later wrote, "would have overcome the depression which was spreading like a starless night over the country."[55] According to the April 4 speech, Davis believed that with the Army of Northern Virginia free to maneuver and join Johnston's force, the Confederates—like Washington's Continentals—could retreat into the interior of the country, lure the Federals away from their bases, prey on their communications, and then, at opportune times and places, "strike in detail the detachments and garrisons of the enemy." Although ignoring the fact that Sherman had recently slashed his way across Georgia and the Carolinas without relying on vulnerable supply lines, the president's Washingtonian approach appeared promising. Illuminating the rationale behind this approach, Gary W. Gallagher noted that throughout the war "a protracted conflict marked by periodic Confederate success on the battlefield [had] more than once threatened to destroy the North's will to continue the war." Far from inciting a guerrilla war, Davis—believing the Confederacy to be the true heir of the Revolution—endeavored to preserve that sacred legacy in 1865 using the same strategy that had helped sustain Washington's army during the dark days of 1776.[56]

Ulysses S. Grant thwarted Davis's scheme when he brought the Army of Northern Virginia to its knees on April 9. Unofficial reports of Lee's surrender at Appomattox reached Danville the next day. Although Davis claimed that the war would continue without Lee, he had staked much on the Virginia army's survival. "Had that army held together," the Southern president later lamented, "I am now confident we could have successfully executed the plan . . . and would have been today on the high road to independence."[57]

The rumors of disaster in Virginia forced the president and his entourage into North Carolina, where the Army of Tennessee still confronted Sherman. Despite Lee's reported disaster, Davis still held out hope that the general might elude Grant's grasp and come south. Even the chilly reception from the townspeople at Greensboro, the new government seat, failed to dampen Davis's defiant attitude.[58] As long as armies remained in the field, the president remained sanguine of success. Writing to North Carolina governor Zebulon Vance on April 11, he again revealed that as long as the Confederacy had an organized army somewhere, the cause was not lost. "An army holding its position with determination to fight on, and manifest ability to maintain the struggle," he urged, "will attract all the scattered soldiers and daily and rapidly gather strength."[59] But in his attempt to salvage Confederate fortunes, Davis had obviously forgotten recent history. During Gen. Braxton Bragg's invasion of Kentucky in 1862, a time when the Confederate cause appeared fairly robust, Kentuckians failed to turn out as expected to aid Southern forces in "liberating" their state. This example of lukewarm Confederate nationalism, the existence of sizable pro-Union populations in many key states, and the sheer depth of Confederate war weariness, which Davis had witnessed firsthand during his recent journeys, boded ill for the president's phoenix-like vision of the future.[60] These omens, however, failed to dampen Davis's defiant spirit.

After receiving official confirmation of Lee's surrender on April 12, Davis, Johnston, and Gen. P. G. T. Beauregard met with the Confederate cabinet to discuss the situation. If Davis was determined to shift the war toward a guerrilla approach, this official gathering would have been an appropriate forum for debating such a possibility. But the guerrilla option was never mentioned, let alone discussed. The president did express confidence that the South could "whip the enemy yet, if our people turn out."[61] But by "our people" he was referring to deserters and others currently absent from the ranks, not to a general uprising by the citizenry. On numerous occasions, including just before the cabinet meeting, Davis had stressed the importance of persuading deserters and others who had avoided service to fill the ranks and fight. Drawing these men to the colors constituted a critical element in his plan. The president insisted later that "if the men who 'straggled,' . . . had come back with their arms and with a disposition to fight we might have repaired [the] damage" caused by Lee's capitulation.[62] Nevertheless, with Johnston's men and those still with Richard Taylor, Dabney Maury, and Nathan Bedford Forrest in Alabama and Mississippi, Davis hoped to create "an army large enough to attract stragglers, and revive the drooping spirits of the country." With this combined force, Davis planned to fight his way to the Mississippi River and eventually join Gen. Kirby Smith's army in Louisiana.[63]

As the hope and the means of attaining Southern nationhood crumbled around him, Davis remained convinced that keeping the armies intact constituted the wisest policy. He believed that even if the Confederates lost their bid for independence (a point he was not yet willing to concede), having national forces in the field during peace talks would allow the South to negotiate from a position of unity and strength. "It seemed to me," he wrote later, "that certainly better terms for our country could be secured by keeping organized armies in the field than by laying down our arms and trusting to the magnanimity of the victor."[64] The president was not alone in this sentiment. After Lee's surrender, Kirby Smith urged the Trans-Mississippi Confederates to remain in the ranks because "the numbers, the discipline, and the efficiency of the army, will secure to our country terms that a proud people can with honor accept."[65] Taylor believed that "remaining together in an organized state" would enable Confederate forces in the West to "lay down our arms as soldiers of a national cause with the preservation of military honor."[66] Whether for independence or honorable terms, Davis pinned his hopes on a conventional solution, even while the means to achieve it grew weaker by the hour.

The cabinet meeting, in which Johnston, Beauregard, and most of the cabinet officers recommended ending hostilities and initiating peace talks, ended with Davis reluctantly authorizing the negotiations with Sherman. Still unwilling to submit and confident that the Federals would rebuff the peace overture, the president left Greensboro determined to reach the Trans-Mississippi theater. After establishing another temporary capital in Charlotte, North Carolina, on April 19, Davis spent much of his time on government business and in cobbling together scattered regular units in the area for a conventional defense, not in exhorting the local citizens to arm themselves and prepare for a guerrilla war.[67] In the midst of these preparations, the president and cabinet secretaries Judah P. Benjamin (state), John C. Breckinridge (war), Stephen R. Mallory (navy), George Davis (attorney general), and John H. Reagan (postmaster general) received the shocking news not only of the assassination of Abraham Lincoln but also that Sherman and Johnston had agreed to surrender terms on April 18. The settlement encompassed far more than just the capitulation of Johnston's army, however, as it recognized the legitimacy of the present state governments, guaranteed the rights of Southerners under the U.S. Constitution, and promised amnesty for many who had participated in the rebellion. After Johnston relayed the contents of the agreement to Charlotte, Davis requested that each cabinet officer evaluate the terms in writing, specifically addressing whether they should be accepted and, if so, how they should be implemented.[68]

In the end, the cabinet unanimously urged the acceptance of Sherman's magnanimous terms and each member provided a realistic and dispassionate assessment of the Confederacy's dire predicament. They agreed with the president that only with organized and cohesive armies could the South hope to achieve independence or receive honorable terms. But they also realized that the wretched condition of the Confederate armies and the sagging spirits of the populace had destroyed any hope of forcing more favorable concessions from the North. Contrary to Davis's view, the cabinet saw little chance that a patriotic revival would sweep through the Confederacy, fill the ranks with recruits, and spur them to drive out the invaders. Rampant desertion and the failure of recruiting and conscription provided ample evidence that the people had had enough. "They are weary of war and desire peace," concluded Mallory.[69]

In his instructions to the cabinet Davis never mentioned the guerrilla option. Three members, however, broached the subject on their own, and each rejected it. Reflecting the popular disdain for guerrillas, Breckinridge observed that, if prolonged, the conflict would "lose entirely the dignity of regular warfare" and "degenerate into that irregular and secondary stage, out of which greater evils flow to the South, than to the enemy." While congratulating Davis on his unwavering defense of "the cause of the Confederate States while the means of *organized resistance* remained," the secretary of war advised him to end the war on honorable terms.[70] Benjamin noted that turning to partisan war promised only to protract the suffering of the Southern people with no significant military or political dividend. He also doubted that the populace would support such a war, particularly when Sherman offered terms that were neither dishonorable nor degrading.[71] Mallory offered perhaps the most intriguing reason why a partisan conflict was unwarranted, if not impossible, even if mandated by the president. "Guerrilla warfare," he wrote, "never has been and never can be carried on by and between peoples of a common origin, language and institutions." If nothing else, this comment proved how truly out of touch the navy secretary was with the nature of the war in such places as Missouri and Middle Tennessee.[72]

Persuaded by their arguments, Davis accepted the Sherman-Johnston cartel. On April 24, however, the president learned that the Federal government, led by Lincoln's successor, Andrew Johnson, had retracted Sherman's generous offer and ordered the resumption of military operations until the Confederates agreed to a settlement based on the Appomattox accords. Johnston reported this news and recommended that his army be disbanded and sent home "to prevent devastation to the country."[73] Breckinridge, who responded for the president, agreed with Johnston but suggested that if disbandment became necessary, the men should be instructed to "save their small-arms and find their way to some appointed rendezvous." He then requested that Johnston "bring off the cavalry and all the men you can mount" for service elsewhere.[74]

At least one historian has interpreted this exchange as another indication of Davis's unabashed advocacy of a Southern guerrilla war. According to Emory Thomas, Breckinridge's dispatch (approved by Davis) constituted nothing short of an order to "begin the war's new phase" and "continue the fight as partisans" and that Johnston, seeing further resistance as useless, defied the directive and surrendered his army instead.[75] But a careful reading of the dispatch reveals that instead of shifting to a partisan strategy, Davis envisioned that Johnston's infantry would temporarily disband, slip through Sherman's fingers, reform as an organized body "at some appointed rendezvous," and, along with the large mounted force cobbled together from various sources, cut their way to the Trans-Mississippi theater. "Such a force," wrote Breckinridge in the same dispatch, "could march away from Sherman and be strong enough to encounter anything between us and the Southwest."[76] Contrary to Thomas's view, Davis did not order Johnston to commence guerrilla operations but offered a plan to liberate the Army of Tennessee and allow it to fight another day as an organized force.

With the aid of Johnston's army and the troops in the Trans-Mississippi, Davis hoped to prolong the war until the Federals acknowledged the constitutional rights of the states and guaranteed the protection of Southern property. "The war had now shrunk into narrow proportions," he later wrote, "but the important consideration remained *to so conduct it* that, if failing to secure our independence, we might obtain a treaty or quasi-treaty of peace which would secure to the Southern states their political rights, and to the people thereof immunity from plunder of their private property." Again, Davis remained committed to conducting a conventional war because that course offered the best means of attaining the South's political and social goals, just as it had from the beginning of the conflict.[77]

Johnston rejected Davis's plan *not* because it called for a guerrilla war but because the escort the president hoped to gather for the journey to the Trans-Mississippi would have been, in Johnston's opinion, "too heavy for flight, and not strong enough to force a way for him." Moreover, the general believed that the scheme would have "spread ruin" across the South as the Federal armies pursued the column. Seeing further resistance as futile, Johnston surrendered his army to Sherman on April 26.[78] Dismayed by his subordinate's action, Davis proceeded on toward the Trans-Mississippi vowing to "remain with the last organized band upholding the flag." Later, when the president and his ever-shrinking entourage entered South Carolina, Breckinridge and Reagan urged him to head for Florida and commandeer a ship to Mexico. "I shall not leave Confederate soil while a Confederate regiment is on it," was his caustic reply.[79] A few weeks after Federal cavalry ended her husband's flight, Varina Davis verified that his main objective all along had been "to escape from the surrendered territory in order to renew the struggle in the country still ours."[80]

Some historians believe that by this time Davis had fully accepted the guerrilla option. If so, it seems odd that he had yet to make a concerted effort to rally the Southern people behind the concept. If he intended to rekindle the smoldering embers of anger and defiance and induce the citizenry to become guerrillas, South Carolina—still reeling from Sherman's recent visit—would have been fertile soil for such a plea. Convinced that "no prospect of a successful resistance east of the Mississippi" remained, however, Davis slipped silently through the Palmetto State and into Georgia. The journey to reach the last remaining organized Southern forces, his final hope for keeping the Confederacy alive, ended when Federal cavalry captured his party near Irwinville, Georgia, on May 10.[81]

Toward the end, Davis made some statements that could be interpreted as advocating guerrilla warfare. For example, on April 23 he evinced concern about continuing the war because the "few brave patriots" who fought on would surely die in vain "unless the people would rise *en-masse* to sustain them." Later, during a meeting with several Confederate officers in South Carolina, the president lapsed into a discussion of the desperate days of the American Revolution and expressed confidence that even an army of only three thousand men would be sufficient to provide a "nucleus around which the whole people will rally." These statements, however, do not show Davis turning the corner toward a formal policy of guerrilla warfare. On the contrary, the president remained optimistic that once the Southern people realized the Confederacy lived on through its armies, they would gladly renew their support for the cause, much as their ancestors had rallied around the Continental army in its darkest hours. He believed to the bitter end that once the "panic" that had sapped Southern patriotism subsided, the people would again flock to the colors, replenish and reinvigorate the armies, and ultimately crown the South with victory. Above all else, these statements reflect more Davis's feeble grasp on reality than his desire to initiate a general guerrilla war.[82]

In the final analysis, even as the Confederacy slid toward extinction, Davis did not, as some have argued, become an unabashed advocate of guerrilla war. Like Washington, the Confederate president believed that only through conventional armies could the South achieve its political objectives and take its place among the pantheon of *civilized* nations—even in defeat.[83] In fact, his April 4 proclamation, viewed by many historians as a call for partisan warfare, was focused on the *preservation* of conventional forces as a psychological rallying point for Southerners and an irresistible magnet for the thousands of Confederate soldiers who had earlier abandoned the fight and gone home. As time passed and the goal of independence became untenable, Davis remained convinced that only through organized and disciplined armies operating under nationally constituted authority could Southerners protect their rights and property and secure the postwar dominance of Southern elites, not to mention maintain the white-dominated racial hierarchy in the region. These constituted sacred elements that an unpredictable guerrilla war, waged on Southern soil, would likely alter or destroy. Given these insights, perhaps a fellow Southerner's thoughts expressed near war's end best reflected Davis's true attitude toward the guerrilla option. Resorting to "irregular warfare in detached bands," observed a Virginian, promised only to "reduce the country to anarchy, without a single element of settlement."[84] In the end, Jefferson Davis retreated from the "absolute edge of no return" rather than send his beloved South plunging over the "world's roaring rim."

Notes

1. William Faulkner, *Intruder in the Dust* (New York: Random House, 1948), 194–95.

2. In 1862 Dr. Francis Lieber acknowledged that, although technically distinct, the terms *guerrillas* and *partisans* were seen by most as synonomous. I have followed contemporary practice and use the terms interchangeably. See Francis Lieber to Henry W. Halleck, August 6, 1862, in *The War of the Rebellion: The Official Records of the Union and Confederate Armies* (OR henceforth), 128 vols. (Washington DC: Government Printing Office, 1880–1901), Ser. III, 2:301–9 (henceforth all references are to Ser. I unless noted). See also the definitions provided in Col. H. L. Scott, *Military Dictionary* (1861; rpt. New York: Greenwood Press, 1968), 327, 453.

3. John W. Shy, *A People Numerous and Armed: Reflections on the Military Struggle for American Independence*, rev. ed. (Ann Arbor: University of Michigan Press, 1990), 284; Richard E. Beringer, Herman Hattaway, Archer Jones, and William N. Still Jr., *Why the South Lost the Civil War* (Athens: University of Georgia Press, 1986), 343; Reid Mitchell, "The Perseverence of Soldiers," in *Why the Confederacy Lost*, ed. Gabor S. Boritt (New York: Oxford University Press, 1992), 124–25. Gary W. Gallagher has shed much needed light on the complex question of why the Confederacy did not pursue the guerrilla option. See Gallagher, *The Confederate War* (Cambridge MA: Harvard University Press, 1997).

4. For prominent examples, see Emory M. Thomas, *The Confederate Nation, 1861–1865* (New York: Harper & Row, 1979), 301; Thomas, *The Confederacy as a*

Revolutionary Experience (Columbia: University of South Carolina Press, 1971), 51; William C. Davis, *Jefferson Davis: The Man and His Hour* (New York: HarperCollins, 1991), 608–9; and Michael B. Ballard, *A Long Shadow: Jefferson Davis and the Final Days of the Confederacy* (Jackson: University Press of Mississippi, 1986), 56–57.

5. Thomas, *Confederate Nation*, 304.

6. Carl von Clausewitz, *On War*, ed. and trans. Michael Howard and Peter Paret (Princeton: Princeton University Press, 1976), 87.

7. Ballard, *Long Shadow*, 56.

8. Davis to "The People of the Confederate States of America," April 4, 1865, in Dunbar H. Rowland, ed., *Jefferson Davis, Constitutionalist: His Letters, Papers, and Speeches*, 10 vols. (Jackson: Mississippi Department of Archives and History, 1923), 6:529–31 (henceforth all references are to volume 6 unless noted).

9. Thomas, *The Confederacy as a Revolutionary Experience*, 51.

10. Davis, *Jefferson Davis*, 608.

11. Richard L. Kerby, "Why the Confederacy Lost," *Review of Politics* 35 (July 1973): 344–45. Kerby ignores the Confederacy's political and military situation in 1861, the South's passionate desire to "whip" the Yankees on the battlefield, and its decided distaste for generals who retreated rather than confront the enemy. Of the historians who contend that the Confederacy could have won a guerrilla war, those writing after the 1960s were undoubtedly influenced by the American experience in Vietnam, a conflict that had seemingly demonstrated the potency of "people's war" when waged by the weaker belligerent against a numerically superior, resource-rich, and technologically advanced foe.

12. Grady McWhiney, "Jefferson Davis and the Art of War," *Civil War History* 21 (June 1975): 105, 111.

13. Gallagher, *Confederate War*, 86–87.

14. Quoted in George C. Rable, *The Confederate Republic: A Revolution Against Politics* (Chapel Hill: University of North Carolina Press, 1994), 68.

15. Davis to Lt. Col. C. H. Lynch and Others, April 18, 1865, in Rowland, ed., *Jefferson Davis*, 548–49.

16. Rowland, ed., *Jefferson Davis*, 549.

17. Rable, *Confederate Republic*, 285. For example, Davis rejected Virginia governor William Smith's request for authority over the remaining Confederate forces in the state. See William Smith to John C. Breckinridge, April 16, 1865, OR, 51: pt. 2, 1069. John A. Campbell to Breckinridge, March 5, 1865, OR, 51: pt. 2, 1066–67.

18. Michael Fellman, *Inside War: The Guerrilla Conflict in Missouri During the American Civil War* (New York: Oxford University Press, 1989); Ballard, *Long Shadow*, 61.

19. Rable, *Confederate Republic*, 265.

20. Don Higginbotham, *War and Society in Revolutionary America: The Wider Dimensions of the Conflict* (Columbia: University of South Carolina Press, 1988), 159.

21. Quoted in Nathaniel Cheairs Hughes Jr., *General William J. Hardee, Old Reliable* (Baton Rouge: Louisiana State University Press, 1965), 297.

22. Rable, *Confederate Republic*, 273. Paul D. Escott claimed that widespread desertions doomed the Confederacy because "the South could not achieve nationhood without an army" (*After Secession: Jefferson Davis and the Failure of Confederate Nationalism* [Baton Rouge: Louisiana State University Press, 1978], 128). See also Thomas, *Confederate Nation*, 249–50.

23. Not a few Southerners had pinned all their hopes on the Army of Northern Virginia. Once Lee surrendered, many resigned themselves to defeat even though the Army of Tennessee and other scattered forces remained in existence. See Gary W. Gallagher, " 'Upon Their Success Hang Momentous Interests': Generals," in *Why the Confederacy Lost*, ed. Boritt, 102–3, 107. For a fuller discussion of these issues, see Gallagher, *Confederate War*.

24. Robert E. Lee to Samuel Cooper, April 1, 1865, in Clifford Dowdey and Louis H. Manarin, eds., *The Wartime Papers of R. E. Lee* (Boston: Little, Brown, 1961), 939.

25. General Orders No. 30, April 28, 1862, OR, Ser. IV, 1:1094–95.

26. OR, Ser. IV, 1:689.

27. Henry Heth to John Letcher, April 2, 1862, OR, 51: pt. 2, 526; Thomas L. Rosser to Lee, January 11, 1864, OR, 33:1081; James A. Seddon to Davis, November 26, 1863, OR, Ser. IV, 2:1003.

28. For the importance of honor to Southerners, see Bertram Wyatt-Brown, *Southern Honor: Ethics and Behavior in the Old South* (New York: Oxford University Press, 1982).

29. Thomas, *Confederate Nation*, 247; Walter Taylor to Bettie Saunders, March 5, 1865, in Walter Taylor, *Lee's Adjutant: The Wartime Letters of Colonel Walter Herron Taylor, 1862–1865*, ed. R. Lockwood Tower (Columbia: University of South Carolina Press, 1995), 231.

30. Hughes, *General William J. Hardee*, 297; Richard Taylor to Dabney H. Maury, May 3, 1865, OR, 49: pt. 2, 1278–80.

31. Quoted in Gaines M. Foster, *Ghosts of the Confederacy: Defeat, the Lost Cause, and the Emergence of the New South* (New York: Oxford University Press, 1987), 12.

32. C. Franklin to Davis, November 6, 1863, OR, 22: pt. 2, 1059–60.

33. For an excellent discussion of the nature of guerrilla warfare and the drift toward lawless banditry by war's end in Union-occupied Middle Tennessee, see Stephen V.

Ash, *Middle Tennessee Society Transformed, 1860–1870: War and Peace in the Upper South* (Baton Rouge: Louisiana State University Press, 1988).

34. Fellman, *Inside War*, 112.

35. Quoted in Rable, *Confederate Republic*, 169.

36. George M. Fredrickson, "Why the Confederacy Did Not Fight a Guerrilla War after the Fall of Richmond: A Comparative View," Thirth-fifth Annual Robert Fortenbaugh Memorial Lecture, Gettysburg College, 1996. The author wishes to thank Professor Gabor Boritt for providing a copy of the lecture.

37. Campbell to John Breckinridge, March 5, 1865, OR, 51: pt. 2, 1067.

38. Thomas, *Confederate Nation*, 301; Beringer et al., *Why the South Lost*, 338–43; Shy, *People Numerous and Armed*, 284.

39. Gunther E. Rothenberg, *The Art of Warfare in the Age of Napoleon* (Bloomington: Indiana University Press, 1978), 156.

40. Baron Antoine Henri Jomini, *The Art of War*, trans. Capt. G. H. Mendell and Lt. W. P. Craighill (1862; rpt. Westport CT: Greenwood Press, 1971), 29–53.

41. McWhiney, "Jefferson Davis and the Art of War," 103.

42. Jomini, *Art of War*, 33–34.

43. Herman Hattaway and Archer Jones, *How the North Won: A Military History of the Civil War* (Urbana: University of Illinois Press, 1983), 701–2; William T. Sherman to Mrs. Sherman, July 26, 1864 in M. A. DeWolfe, ed., *The Home Letters of General Sherman* (New York: Charles Scribner's Sons, 1909), 301.

44. Jomini, *Art of War*, 34–35.

45. Davis to Hugh Davis, January 8, 1865, in Hudson Strode, ed., *Jefferson Davis, Private Letters, 1823–1889* (New York: Harcourt Brace, 1966), 140.

46. Hattaway and Jones, *How the North Won*, 702.

47. Thomas, *The Confederacy as a Revolutionary Experience*, 44–45; Rable, *Confederate Republic*, 122–23, 131.

48. See Russell F. Weigley, *The American Way of War: A History of United States Military Strategy and Policy* (Bloomington: Indiana University Press, 1977), 3–17; Mark Grimsley, *The Hard Hand of War: Union Military Policy Toward Southern Civilians, 1861–1865* (Cambridge: Cambridge University Press, 1995), 18–19; Rothenberg, *Art of Warfare*, 156–57; Gerard Chaliand, ed., *Guerrilla Strategies: An Historical Anthology from the Long March to Afghanistan* (Berkeley: University of California Press, 1982), 2.

49. Even the Vietnam War, an oft-cited example of the power of guerrilla warfare when used by the weaker side, was not decided by guerrillas alone. When the end came in 1975, it was not the Vietcong but North Vietnamese regulars and tanks that rolled over the South Vietnamese army and into Saigon.

50. Davis's Message to Congress, November 7, 1864, in Rowland, ed., *Jefferson Davis*, 386.

51. Weigley, *American Way of War*, 12; Don Higginbotham, *The War of American Independence: Military Attitudes, Policies, and Practice, 1763–1789* (1971; rpt. Boston: Northeastern University Press, 1983), 414.

52. Higginbotham, *War and Society*, 98. See also Davis, *Jefferson Davis*, 616.

53. Weigley, *American Way of War*, 15.

54. Weigley, *American Way of War*, 15; Charles Royster, *A Revolutionary People at War: The Continental Army and American Character, 1775–1783* (New York: Norton, 1979), 118–19. See also John Morgan Dederer, *Making Bricks Without Straw: Nathanael Greene's Southern Campaign and Mao Tse-Tung's Mobile War* (Manhattan KS: Sunflower University Press, 1983), 13–14.

55. On the manpower problem, see Davis's speeches in late 1864 in Rowland, ed., *Jefferson Davis*, 342–43, 346, 355, 358–59; Jefferson Davis, *The Rise and Fall of the Confederate Government*, 2 vols. (New York: D. Appleton, 1912), 2:693 (henceforth all references are to volume 2 unless noted).

56. Davis to "The People of the Confederate States of America," April 4, 1865, in Rowland, ed., *Jefferson Davis*, 530; Gallagher, "Upon Their Success," 108.

57. Davis, *Jefferson Davis*, 612; Davis to Mrs. Davis, April 23, 1865, in Rowland, ed., *Jefferson Davis*, 559.

58. Davis, *Jefferson Davis*, 615.

59. Quoted in Davis, *Jefferson Davis*, 614.

60. James M. McPherson, *Battle Cry of Freedom: The Civil War Era* (New York: Oxford University Press, 1988), 516–18.

61. Davis, *Jefferson Davis*, 614–16; Ballard, *Long Shadow*, 80–83; Stephen R. Mallory, "Last Days of the Confederate Government," *McClure's Magazine* 16 (December 1900): 240.

62. See Davis's speeches in Rowland, ed., *Jefferson Davis*, 342–43, 346, 355, 358–59; Davis, *Jefferson Davis*, 614–15; Davis to Varina Davis, April 23, 1865, in Rowland, *Jefferson Davis*, 559–60.

63. Davis, *Rise and Fall*, 679, 696; Davis, *Jefferson Davis*, 621.

64. Davis, *Jefferson Davis*, 681; Davis, *Rise and Fall*, 681.

65. E. Kirby Smith to Soldiers of the Trans-Mississippi Army, April 21, 1865, OR, 48: pt. 2, 1284.

66. Richard Taylor to Dabney H. Maury, May 2, 1865, OR, 49: pt. 2, 1275.

67. Ballard, *Long Shadow*, 98–105; Davis, *Jefferson Davis*, 619–23.

68. Ballard, *Long Shadow*, 104; Sherman to Ulysses S. Grant and Henry W. Halleck, April 18, 1865, OR, 47: pt. 3, 243–44.

69. Stephen R. Mallory to Davis, April 24, 1865, in Rowland, ed., *Jefferson Davis*, 574.

70. John C. Breckinridge to Davis, April 23, 1865, in Rowland, ed., *Jefferson Davis*, 572–73; emphasis added.

71. Judah P. Benjamin to Davis, April 22, 1865, in Rowland, ed., *Jefferson Davis*, 569–72.

72. Mallory to Davis, April 24, 1865, in Rowland, ed., *Jefferson Davis*, 574–76.

73. Davis, *Jefferson Davis*, 625; Craig L. Symonds, *Joseph E. Johnston: A Civil War Biography* (New York: Norton, 1992), 356–57; Joseph E. Johnston to Breckinridge, April 24, 1865, OR, 47: pt. 3, 835.

74. Breckinridge to Johnston, April 24, 1865, OR, 47: pt. 3, 835.

75. Thomas, *Confederate Nation*, 304.

76. Breckinridge to Johnston, April 24, 1865, OR, 47: pt. 3, 835; Davis, *Rise and Fall*, 689.

77. Davis, *Rise and Fall*, 696, 683–84; emphasis added.

78. Symonds, *Joseph E. Johnston*, 357; Joseph E. Johnston, *Narrative of Military Operations* (1874; rpt. Bloomington: Indiana University Press, 1959), 411–12.

79. Davis, *Jefferson Davis*, 619; Burton N. Harrison, "The Capture of Jefferson Davis," *Century Magazine* 27 (November 1883): 136; John H. Reagan, *Memoirs* (New York: Neale, 1906), 212.

80. Varina Davis to "Captain of English Man of War," May 23, 1865, Edwin M. Stanton Papers, Library of Congress, Washington DC.

81. Davis, *Rise and Fall*, 697; Ballard, *Long Shadow*, 141–44; Harrison, "Capture of Jefferson Davis," 142–45.

82. Davis to Varina Davis, April 23, 1865, in Rowland, ed., *Jefferson Davis*, 560; Davis, *Jefferson Davis*, 628–30.

83. Undoubtedly, Davis's rejection of the guerrilla option and the fact that most Confederates surrendered instead of "taking to the hills" made it easier for "Lost Cause" enthusiasts to ennoble the Southern cause in the postwar era.

84. Quoted in Foster, *Ghosts of the Confederacy*, 12.

George C. Rable

Despair, Hope, and Delusion

The Collapse of Confederate Morale Reexamined

Thy wish was father . . . to that thought. – *William Shakespeare*

Men willingly believe what they wish. – *Julius Caesar*

I strongly wish for what I faintly hope:
Like the day-dreams of melancholy men, I think and think on things impossible,
Yet love to wander in that golden maze. – *John Dryden*

On January 1, 1865, an Alabama preacher's wife sat down to write in her diary. How different this New Year's Day was compared to the holiday before the war; even the children seemed to feel the sense of impending gloom that hung over the household and were unusually quiet. Having just recovered from "another of my nervous attacks," she posed a plaintive question: "When each day brings with it such terrible and startling events, what may be the record of the coming year?" Anxious Confederates prayed for peace, sometimes cursed Northern and Southern politicians alike, but longed for reassurance that the Confederacy would somehow survive another year. One thing was sure—the war would go on—though for how long was anyone's guess. Many soldiers and civilians simply yearned for accurate news. "Everything is uncertain," wrote a Marietta, Georgia, woman who watched her neighbors return to homes that had been wrecked by Maj. Gen. William T. Sherman's troops during the summer of 1864. "We hear thousands of rumors—but nothing reliable."[1]

The same was true in the Confederate capital. The government reportedly could no longer feed Gen. Robert E. Lee's Army of Northern Virginia, and street gossip hinted at the imminent evacuation of Richmond. Recent visitors to the gulf states reported the people there utterly demoralized. Even the resilient and dutiful Lee appeared to despair of the cause.[2]

Whether the men in the ranks would stick it out for another spring and summer remained even more doubtful. Veterans who had served for three or more years likely thought they had endured enough; new volunteers and conscripts were in short supply. The devotion of Lee's soldiers would be severely tested again, and they knew it. As he prepared to return from a holiday furlough, a Virginia artilleryman found "many sad and hopeless thoughts running through my mind." He vowed to "do my whole duty to my God, my country, and my fellow man" but could not suppress dark meditations on the future. Cries for peace echoed through the camps around Richmond, and if anything, the western troops were yet more disheartened after Gen. John B. Hood's defeats at Franklin and Nashville. When civilians heard about soldiers suffering from cold and hunger, their devotion to the cause wavered. Even normally stalwart women no longer bothered to conceal their doubts and fears from their husbands. "I am very low down," Kate Peddy wrote from Franklin, Georgia, "We shurely [are] on the verge of ruin. I cannot see one glimmering ray of hope that we will ever have any peace. Everyone is whipped now."[3]

This evidence buttresses the argument made by Bell Wiley over forty years ago that from November 1864 onward Confederate morale plummeted. Although Wiley admitted that there were die-hards in the army and on the home front who never lost faith in the ultimate triumph of the cause, his famous essay "The Waning of Southern Will" treated the mood of both soldiers and civilians in a linear fashion. He even presented a simple drawing showing the ups and downs of Confederate morale.[4] This fever-graph approach did little justice to either the complexity of the question or the inherent difficulty of assessing—much less measuring—the mood of a large and diverse population.

Wiley's study and subsequent ones have assumed that morale rose and fell in response to military events and conditions at home. This was true, however, only in the broadest sense. Some soldiers, civilians, and newspapers sounded pessimistic regardless of what was happening on the battlefield or, more commonly, excessively sanguine and seemingly oblivious to setbacks and obstacles. Such had been the case throughout the war. Gary Gallagher, for example, has shown that Confederates viewed Gettysburg as either a Southern victory or at least not a significant defeat for several months after the battle.[5] At the beginning of 1865, many Confederates both inside and outside the army still believed their fledgling nation could win its independence.

Imagination and rationalization encouraged wishful thinking about the immediate future. Beset by swirling rumors and false reports of Federal defeats, unswerving patriots found grounds for hope during the war's gloomi-est days. Thus morale did not collapse in 1865, as has been commonly asserted. Commitment to the Confederacy proved remarkably resilient, yet events that caused some people to despair only seemed to redouble the enthusiasm of others. Rationalizations and wishful thinking helped citizens hang onto hope even in the absence of any tangible reasons to do so.

Obviously, 1864 was a disastrous year for Confederate arms. As the year ended on a "chill and damp day" in Columbia, South Carolina, seventeen-year-old Emma LeConte worried that Sherman's troops were "preparing to hurl destruction upon the State they hate most of all." Physically and emotionally exhausted people had few psychological reserves left except a "dogged, sullen resistance," yet she believed in a "Providence who fights for those who are struggling for freedom." New Year's Day sunshine brightened her mood and helped her "throw off the sad memories I was brooding over and hope for better things." Newspapers across the Confederacy echoed and amplified these sentiments. Despite setbacks, the Lord would still bless the Southern people, a Richmond editor maintained. After all, Lee's men were still holding their lines around Petersburg, and Grant's repeated efforts to flank them out of Richmond had failed. The Yankees had sustained heavy losses without capturing the Confederate capital. The Southern people, the *Richmond Whig* declared, stealing a phrase from John Bunyan, should therefore drag themselves from their "slough of despond." Indeed, civilian determination remained the key to victory. According to the *Lynchburg Virginian*, it was simply a matter of will: "Let every man resolve to conquer or perish, and when this resolution shall be made known at the North, peace and independence will be virtually achieved."[6]

Confederates had endured great hardship but now presumably stood on the threshold of achieving independence. The armies were better supplied than at the beginning of the war, a Georgia editor claimed, and there were enough men in the ranks to defeat the Federals. The Southern people had proven their mettle by making countless sacrifices for the cause. Even a recent surge in gold prices and the steady depreciation of Confederate currency were not reasons to despair. Gold was but a single item of commerce, and the Southern states' real wealth lay in fertile land and productive slaves. Victory did not always go to the side with the warmest uniforms, most guns, or even strongest divisions. The Yankees had placed too much faith in their superior numbers and had forgotten how often weaker nations prevailed in protracted wars.[7]

Nor was the military situation nearly as gloomy as the ever-present Cassandras believed. On New Year's Day, a rumor circulated in Richmond that General Hood was no longer retreating with his tattered legions but had soundly whipped the Federals under Maj. Gen. George H. Thomas. Although many people had grown skeptical of such reports, the war-weary admitted that any good news—whether reliable or not—lifted their spirits.[8] Even the War Department clerk John Beauchamp Jones, who recorded events in his diary with a world-weary cynicism and who doubted that Grant's spring offensive could be stopped, noted how much faith everyone—including himself—still had in General Lee. One of Lee's staff officers was sure that the army would come through the spring campaign "with flying colors." Regimental and brigade meetings deplored talk of submission and expressed confidence that the new year would mark a triumph for Confederate arms. Resolutions routinely praised Lee and President Jefferson Davis while denouncing any editors, politicians, or demagogues who attempted to divide the people in this hour of peril. Newspapers and members of Congress presented reports of these meetings as evidence of the army's unswerving determination to fight on. And optimism would come easier as the weather improved. On a still wintry but sunny day, a Texas private in the Army of Northern Virginia imagined returning home "to chat over many dangers and difficulties . . . under the FREE and independent FLAG of the SOUTHERN CONFEDERACY."[9]

At this stage of the war, Confederates often exaggerated the importance of relatively minor victories. When an amphibious Federal assault on Fort Fisher near Wilmington, North Carolina, failed miserably on Christmas Day 1864, many Rebels rejoiced as if a great battle had been won. Editors especially relished the defeat of their bête noire Benjamin F. Butler—the scourge of New Orleans women but a general who was incompetent to lead troops against Southern men. The scattering of the Federal fleet was interpreted as yet another sign of divine favor. The Almighty had sent a gale to defeat the enemy's "great Armada," North Carolinian Catherine Edmondston maintained; "God's hand" had been apparent" through the entire operation. With more hopefulness than discernment, Confederate minister James M. Mason wrote from London that the Federal repulse in North Carolina would offset Sherman's capture of Savannah and Hood's recent defeats in shaping European opinion about Confederate prospects.[10]

"The soldiers are not demoralized," Mary Chesnut declared—though with how much conviction is difficult to say. As troops changed trains in Columbia, South Carolina, she commented, "Their shouts as they go by gladden my heart." And if the soldiers had not given up hope, neither should the people at home. Indeed, the men's sterling example should silence the croakers and inspire the downhearted. In Richmond, Congressman Warren Akin of Georgia heard that General Lee saw no reason for gloom because the army was in better shape than it had been a year before.[11]

Whether Lee either believed this or made such a statement is doubtful. In early February, his thinly clad men were shivering in the Petersburg trenches and some had been without meat for three days. Yet even officers who should have known better still maintained that supply problems could be easily remedied. There would be more than enough food, Lt. Gen. James Longstreet suggested, if the government would only pay for provisions in gold. Farmers would then eagerly cross enemy lines to bring in their produce. Lee patiently explained to Longstreet that the treasury did not have the gold.[12]

Poorly clothed and fed troops, who had not been paid recently and who had learned about suffering back home, often deserted. President Jefferson Davis agreed to extend a thirty-day amnesty for all deserters in hopes of reversing this flow, but Lee's use of words and phrases such as "perhaps" and "may expect" implies that no great results were anticipated. Lee claimed that hundreds of men had deserted, but the actual numbers are elusive. One Mississippi soldier doubted that the officers had reported all the men who had left. In late March Lee warned his troops—and the note of desperation was painfully clear—that recommending desertion even in jest was a capital offense.[13]

Newspaper editors and others pressed the government to strengthen the army but offered no practical means. Despite Secretary of War James A. Seddon's call for more vigorous enforcement of the Conscription Acts, there were few able-bodied fellows left to draft. An imaginative North Carolinian urged President Davis to offer fifty acres and a slave to all volunteers. This would give more white men a direct interest in slavery and scotch talk of a "rich man's war and a poor man's fight." Should the same terms be tendered to enemy deserters, half of Grant's and Sherman's men would supposedly flock to the Confederate ranks; "we can command thousands of men from Ireland, Germany, Poland, Austria, England, and France by offering them a home in the sunny South and a servant." Yet politicians still fussed over draft exemptions for overseers, legislatures still tried to shield state officials from the draft, and die-hard libertarians still argued that the government should rely on volunteers.[14]

The course of the war soon caught up with these stale arguments, and events overtook the dreams of Confederates who remained convinced that somehow the contest could be won despite the long odds. After the recent crowing over the defeat of Butler, the fall of Fort Fisher on January 15 seemed a particularly devastating blow to public confidence. The anticipated loss of the port of Wilmington would make the Federal blockade virtually complete. As a consequence, the sale of taxable Confederate bonds had ceased, Treasury Secretary George A. Trenholm admitted to Congress. Words such as "disaster," "gloom," and "depression" appeared in many comments about this stunning and unexpected loss.[15]

Even such a military catastrophe, however, did not radically change the thinking of fervent patriots who quickly recovered their psychological equilibrium. Several editors maintained that the end of blockade running could prove a blessing because all the Confederacy's resources would now be devoted to fighting Union armies in the interior. Some ladies might not be able to buy hat pins, ribbons, or fancy laces, but the loss of seaboard cities would hardly prove fatal. Congress had recently declared that the war must continue, and the Southern people were standing firm, Mason wrote cheerfully from London.[16] Holding Fort Fisher had once seemed a major accomplishment, but its loss was now dismissed as a matter of minor importance.

Sherman's devastation of Georgia and the beginning of his march into the Carolinas posed a much larger challenge for Confederates trying to look on the bright side of things. What Mark Grimsley has termed a "hard war" against Southern civilians had perhaps so destroyed people's psychological equilibrium that they became more prone to grasping at flimsy rationalizations and indulging in wishful thinking. Or perhaps their anger redoubled their determination. Whichever the case might be, even the optimists agreed that somehow Sherman must be stopped. South Carolina governor Andrew G. Magrath advised his state's congressmen and senators to demand more troops for the defense of Charleston. Conferring with President Davis, however, accomplished nothing because Lee feared that weakening his army would doom Richmond. Turning Lee's argument on its head, Magrath told Davis that if Charleston fell, so would the capital. "I know there are some who have a vague idea that the cause is not lost while there is an Army," he observed pointedly. "Such persons however argue from their hopes, not from facts. You can not have an Army if you lose the states which give you the men & the means . . . [to] support the army."[17]

Not only did many Confederates claim that the loss of cities and even states would not be calamitous, but some hung their hopes on the merest rumor that Sherman had been delayed in his drive through South Carolina. "So

I indulge fond fancies—to have the pang of ruin come once more," Mary Chesnut perceptively confessed. In Columbia, several women organized a bazaar to raise money for soldiers' families. Grace Elmore thought the people resembled those French aristocrats imprisoned in the Bastille who had adopted a "philosophical" attitude and had focused on anything that seemed "cheerful and bright" to help them forget their troubles. "We romp with children, receive our friends, and eat our dinner, just as tho' Sherman were a thousand miles away instead of only two hundred." As blue columns feinted toward Charleston and then advanced on the South Carolina capital, false reports that Confederate cavalry had slowed the Federal juggernaut and that the city was still holding out offered a few moments of cheer during an otherwise bleak month. When news finally arrived that Columbia had been captured and burned, Catherine Edmondston refused to believe it, then hoped it was mere rumor, but finally acknowledged that only God could save the Confederacy.[18]

This reluctance to face reality only intensified the anguish—especially when Charleston was evacuated on the same day as Columbia's capitulation. From South Carolina civilians who feared that Federal raiders might rampage across the entire state, to a Charleston refugee who believed that Lee's army was now doomed, to a War Department official who worried that the Confederacy's end was "swiftly approaching," a pervading sense of hopelessness began to spread. Failing to take much comfort in the fact that her husband was still safe, Mary Chesnut offered a terse epitaph: "Our world has gone to destruction."[19]

Soon Sherman would be in North Carolina. Perhaps muddy roads would slow his progress, and Lee hoped that Gen. P. G. T. Beauregard's troops could "destroy or remove all provisions in his [Sherman's] route." Lee planned to gather the scattered Confederate forces and strike a blow before Sherman could join Grant.[20] So far, as several editors pointed out, Sherman had been a successful "raider," but whether he was a "fighter" remained to be seen. His campaigns in Georgia and South Carolina had created a "braggart confidence" among the Federals, the *Richmond Whig* sniffed. But from now on, the Confederate press should supply no information on his movements to the Yankees.

"We intend to tell them only one thing . . . that Sherman's army will be met, defeated, and probably destroyed." Why the editor bothered to add the qualifier "probably" is a mystery. Sherman would soon overtake the retreating Confederates, but then Beauregard would suddenly turn and maul him. With

Sherman whipped, the Yankees would be finished. According to a patriotic Tennessee refugee, God simply would not allow Sherman to continue on his path of destruction and terror. And the Lord's instrument, as always, would be General Lee. Richmond might be temporarily lost, but Lee would crush Sherman, the capital would be liberated, and Southern independence won. Thus Col. Walter Taylor sketched out the fantastic possibilities.[21]

If the armies could still be supplied with food and arms and Lee remained the Southern nation's invincible guardian, the explanation for all the recent disasters must lie elsewhere. For disgruntled Confederates searching for a scapegoat, Jefferson Davis filled the bill. The president's patriotism was undeniable, but so was his failure as a political and military leader. Davis's poor health, strong prejudices, and forbidding personality hampered his ability to work with prickly, egotistical generals and politicians. He became obsessed with having the last word in any controversy and spent too much time worrying about administrative details. His relationship with Congress had deteriorated to the point that a routine motion in the House of Representatives to pay a courtesy call at the Executive Mansion was met with cries of "no, no," and had to be decided by a roll-call vote.

Old nemeses such as Vice-President Alexander H. Stephens and Governor Joseph E. Brown of Georgia relentlessly blasted Davis and blamed him for each defeat. Newspaper critics exhausted their acerbic vocabularies in attacking the administration. Out of patience with libertarian hairsplitters, the president waspishly accused his enemies of "magnifying every reverse" to sow the "seeds of disintegration." Yet even to his own cabinet, Davis seemed to be a man adrift with no plan to stop the Federal offensives now striking at the very heart of the Confederacy. In early January a Georgia regiment reportedly cheered the false rumor that the president had died.[22]

Denying that their attacks heartened the enemy and depressed the Southern people, Davis's critics blamed public demoralization on what a Richmond editor termed the "prevailing mismanagement and incompetence on the part of the Executive authority." All that was needed was sufficient energy and judgment to muster the Confederacy's material and human resources for a final stand against the Yankees. The missing element was leadership. Speaker of the House Thomas S. Bocock of Virginia warned the president that Congress had lost confidence in the cabinet. When the ailing and unhappy Seddon asked to leave the administration in late January, Davis hesitated to accept the resignation for fear of appearing to cave under congressional pressure. Yet he had little choice but to accede and therefore chose the capable John C. Breckinridge as his new secretary of war. The president's enemies would not be mollified, however, and Robert Toombs declared that "nothing can save us but the overthrow of Davis, and that must come quickly to be of any service."[23]

By February and March public frustration with Congress had also reached a boiling point. Endless and often tedious debate while enemy armies drove deeper into Confederate territory had not impressed anyone. To frustrated patriots, Congress seemed dominated by second-raters and laggards. A pack of "cowards," thundered Chief of Ordnance Josiah Gorgas, who fantasized about a few senators being "taken out & hung or shot." To Catherine Edmondston, the deficiencies of the political class were palpable: "When we gain our Independence it will be in spite of our rulers!" The conditional "when" was significant because her statement assumed that only a few shortsighted congressmen stood in the way of victory. Nor was she alone in holding such views. To a Rome, Georgia, editor the solution to the nation's woes was equally obvious: "If Congress would . . . say, this is a war in which every man that is physically able should fight his equal share and every man who is pecuniarily able, shall pay his equal share of expenses—the people should be satisfied and contented, and press the work through with a hearty good will."[24]

If the people were demoralized, were not their leaders to blame? Should the war be lost, would not the politicians be held responsible? "The revolution has not produced a man," one disaffected congressman groused. Loose talk about the need for a dictator had long circulated in Richmond, though as Gorgas wisely pointed out, whether anyone else would have made a better president than Davis was difficult to say. To the most ardent Confederate nationalists, victory was still attainable if ordinary citizens did not give up hope. Even the naysayers never seemed to lose faith in the common people, and a reversal of fortune might still be possible given better leadership.[25]

Disenchantment with the administration appeared to be confined mainly to elite circles. One editor dismissed Davis's critics as "malcontents, traducers, friends of the North in disguise; and a host of sickly, timid, apprehensive men who have become their dupes and instruments." The president appeared to be much more unpopular with certain politicians and generals than with the public at large. Admirers still compared him to George Washington, a leader who had been greatly maligned during the darkest days of an earlier revolution. Indeed, many newspapers remained loyal to the administration and sanguine about Confederate prospects right up to the end. But then, this was an era in which true cynicism was rare and patriotism was a common and simple emotion. "I love and honor my president and I trust my generals," Mary Chesnut declared, and many ordinary citizens would have echoed these sentiments.[26]

Such talk was easy enough for civilians far removed from combat. After listening to a female cousin denounce "whitelivered men," a Confederate artilleryman wondered "how she would face a Yankee battery." Yet this same soldier refused to abandon his post. He prayed for strength although he hardly expected to live through another year of war. Simple assertions that God favored the Confederacy had given way to a more complex theology in which the Almighty might use the devilish Yankees to scourge Southern sinners.[27]

Perhaps the generals and politicians were not entirely responsible for all the recent losses; perhaps the people themselves had failed the test of public virtue. "Immorality sweeps over the land and religion burns dimly in the misty atmosphere," a Tennessee woman lamented. Selfishness, hoarding and extortion had wrecked the economy. "There is no forgiveness for political sins," a South Carolina editor warned, "and the results will as certainly follow as if there had been no repentance." Among people who had somehow managed to evade wartime sacrifices, a shocking decadence prevailed. The usual round of New Year's receptions and dress balls occurred; the partygoers feasted on delicacies while Confederate soldiers went hungry. The Richmond elite appeared determined to dance on the nation's grave. After an evening of cards and light conversation, however, a Tennessee woman who was a refugee in a small Georgia town defended such entertainment as a psychological necessity: "The only thing I like about it is I never have a moment to think, and that certainly appears to me like a blessing now. Were I to think much I would go crazy."[28]

Simply reading newspapers, or listening to soldiers, or trying to buy food gave Confederates reasons for despair. Yet by not thinking about such things too much or too clearly, they clung to delusive hopes. Even those who had not brushed up on their Shakespeare recently were familiar with the catchphrase about making the wish father to the thought. And the greater their devotion to the Southern cause, the more likely they were to ignore or explain away unpleasant realities. As social psychologists and political scientists have discovered, wishful thinking in a political context helps people cope with current difficulties and fear of the future by shutting out disturbing facts and events. Even when citizens have access to accurate information, wishful thinking still shapes expectations.[29] Although modern studies have described wishful thinking as pervasive among voters, the distortion of political reality in most cases is limited. During the Confederacy's final days, however, wishful thinking among white Southerners sometimes became a blindness to reality that turned into sheer fantasy about how independence could still be won.

As the military situation deteriorated, many people searched desperately not only for explanations and scapegoats but for a deus ex machina. Senator Louis T. Wigfall had consistently supported Gen. Joseph E. Johnston in a running feud with Jefferson Davis. Mary Chesnut satirized the Texan's position: "Make Joe Johnston dictator, and all will be well." Johnston remained a popular figure in Congress and among Confederates generally. Davis's critics had long castigated the president for preventing Johnston from displaying his military genius and were quick to describe all the victories that would have been won had Johnston only been given unfettered responsibility in an important command. Administration opponents still believed that "Uncle Joe" would have held on to Atlanta. Both the House and Senate adopted resolutions calling for Johnston's return to what was left of the Army of Tennessee, and several senators petitioned Lee for the same purpose. Governors and state legislatures agreed that this appointment would redeem Confederate fortunes at the eleventh hour.[30]

Lee had a higher opinion of Johnston than he would ever dare confide to Jefferson Davis. James Longstreet, Wade Hampton, and Howell Cobb all believed that bringing back Johnston would restore public confidence and boost morale among the troops assigned to stop Sherman. After Lee diplomatically persuaded Davis to allow Johnston's return to command, a Georgia surgeon who had served with the Army of Tennessee since Bragg's invasion of Kentucky spoke for the wild-eyed optimists: "Evry face looks bright and cheerfull. You need not doubt our ability to whip Shearman. We will have in a short time a splendid army, better if possible than we have had before." The egotistical Johnston, who in parlor colloquies could wax eloquent on Stonewall Jackson's blunders and Lee's mistakes, thought his reappointment had come too late to do any good and still shied away from responsibility. Even at this desperate stage of the war, both Davis and Johnston remained obsessed with scoring points against each other by dredging up old controversies.[31]

However much faith loyal Confederates still placed in Johnston, it could hardly match their unswerving confidence in Lee. While Lee and his army remained in the field, victory seemed possible, yea probable. Unfortunately, the Confederacy had not fully benefited from the Virginian's talents. As members of Congress grew increasingly critical of the president, they decided that making Lee general in chief could reverse the tide of recent defeats. No longer would strategic blunders undo the best efforts of patriotic soldiers and civilians. According to a Georgia representative, the elevation of Lee would "restore confidence in the army." A plainly irritated Davis informed Virginia legislators that Lee had always declined such expanded responsibilities, but he quickly agreed to make the appointment. Lee tactfully thanked the president, questioned whether he could "accomplish any good," but humbly agreed to try.[32]

Politicians of all stripes hailed Lee's promotion and claimed it would boost public morale. Few decisions made by Jefferson Davis ever received such widespread approval. "This gives universal satisfaction," a corporal in a Virginia battery enthused, "and will silence the voice of croakers and dispel, in a great measure, the gloom which has filled the hearts of the people for some time."[33] The name "Lee" carried talismanic qualities for the rest of the war and well beyond.

Shortly after becoming general in chief Lee became embroiled in a controversy that uncovered the depths of wishful thinking as the Confederacy entered its death throes. From the fall of 1864 onward, as public debate raged on the question of conscripting slaves, rumor had it that Lee favored emancipation. Pressed for his views by members of the Virginia legislature, Lee denied any hostility to slavery but believed the time had come for the Confederacy to use all its manpower. He asserted that "long habits of obedience and subordination, coupled with the moral influence . . . the white man possesses over the black" would readily turn slaves into soldiers. Asking Lee to endorse the enrollment of African American volunteers publicly, Secretary of State Judah Benjamin predicted that thousands of slaves would join the Confederate armies in exchange for freedom.[34]

The advocates of such a policy made the matter sound simple largely because of their racial assumptions. Brig. Gen. Francis A. Shoup, who had recently served as Hood's chief of staff, argued that blacks were accustomed to "hardship and fatigue." Under the command of white officers, they would follow orders and learn to fight well without having to believe in the Confederate cause. Others agreed that with proper discipline, slaves could make efficient soldiers. Although many who favored enlisting blacks advocated freeing those who served faithfully, the more cautious proponents denied that emancipation was necessary. If medieval serfs could be transformed into soldiers, so could Southern slaves—and without changing their status, the *Richmond Enquirer* added. Mary Akin, wife of a Georgia congressman, feared that the black population had been growing so rapidly that it would overwhelm the whites through sheer numbers. Putting male slaves into the army would allow some of the surplus to be killed off. "I want to see them *got rid of* soon," she coldly advised her husband.[35]

Aside from these racial phobias and fantasies, however, even the practical arguments contained large doses of wishful thinking. "We must fight the negro with the negro," a Richmond editor asserted. A Georgian suggested that white soldiers be given furloughs on the understanding that each would return with a black recruit. The implicit (and sometimes explicit) assumption was that African Americans would serve as loyally in the Confederate as in the Union armies, even without the promise of freedom. "Certainly negro slaves have a far stronger interest in defending a country where they have a master and protector and an assured home, than one in which they would be left exposed, without defense, to the cruel benevolence of Yankee abolitionists," the *Richmond Enquirer* declared. In this world of make-believe, having slaves fight to defend slavery made perfect sense. A South Carolina editor even suggested that black men would perform much better for the Confederates than for the Yankees.[36]

If the Federals saw Southern slaves charging them with the stars and bars waving, they could no longer doubt that the Confederates were in earnest. The impact on Northern opinion would be shattering, or so it was hoped. The appearance of black Confederates would quickly demoralize the Yankees. Lincoln would have to raise more troops, and this would surely bankrupt the United States government. With one final exercise in tortured reasoning, the *Richmond Whig* claimed that anyone who still questioned whether slaves should be enrolled had given up on the Southern cause and actually feared the experiment might succeed.[37]

The opposition could easily point out the absurdities and contradictions in these arguments but embraced a different variety of wishful thinking. Congressman Thomas S. Gholson of Virginia turned the racial arguments on their head. African Americans would never make reliable recruits because they were too "licentious and fanatical"; freed from restraint, they would flee to the Yankees. Emancipating slave soldiers amounted to rank abolition, a "confession of weakness" that would inspire the enemy, reduce agricultural production, and depress the country.[38]

Instead, the politicians and generals should be bringing more white men into the ranks, fault-finders should fall silent, and the people should rally to their nation's defense. All that was needed for the triumph of Confederate arms was for free Southern white men to fight for their liberty. Enlisting blacks would cause many veterans to desert, Howell Cobb predicted. He favored raising more white volunteers before "resorting to the suicidal policy of arming our slaves." Although perceptive observers understood that slavery was likely doomed, the ultra-nationalist *Charleston Mercury* warned against destroying the very foundation of the Confederacy. At the other end of the political spectrum, but with equally shallow logic and only a tenuous grasp on reality, the defeatist North Carolina editor William W. Holden claimed that the most ardent secessionists now favored using black soldiers so they would not have to fight themselves. Were these "destructives" to enter the ranks, there would be no need even to discuss slave enlistments. As usual, some politicians preferred to change the subject and indulge their favorite pipe dream. Better leadership—notably the restoration of Johnston to command— would make this dangerous debate unnecessary.[39]

But of course, despite the hopes of the Confederacy's founding fathers, disputes over slavery had never ended. The issue of enrolling and freeing slaves inevitably became entangled with another last-gasp expedient for securing Southern independence. Perhaps if the Confederates agreed to emancipation, the European powers would grant diplomatic recognition and break the blockade. Throughout January the Richmond rumor mills reported that such a deal was being worked out. Gen. Edmund Kirby Smith, commander of the Trans-Mississippi Department, claimed that "nineteenth-twentieths" of the large planters would happily agree to gradual emancipation in exchange for independence and suggested making such a proposition to the French government. Davis was rightly skeptical about the assumption that slavery was the major obstacle to foreign recognition but incredibly enough still claimed that states'-rights objections prevented him from negotiating on this point. The British closely followed the discussions on raising slave regiments but moved no closer to recognition, much less intervention.[40]

From the beginning of the war, foreign recognition had been largely a chimera but one that never disappeared. In January 1865 newspaper reports again claimed the British and French were on the verge of intervention. The most popular rumor was that the Confederacy would receive full diplomatic recognition on March 4—the date of Lincoln's second inauguration—when it no longer could be claimed that Southerners had refused to abide by the results of a legitimate election. On hearing this, young Emma LeConte "jumped up with the first thrill of joy" she had felt for some time. "A bright vista of peace and happiness seemed to open up before my mind's eye." She quickly caught herself, however, and recalled how many times she had been "disappointed and lured on to false hopes by that will-o-the-wisp 'Recognition' and 'Intervention.'" Yet she could not dismiss the possibility out of hand. For Confederates who despaired of the military situation, talk of foreign intervention sparked new hope for winning independence. With all Southern ports now closed, Catherine Edmonston longed to hear reports of a "collision between the Great powers of the Earth & the U S." She admitted it all might be a delusion yet looked forward to March 4 with nervous anticipation. Even Northern military operations were interpreted as signs of Yankee desperation to win some great victory before the magical fourth of March.[41]

Although most Confederates had given up on the British, many still thought the French would intervene in the American war to protect their Mexican interests. Napoleon III's adventurism with Maximilian was cited as solid evidence of his need for Confederate goodwill. To those blinded by this assumption it seemed surprising that the Federals did not immediately recognize Southern independence to avoid entanglement in a foreign war. A captain in Lee's army expected fighting to soon break out between France and the United States.[42]

On January 30, 1865, in an hour-long speech, Congressman Daniel De Jarnette of Virginia put a clever twist on all this speculation. He proposed an alliance with the United States to uphold the Monroe Doctrine and drive the French from Mexico. In turn, the Federals would recognize Confederate independence. This idea rested on the belief that the Yankees' wily secretary of state, William H. Seward, was scrambling to find an ally against the European powers.[43]

The possibility of a diplomatic breakthrough seemed even more plausible after the appearance of that aged Jacksonian politico Francis Preston Blair Sr. in Richmond. Blair had made an unofficial visit to Jefferson Davis, though everyone believed his "mission" involved a potential peace settlement. Meeting with the president on January 12, Blair had proposed a cease-fire followed by a military alliance to enforce the Monroe Doctrine. Blair had no authority to negotiate but promised to discuss this plan with Lincoln. Although expecting little from this quixotic diplomacy, official Richmond viewed Blair's arrival as evidence of Yankee desperation. Once again hopes for peace were raised along with fears that some scheme to reconstruct the old Union might be worked out. A skeptical North Carolina editor advised his readers to view any hint of a peace settlement with caution.[44]

Discussion of European intervention and Blair's sojourn in Richmond, however, dovetailed neatly with renewed calls for peace among Confederates themselves. A majority in Congress reportedly favored sounding out Lincoln, but the peace advocates were neither bold nor unified, and despite the claims bandied about, they were not in the majority. The sticking point as always remained Confederate independence, and a fractious Congress continued to support the war rather than agree to humiliating peace terms. There was also desultory talk of a commercial treaty between the two "nations" that included John C. Calhoun's old proposal for a dual executive and even the establishment of an American "diet" with delegates from both the United States and the Confederate States.[45]

In the absence of congressional unity or any workable plan for ending the war, several governors considered calling for a convention of the states to open peace negotiations. Individual states might even withdraw from the Confederacy. Congressman Warren Akin feared that the Georgia legislature would entertain reconstruction proposals. Should local peace meetings continue, Lincoln would be less willing than ever to recognize Confederate independence. Howell Cobb conceded that his fellow Georgians were becoming more disloyal but did not think that even Joe Brown would desert the Confederacy. When the governor did propose a convention of the states, the state senate condemned the scheme as a "distraction of the public mind from the great business of prosecuting the war with vigor."[46]

Other governors likewise rebuffed Brown's efforts. Magrath maintained that any peace negotiations would have to proceed through the regular government channels rather than through conventions of dubious constitutionality. Vance especially opposed having conventions assemble in Georgia and North Carolina. Such a movement would launch "another revolution" leading to "domestic strife and bloodshed." Any effort to withdraw from the Confederacy would be resisted by a "considerable minority, backed by the army," and this would then create a "state of anarchy more horrible than anything we have yet endured."[47] Despite the deteriorating military situation and general demoralization, editors and politicians still denounced "submission" in general and talk of a separate peace in particular. The Louisiana and Texas legislatures repudiated any suggestion of reconstruction and vowed to continue the war. "Our only hope is to fight until we conquer a peace," a Georgia soldier informed his father. With little prospect for foreign intervention, conventions, or peace negotiations, everything now depended on the "fortitude, courage, and patriotism of soldiers."[48]

By the end of January, however, the chances for peace had seemingly improved. On January 28, Davis appointed three commissioners, Vice-President

Alexander H. Stephens, Senator Robert M. T. Hunter of Virginia, and Assistant Secretary of War John A. Campbell, to meet with Federal officials. Soon the newspapers overflowed with encouraging speculation. Rumor had it that Lincoln would appoint two avowed peace men—former presidents Franklin Pierce and Millard Fillmore—to meet with the Confederates. When the three Southern commissioners passed through the lines at Fort Monroe, reports quickly spread that soldiers on both sides had cheered wildly. An armistice appeared to be in the offing.[49]

The slightest hint of compromise could not help but revive hopes for an end to the fighting. The willingness of the Confederate government to send commissioners should at least silence the disaffected and give pause to administration critics who had often blasted Davis for inflexibility. Negotiations could only help the cause, a Georgia editor claimed, though people should not expect too much. Perhaps the Yankees had grown desperate because of their financial woes and fear of foreign intervention, and if so, a settlement was possible.[50]

Yet even the sanguine wondered if the commissioners could accomplish anything. The word "doubt" appeared most prominently in comments on the impending negotiations. Perhaps peace would come soon, but such hopes had often been dashed before. Lincoln would likely offer no better terms than a restoration of the old Union and an end to slavery. Davis deserved credit for sending the commissioners, but their chances of achieving a diplomatic miracle seemed small.[51]

The treacherous Yankees could hardly be trusted to negotiate in good faith, and there was really little basis for compromise. The Confederates would demand independence and the Federals would insist on emancipation, a South Carolina editor predicted, and so no "honor or advantage" would be gained. According to the *Richmond Whig*, nine of ten Confederates knew that negotiations were only a ploy to subjugate the South. By summer, Lincoln would need three hundred thousand more men to fight, and his great war machine would grind to a halt. Indeed, failure to reach an agreement would be a blessing because people would at last realize that independence could be achieved only by fighting. "Great will be the slaughter," one War Department official admitted gloomily.[52]

When the Confederate commissioners met with Lincoln and Seward aboard a steamer at Hampton Roads on February 3, there were few surprises. The discussion was amicable, but Lincoln remained adamant on the issues of Union and emancipation while the Southerners insisted on independence. The breakdown of negotiations showed how hopeless the situation had become. President Davis remained physically and politically weak; the government appeared to be unraveling; the prospects for stopping Sherman or Grant seemed remote. The only remaining question, according to one depressed bureaucrat, was whether the Confederacy would submit to Northern demands or be overrun. Sharp denunciations of the Yankees appeared in editorials and public speeches, but gasconade would not fill depleted regiments with fresh volunteers. "This cruel, this interminable, this ferocious war goes on," a Richmond mother lamented. "More hearts are to wail, more blood [is to] be shed, and the end is beyond the reach of mortal ken."[53]

Yet to say that morale plummeted for the rest of the war would oversimplify a complex reality. The Hampton Roads debacle certainly disappointed anyone who expected a diplomatic settlement, but it also undermined those Confederates who had been loudly calling for negotiations. The so-called peace men fell silent; "we are all war men henceforth," a Richmond editor declared. The illusion that peace could be secured through bargaining and compromise had nearly vanished. A false report even circulated that Vice-President Stephens was heading home to rally his fellow Georgians. The Southern people must fight for their independence or give up everything for which so many had worked, struggled, sacrificed, and died. Only "villains, poltroons, and traitors" would accept Lincoln's terms, a Georgia editor asserted, but strident rhetoric hardly concealed fears that ordinary soldiers and citizens now despaired of the cause.[54]

Remarkably, however, a great patriotic revival began. Even skeptics conceded that the mood on the streets seemed more cheerful. Knowing the worst about Yankee intentions, the people would display what a North Carolinian called a new "firmness and constancy." Unity and perseverance would become the watchwords, honor and independence the rallying cries. "Let the South be extinct before she should be disgraced," a refugee teacher living in a small Tennessee town declared.[55]

On February 6, Congress received the report of the Confederate commissioners. That evening, despite a heavy snow, nearly ten thousand people gathered at the African Church in Richmond to hear patriotic speeches. The president lampooned Lincoln as "His Majesty Abraham the First" and promised, though in an alarmingly feeble voice, that "before the next summer solstice falls upon us, it will be the enemy who will be asking us for conferences and concessions." Three days later, other leading Confederates harangued another large crowd. Secretary of State Benjamin strongly urged Congress to enroll slave soldiers. Speaking of the glories that would flow from Southern independence, Senator Hunter declared that a "righteous" God would never allow the Southern people to be defeated by the "wicked" Yankees. North Carolina congressman John A. Gilmer, who had been a prominent Whig Unionist and had even been mentioned as a possible member of Lincoln's cabinet, proclaimed that "doubts and divisions" were gone. The Federal armies would soon dwindle, and the Confederacy's condition was far from desperate. For true believers, a nation that had produced Davis, Lee, and Jackson could never be conquered.[56]

Although the delusive quality of this rhetoric is striking, ardent Confederates claimed it was Lincoln who was living in a dream world. The failure of diplomacy would surely hamper northern recruitment efforts. The Federals' insistence on reunion and emancipation would prove a great blessing because it would enrage the Confederate people, prod Congress into passing necessary measures, and perhaps even lead to foreign intervention. Thus one avenue of wishful thinking was closely connected to several others. More than ever dependent on Lee to pull off a strategic miracle, optimists still talked of winning Southern independence on the battlefield. The only choice now was to fight it out, a sentiment repeatedly expressed in the aftermath of Hampton Roads.[57]

"So the carnival of blood will be a 'success,'" War Clerk Jones remarked with rueful ambiguity. No doubt about it, for Confederates, February was a depressing month. Prices soared while morale sagged. Regiments and brigades held meetings to adopt patriotic resolutions, but a Mississippi sergeant suspected they were all "for show." Empty words no longer mattered: "The time for big talk has passed. Disguise the fact as we may, the real sentiment of this brigade and this division is for peace on almost any terms." Calamities multiplied. Hungry soldiers sadly watched their nation shrinking as Federal armies grabbed more territory. The burning of Columbia and the evacuation of Charleston dampened the patriotic revival after Hampton Roads, and Sherman kept advancing.[58]

But just as gloom seemed to be settling in to stay, some ray of hope would break through the dark clouds. From her refuge home in Tyler, Texas, Kate Stone heard that Lee had given Grant a "good drubbing" and that furloughs were now being granted liberally. Yet most Confederates seemed less inclined to swallow such rumors than simply to will themselves into believing that all was not lost. In a month filled with bad news, wishful thinkers discovered new reasons why the Confederacy was bound to prevail. For those familiar with ancient history, examples of successful revolutions in various empires provided comfort. And had not the Romans rallied after the disastrous defeat at Cannae to stop Hannibal and ultimately prevail in the Second Punic War? Just as the civilizations in the warmer Mediterranean areas had ruled Europe's northern "wasteland," so would Southerners eventually triumph over their Northern foes.[59] Even dubious and imperfect historical analogies were better than succumbing to despair.

Several senators suggested that raids be conducted by saboteurs against Northern cities and shipping. "I fear this war will never end," young Abbie Brooks lamented, but she hoped that Southern armies would break into guerrilla bands to harass the horrid Yankees. Although many soldiers knew that the end was near and desertions continued apace, even in the ranks there was an air of unreality. After hearing that the Confederate commissioners had returned from the Hampton Roads conference empty-handed, Stonewall Jackson's mapmaker laconically remarked: "No one seems disappointed." The war would continue, and a Kentucky brigade resolved to fight for ninety-nine years if necessary. With no apparent sense of the cruel irony in the suggestion, the widely read *Richmond Dispatch* recommended the Confederate army as the best school for young boys: "If a Confederate parent now wishes to teach his son the way to live, and the way to die, let him send him . . . to the bronzed and battle-scarred veterans in the front."[60]

How much confidence such strained logic inspired can never be known, but Confederate leaders made one final attempt to rally their people against the Federal onslaught. Several governors issued fire-breathing proclamations. Poverty, starvation, emancipation, and even executions would follow in the wake of a Union triumph, Vance warned. "Let no man mistake the issue now. The line of distinction will be drawn plainly between those who are for their country and those who are against their country. There is no half-way house upon the road. The purifying fire is even now burning through the land, its consuming flames must separate the dross from the true metal." The Confederacy was not whipped, the governor bravely claimed, so long as there were thousands of names on the army's rolls and a supposed abundance of supplies. Even as Sherman's troops approached the Tar Heel State, Vance promised Lee to hold meetings for "reviving public sentiment." The governor's political opponents ridiculed these last-ditch efforts, but Catherine Edmondston disdained the naysayers. "We will succeed!" she maintained. "We will yet leave a fair inheritance free & independent to our children."[61]

In other states attempts to rekindle patriotism ranged from the subdued to the absurd. Magrath calmly suggested that the citizens of South Carolina, the birthplace of secession, end all factious bickering and unite against the common enemy. Alabama governor Thomas Hill Watts claimed the Confederates now controlled more territory than they had a year before, but he did not mention that most of it was in the Trans-Mississippi. Yet amazingly, such assurances were echoed outside official circles. The die-hards could still envision a popular uprising that would send the skulkers and deserters back into the armies. A public meeting in Lynchburg, Virginia, expressed confidence in Lee and vowed to continue the fight. Richmond's leading clergymen appealed to "citizens in their comfortable homes, exempt from the privations and perils of the field" to donate provisions for the soldiers. Claiming there was more than enough food in Virginia and North Carolina to feed the troops, they still expected the Confederate cause to be crowned with success.[62]

A belief that somehow independence could yet be won persisted but now depended much more on abstract assertions than faith in any tangible means of deliverance. Defeat was simply unthinkable because its horrors were so unimaginable. For some months, leading Confederates had relied on fear to sustain public enthusiasm for the war. If people could only see the danger, the croakers would fall silent. Warnings about Southern lands being confiscated and people being taxed to pay the Yankee war debt became commonplace. Hypocritical abolitionists in truth worshiped the "almighty dollar" but also would put black men in Congress to rule over their former masters.[63]

In a slaveholding society, the word "subjugation" naturally conjured up visions of white people being "enslaved." Nor would the calamity stop with the mere loss of freedom. The victorious Federals would replace Southern grace and gentility with what a Richmond editor politely termed "New England notions and habits." Senator Williamson S. Oldham of Texas, however, minced no words. A defeated people would be governed by a "triumvirate, consisting of the whining, canting, hypocritical Yankee, the red republican, infidel German, and . . . the African negro." Oppression, impoverishment, and even rape would likely follow.[64]

The horrors of subjugation would fall especially hard on women. The racial and sexual implications of former slaves having the upper hand over their onetime mistresses were frightening. The very foundations of the classic Southern household—a household resting on slave labor—would crumble. "The man who talks of peace now," a Richmond editor declared with a surprisingly blunt appeal to class privilege, "now means to send his mother to the kitchen, his wife to the slops of the bed chamber, his daughters to the wash tub, and his sisters to the scrubbing brush."[65]

These supposedly delicate women hardly deserved such a fate because, according to Confederate propaganda, they had been the most ardent patriots. In a typical tribute, Governor Henry Watkins Allen of Louisiana praised the "Ladies of Natchitoches" whose example of "Christian heroism" would help secure Southern independence. Such statements had long become staples of Confederate discourse, but in the spring of 1865, they acquired a sharper, more desperate edge. Women talked of holding meetings to pass resolutions in support of the army. Such behavior challenged gender conventions in a limited way, but one "Lady of Virginia" even vowed to take up arms if cowardly men faltered.[66] Whatever the longer-range implications, defeat somehow could be staved off so long as the women of the South remained steadfast.

Or so long as God favored the Confederacy. As the war dragged on, however, divine assistance seemed more uncertain. The devout found explanations and perhaps some consolation for their travail in the Bible. Not surprisingly, by early 1865, they turned to Psalms, Lamentations, and especially Job for comfort. "God teaches us patience and resignation, and may the rod of affliction soon be stayed," a Mississippi sergeant prayed. Just as the Lord had often chastised the children of Israel, so now he must punish the Southern people for their sins, and just as he had sent various heathenish tribes against his chosen ones, so now he permitted the godless Yankees temporarily to gain the upper hand against the Confederates. Once the Southern nation was sufficiently humbled, divine wrath would give way to divine mercy. Walking through the ruins of Columbia, however, Grace Elmore could not help but wail, "how long, oh Lord, how long?" Civilians and soldiers alike struggled to hold on to their stoic faith, to utter those familiar words, "Thy will be done."[67]

Aside from individual expressions of faith, Confederate civil religion also served to sustain public morale. In a late January proclamation calling for a day of "fasting, humiliation, and prayer," Jefferson Davis resorted to familiar evangelical formulas. "In a season of adversity and public trial," all persons should "acknowledge our dependence on His mercy, and to bow in humble submission before His footstool, confessing our manifold sins, supplicating His gracious pardon, imploring His divine help, and devoutly rendering thanks for the many and great blessings which He has vouchsafed to us." In the midst of their suffering, the Southern people should "recognize in His chastening hand the correction of a Father" and pray that the "Lord of Hosts" would protect Confederate armies against their enemies. As a South Carolina editor pithily commented, "man's extremity is God's opportunity." Despite a certain cynicism in some quarters, Confederates—albeit mostly women— gathered in prayer meetings on March 9 to petition for the deliverance of their beleaguered nation.[68]

The Lord had allowed the Federal armies to punish Southerners for their sins, but soon the tide would be reversed. Confederates kept asserting that their enemies were about to falter. Many believed the Yankees were running out of men and that by summer their armies would be seriously depleted. The Northern draft remained unpopular, and already Lincoln had been forced to enroll "confessed thieves, professional deserters, escaped convicts, lunatics, idiots, and cripples." Even if more men could be conscripted, the war would soon force the Federal government into bankruptcy; the Yankees were beggaring themselves to make one great push for victory. Reports that the Federals had lost territory and that Union armies too faced rising desertion rates appeared in Confederate newspapers. Of course, the boastful Yankees, according to one Richmond editor, had always admired P. T. Barnum as much as George Washington. Such irresistible logic—at least for the optimists— meant that the Federals were about to receive their just deserts. On the day before the Confederate capital was evacuated, the editor of the *Richmond Whig* summarized the theological, political, and military assumptions that undergirded these arguments: "The pride that goes before a fall and the madness that precedes destruction are full to overflowing, ripe to rottenness with our enemy—We have but to perform well and bravely now the part assigned to us, as the instruments of Providence, to bring on the promised consummation."[69]

For such a dramatic deliverance, there was abundant precedent not only in sacred but also in secular history. Confederate leaders had often declared themselves the true heirs of the founding fathers, and therefore parallels between the American and Confederate revolutions were commonly drawn. Appeals to the spirit of 1776 appeared in both public and private discourse. Clever propagandists searched for comparisons: perhaps Sherman would share the fate of Gen. John Burgoyne; croakers were no more numerous now than in the 1770s; Confederates reverted to the term "Tory" when denouncing the "traitors" of their day. Suddenly familiar stories of George Washington became real to a generation that now understood their forefathers' sacrifices. In short, the Confederacy was enduring its own Valley Forge.[70]

By the beginning of 1865, however, the events of 1780 and 1781 provided the most inspiring examples. Hood's losses in Tennessee had been no less disastrous than Horatio Gates's defeat at Camden, South Carolina. Johnston's army in North Carolina was surely in better shape than General Nathanael Greene's had been at the end of 1780. Like the Federals, the British had captured Savannah and Charleston, but it had done them little good. While Washington's army had remained in the field, there had been hope, and the same would hold true for Lee's army. The miraculous defeat of Cornwallis at Yorktown should inspire Confederates to follow in the footsteps of stalwart patriots who had refused to give up in the darkest days of an earlier revolution.[71]

But such historical analogies sometimes offered cold comfort. To quote Patrick Henry on the choices of "liberty" or "death" could arouse great anxiety, especially on a dark winter day. March was proving to be an especially gloomy month. Maj. Gen. Philip Sheridan was driving the remnants of Maj. Gen. Jubal Early's army from the Shenandoah Valley. Sherman was advancing into North Carolina, and Johnston was trying to gather his scattered forces for one great battle. Desperate citizens clung to their belief that the righteousness of the Confederate cause made any final defeat impossible. More than ever, success depended on the popular will, as Lee still claimed. Hopeful—though always vague—reports of an improved public spirit circulated throughout the month.[72]

Army morale remained high—or so many Confederates tried to believe— and regimental meetings produced the usual pledges to keep fighting. If only some brigades could be detached from Lee's army, Johnston might be able to stop Sherman. Throughout the month rumors had Sherman whipped at least half a dozen times. After the battle of Bentonville on March 19, the first reports trumpeted a decisive Confederate victory, and even when it was apparent that Johnston had only temporarily checked the Federals, the newspapers remained upbeat. "Let us deserve success, and with this campaign it may yet be ours," a Richmond editor exulted.[73]

On three occasions a Tennessee refugee living in Eatonton, Georgia, heard that Lee had defeated Grant. In mid-March, the *Richmond Dispatch* pointedly noted how often the Federals had already failed in their campaigns to capture Petersburg. Yet as early as mid-February, intense discussions began about the possibility of abandoning the capital. Lee could shift his army south, compel the enemy to lengthen its lines of communication, and concentrate all Confederate forces against Sherman. All the major cities might be lost, newly appointed secretary of war John C. Breckinridge suggested, but ardent patriots had always been able to rationalize such setbacks. After Savannah had fallen to Sherman, a Richmond editor had dismissed the place as a "Yankee town" filled with too many "trading adventurers." Coastal cities had always been vulnerable, but it was doubtful that the Federals could ever conquer the vast Confederate interior or would ever have enough troops to occupy such an expanse.[74]

Similar reasoning readily applied to the possible abandonment of Richmond. Again according to the Pollyannas, so long as the people kept up their spirits, the mere loss of the capital would not be fatal. Soldiers and citizens would suffer, War Clerk Jones conceded, but would manage to "subsist until harvest; meantime the God of battles may change the face of affairs, or France may come to our relief." Josiah Gorgas still hoped that Lee would somehow unite with Johnston to crush either Sherman or Grant. Three days before the evacuation, the Richmond press remained confident that the city could hold out. People had heard rumors about the fall of Richmond so often they had stopped believing them. Besides, the Federals were bringing a much smaller force against the city than the previous year, and if Lee had beaten Grant in the open field before, how much stronger would his army be entrenched in the defenses of Petersburg and Richmond.[75]

Such thinking made news of Richmond's fall, when it finally came, all the harder to swallow. For women living as refugees or on isolated farms and plantations whose spirits had often soared with the most improbable rumors, this final blow fell particularly hard. Their minds reeled and they had trouble grasping what this great disaster might mean.[76]

Yet the evacuation of the capital hardly dashed all hopes. In an address issued from Danville, Virginia, Jefferson Davis warned against "allow[ing] our energies to falter, our spirits to grow faint, or our efforts to become relaxed." No longer would Lee's army be "trammeled" by having to defend Richmond. "Relieved from the necessity of guarding cities and particular points," the troops could now move freely, striking the enemy at will and operating where supplies were more abundant. All that was needed was an "unquenchable resolve." The president probably manifested as much wild-eyed optimism as any Confederate: "Let us but will it, and we are free." Echoing Davis's reasoning and the teachings of the famous Swiss military theorist Baron Antoine Henri Jomini, a Georgia editor suggested that Lee would now have the advantage of "interior lines." Even though more territory would fall under enemy control, "the Confederacy will be stronger than ever." The Yankees' capture of Richmond was therefore "certain to result in good for our cause."[77]

Efforts to shore up public morale surprisingly persisted. People should be of good cheer despite the loss of the capital. "We never can consent to become the willing slaves of the hateful Yankee race," the *Edgefield Advertiser* bravely declared. Even Catherine Edmondston, who had so grieved over the first reports of Richmond's evacuation, quickly recovered her usual confidence: "If we but stand by our President & our Army and present a stubborn dogged resistance, we will yet conquer." Clichés about the darkest hours coming just before the dawn persisted as did expectations that the Yankees would soon, in the words of a Texas private serving in the Trans-Mississippi, "meet with tremendous and overwhelming reverses, and that too at a moment when least expected."[78]

But it was not to be, and on April 9, Lee surrendered the Army of Northern Virginia. How could the Lord allow the wicked to triumph? Had all the precious blood been spilled in vain? Inveterate diarists either fell silent or scribbled rambling, disjointed entries. Reality was so hard to grasp, and to those who had remained faithful during four hard years of war, it all seemed like a dream.[79] Yet the chimera of independence did not immediately disappear. Lee had surrendered, but the Southern people had not capitulated—the hopeful still leaned on that old and now shattered reed. Confederates had "depended too much on Lee and too little on God," a pious refugee concluded. Joe Johnston remained in the field so all was not quite lost. Perhaps Confederates in the Trans-Mississippi could still hold out. Although Lee would have none of it, a few leaders discussed the possibility of guerrilla warfare. Maj. Gen. Wade Hampton suggested to Jefferson Davis that men from the Army of Northern Virginia now join cavalry units because so long as troops remained in the field, the hope of European intervention stayed alive.[80]

Incredible rumors still circulated and even found believers. Beauregard had supposedly been killed in a great battle, or perhaps it had been Sherman. In an address to his command on April 25, Lt. Gen. Nathan Bedford Forrest claimed that Lee had not really surrendered and that Grant had recently lost a hundred thousand men in battle or by desertion. Following Lincoln's assassination, the most widely circulated tales concerned a war between France and the United States or a treaty recognizing Confederate independence.[81]

Yet finally even the most sanguine had to face facts—or at least some of them. After learning that Davis had been captured, Ellen Renshaw House admitted that the Confederacy was dead. "All our sacrifices, all the blood shed has been for nothing," she wrote in a diary that usually overflowed with determination and optimism. "The southern people have no one but themselves to thank for it. They did not deserve their freedom or they would have gained it." Even in defeat, many Confederates could imagine a different outcome. As one psychological study has noted, "people can enjoy the experience of wishful thinking as long as they are willing to pay the price of painful disappointment when reality does not unfold as expected."[82]

The problem all along had been much more complicated than a mere loss of public confidence in the Confederate cause. To say that Confederate morale collapsed in the spring of 1865 is to tell at best a partial truth. Rather, the persistence of unrealistic expectations, wild fantasies, and false hopes sustained the will to continue the war but at an increasingly horrible physical and psychological cost. Did Confederates really believe their own delusive statements? The answer hardly matters. Rationalizing and making excuses had almost become like a narcotic, dangerous and addictive but also attractive to patriots hoping against hope for a different outcome. Many comments made and arguments offered during the final months of the war took on a surreal quality that ill-prepared people for the Confederacy's demise.

This air of unreality would unfortunately suffuse Southern thought for the next several decades and beyond, casting a long shadow over those who experienced a crushing defeat without either acknowledging it or reckoning with its causes. By refusing to admit even to themselves that the cause was being lost, many officers, politicians, and generals—not to mention ordinary soldiers and citizens—were already laying the foundation for the cult of the so-called Lost Cause.

Notes

1. "Civil War Days in Huntsville; A Diary by Mrs. W. D. Chadick," *Alabama Historical Quarterly* 9 (1947): 298; Virginia Clay Diary, January 1, 1865, Clement Claiborne Clay Papers, William R. Perkins Library, Duke University, Durham NC; John W. Brown Diary, January 1, 1865, Southern Historical Collection, University of North Carolina (hereafter cited as SHC); T. Conn Bryan, ed., "A Georgia Woman's Civil War Dairy: The Journal of Minerva Leah Rowles McClatchey," *Georgia Historical Quarterly* 51 (1967): 212–13. I thank Gary W. Gallagher for a very helpful reading of an early version of this essay. I was of course later delighted to read Gallagher's *The Confederate War* (Cambridge MA: Harvard University Press, 1997), which much more fully analyzes many of the questions addressed more modestly in this essay.

2. *War of the Rebellion: A Compilation of the Official Records of the Union and Confederate Armies*, 128 vols. (Washington DC: U.S. Government Printing Office,

1880–1901), Ser. I, 46: pt. 2, 1035 (hereinafter OR); Warren Akin, *Letters of Warren Akin*, ed. Bell I. Wiley (Athens: University of Georgia Press, 1959), 68; Josiah Gorgas, *The Journals of Josiah Gorgas, 1857–1878*, ed. Sarah Woolfolk Wiggins (Tuscaloosa: University of Alabama Press, 1995), 148; John Beauchamp Jones, *A Rebel War Clerk's Diary at the Confederate States Capital*, 2 vols. (Philadelphia: J. B. Lippincott, 1866), 2:373, 385; Robert Garlick Hill Kean, *Inside the Confederate Government: The Diary of Robert Garlick Hill Kean*, ed. Edward Younger (New York: Oxford University Press, 1957), 186.

3. Henry Robinson Berkeley, *Four Years in the Confederate Artillery: The Diary of Private Henry Robinson Berkeley*, ed. William H. Runge (Chapel Hill: University of North Carolina Press, 1961), 116; Jones, *Rebel War Clerk's Diary*, 2:396; Robert Patrick, *Reluctant Rebel: The Secret Diary of Robert Patrick, 1861–1865* (Baton Rouge: Louisiana State University Press, 1959), 250; Catherine Ann Devereux Edmondston, *"Journal of a Secesh Lady": The Diary of Catherine Ann Devereux Edmondston, 1860–1866*, ed. Beth G. Crabtree and James W. Patton (Raleigh: North Carolina Division of Archives and History, 1979), 660; George Peddy Cuttino, ed., *Saddle Bag and Spinning Wheel: Being the Civil War Letters of George W. Peddy, M.D. and His Wife Kate Featherston Peddy* (Macon GA: Mercer University Press, 1981), 300.

4. Bell I. Wiley, *The Road to Appomattox* (Memphis TN: Memphis State College Press, 1956), 43–75.

5. Gary W. Gallagher, "Lee's Army Has Not Lost Any of Its Prestige: The Impact of Gettysburg on the Army of Northern Virginia and the Confederate Home Front," in Gallagher, ed., *The Third Day at Gettysburg and Beyond* (Chapel Hill: University of North Carolina Press, 1994), 1–30.

6. Emma LeConte, *When the World Ended: The Diary of Emma LeConte*, ed. Earl Schenck Miers (New York: Oxford University Press, 1957), 3, 5; *Richmond Daily Dispatch*, January 2, 1865; *Richmond Daily Whig*, January 1–2, 1865; *Macon (GA) Daily Telegraph and Confederate*, January 5, 1865; *Lynchburg Virginian*, January 2, 14, 1865.

7. *Macon (GA) Daily Telegraph and Confederate*, January 10, 12, 1865; Kean, *Inside the Confederate Government*, 184; *Richmond Daily Whig*, January 13, 1865.

8. Jones, *Rebel War Clerk's Diary*, 2:371; *Richmond Daily Dispatch*, January 5, 28, 1865; Edmondston, *"Journal of a Secesh Lady,"* 653.

9. Jones, *Rebel War Clerk's Diary*, 2:397; Walter Taylor, *Lee's Adjutant: The Wartime Letters of Colonel Walter Herron Taylor, 1862–1865*, ed. R. Lockwood Tower (Columbia: University of South Carolina Press, 1995), 216, 223; *Richmond Daily Dispatch*, January 28, February 14, 22, 28, 1865; *Richmond Daily Whig*, January 30, 1865;

Franklin Lafayette Riley, *Grandfather's Journal: Company B. Sixteenth Mississippi Infantry Volunteers*, ed. Austin C. Dobbins (Dayton OH: Morningside, 1988), 232–33; *Richmond Daily Sentinel*, January 31, March 1, 1865; "Proceedings of the Second Congress, Second Session in Part," *Southern Historical Society Papers* 52 (1959): 307; W. W. Heartsill, *Fourteen Hundred and 91 Days in the Confederate Army: A Journal Kept* by *W. W. Heartsill*, ed. Bell Irvin Wiley (Wilmington NC: Broadfoot, 1987), 232. It may be significant that the always optimistic *Richmond Dispatch* had the largest circulation of any newspaper in the capital. See J. Cutler Andrews, *The South Reports the Civil War* (Princeton: Princeton University Press, 1970), 32.

10. Riley, *Grandfather's Journal*, 227; Kean, *Inside the Confederate Government*, 183; Ellen Renshaw House, *A Very Violent Rebel: The Civil War Diary of Ellen Renshaw House*, ed. Daniel E. Sutherland (Knoxville: University of Tennessee Press, 1996), 139; *Richmond Daily Whig*, January 3, 7, 1865; Gorgas, *Journals of Josiah Gorgas*, 148; Edmondston, *"Journal of a Secesh Lady,"* 653; *Official Records of the Union and Confederate Navies in the War of the Rebellion*, 31 vols. (Washington DC: U.S. Government Printing Office, 1894–1922), Ser. II, 3: 1259 (hereafter ORN).

11. C. Vann Woodward, ed., *Mary Chesnut's Civil War* (New Haven: Yale University Press, 1981), 703; *Wilmington (NC) Daily Journal*, January 4, 1865; *Richmond Daily Sentinel*, January 4, 1865; Akin, *Letters of Warren Akin*, 77.

12. OR, ser. I, 46: pt. 2, 1209, 1211–14, 1233–34, 1250–51. Longstreet's biographers have studiously ignored this bizarre proposal.

13. Clifford Dowdey and Louis H. Manarin, eds., *The Wartime Papers of R. E. Lee* (New York: Bramhall House, 1961), 886, 892, 910, 918; Riley, *Grandfather's Journal*, 233; OR, ser. I, 46: pt. 2, 1254, 1265, 1270, pt. 3, 1356–57.

14. *Richmond Daily Whig*, January 11, 1865; *Macon (GA) Daily Telegraph and Confederate*, January 19, 1865; OR, ser. I, 47: pt. 2, 982–83, ser. IV, 3: 1041–42; William Porcher Miles to Thomas D. McDowell, January 1, 1865, McDowell Papers, SHC; *Acts Passed by the Seventh Legislature of the State of Louisiana, at Its Second Session, Held and Begun in the City of Shreveport, on the 16th Day of January 1865* (Shreveport LA: Printed at the South-Western, [1865]), 57–58; *Acts of the General Assembly of the State of Georgia Passed in Milledgeville, at an Annual Session in November, 1864* also *Extra Session of 1865, at Macon* (Milledgeville GA: Boughton, Barnes, and Moore, 1865), 84; *Milledgeville (GA) Confederate Union*, March 7, 1865. During the debate on enrolling slave soldiers in the Confederate army, a Tennessee congressman suggested that a slave be given to each white soldier as a bounty for staying in the field ("Proceedings of Congress," 293–95).

15. Judith White Brockenbrough McGuire, *Diary of a Southern Refugee*, 2d ed. (New York: E. J. Hale and Son, 1867), 331; John Rozier, ed., The *Granite Farm Letters:*

The Civil War Correspondence of Edgeworth and Sallie Bird (Athens: University of Georgia Press, 1988), 236–37; John Walters, *Norfolk Blues: The Civil War Diary of the Norfolk Light Artillery Blues* (Shippensburg PA: Burd Street Press, 1997), 189; Gorgas, *Journals of Josiah Gorgas*, 149; OR, ser. IV, 3: 1033. A bitter debate immediately erupted over the roles of Gen. Braxton Bragg and Maj. Gen. William H. C. Whiting in the loss of Fort Fisher. See *Wilmington (NC) Daily Journal*, January 17, 1865; Edmondston, *"Journal of a Secesh Lady,"* 657, 663; *Lynchburg Virginian*, January 24, 1865.

16. *Richmond Daily Whig*, January 17, February 22, 1865; *Richmond Daily Sentinel*, January 19, 1865; *Atlanta (Macon GA) Southern Confederacy*, January 20, 1865; *Lynchburg Virginian*, February 25, 1865; ORN, ser. II, 3:1260.

17. Mark Grimsley, *The Hard Hand of War: Union Military Policy Toward Southern Civilians, 1861–1865* (Cambridge: Cambridge University Press, 1995); *Wilmington (NC) Daily Journal*, January 9, 1865; Andrew G. Magrath to Robert W. Barnwell, December 3, 1864, Barnwell to Magrath, January 9, 1865, William Porcher Miles to Magrath, January 15, 1865, Magrath Papers, South Caroliniana Library, University of South Carolina [hereafter cited as SCL]; Dowdey and Manarin, eds., *Wartime Papers*, 885–86. The original of Magrath's letter to Davis is more sharply worded than the version printed in the *Official Records*. See Magrath to Davis, January 22, 1865, Davis Papers, Special Collections, Robert W. Woodruff Library, Emory University; OR, ser. I, 47: pt. 2, 1035–36. Expecting little assistance from the Confederate government, Magrath tried to coordinate defense preparations with the governors of Georgia and North Carolina. See Magrath to Zebulon Vance, January 11, 1865, Magrath to Joseph E. Brown, January 26, 1865, Magrath Papers.

18. Mary Boykin Chesnut, *The Private Mary Chesnut: The Unpublished Civil War Diaries*, ed. C. Vann Woodward and Elisabeth Muhlenfeld (New York: Oxford University Press, 1984), 232; Grace Elmore Diary, January 4, 1865, SHC; Ella Gertrude Clanton Thomas, *The Secret Eye: The Journal of Ella Gertrude Clanton Thomas*, ed. Virginia Ingraham Burr (Chapel Hill: University of North Carolina Press, 1990), 256; Mrs. Thomas Taylor et al., eds., *South Carolina Women in the Confederacy*, 2 vols. (Columbia SC: State Company, 1903–7), 1:272; Edmondston, *"Journal of a Secesh Lady,"* 670. After reading some confident statements from the Columbia press in mid-February, Edmund Ruffin astutely commented: "In general, such preliminary boasts of newspapers are worthless—& are never louder than when just preceding an expected retreat, or surrender." Yet even the sophisticated Ruffin claimed to "confide in the people" and hoped that this time Confederate forces would stop Sherman. See Edmund Ruffin, *The Diary of Edmund Ruffin*, ed. William Kauffman Scarborough, 3 vols. (Baton Rouge: Louisiana State University Press, 1972–89), 3:752–53.

19. Floride Clemson, *A Rebel Came Home: The Diary and Letters of Floride Clemson*, rev. ed., ed. Charles M. McGee Jr. and Ernest M. Lander Jr. (Columbia: University of South Carolina Press, 1989), 76; Emma Holmes, *The Diary of Miss Emma Holmes, 1861–1866*, ed. John F. Marszalek (Baton Rouge: Louisiana State University Press, 1979), 397–98; Kean, *Inside the Confederate Government*, 200; Jones, *Rebel War Clerk's Diary*, 2:425; Woodward, ed., *Mary Chesnut's Civil War*, 737.

20. Gorgas, *Journals of Josiah Gorgas*, 152; Dowdey and Manarin, eds., *Wartime Papers*, 995, 999.

21. *Macon (GA) Daily Telegraph and Confederate*, February 23, 1865; *Richmond Daily Sentinel*, February 25, March 1, 1865; *Richmond Daily Whig*, February 24, 27, 1865; Gorgas, *Journals of Josiah Gorgas*, 153; House, *Very Violent Rebel*, 149; Edmondston, "*Journal of a Secesh Lady*," 673–74; Taylor, *Lee's Adjutant*, 227.

22. Jones, *Rebel War Clerk's Diary*, 2:372, 385; William A. Graham, *The Papers of William Alexander Graham*, ed. Max R. Williams and J. G. de Roulhac Hamilton, 6 vols. (Raleigh NC: State Department of Archives and History, 1957–76), 6:256–57; Gorgas, *Journals of Josiah Gorgas*, 147; "Proceedings of Congress," 76–77; OR, Ser. I, 52: pt. 2, 807; Dunbar Rowland, ed., *Jefferson Davis, Constitutionalist: His Letters, Papers, and Speeches*, 10 vols. (Jackson MS: Department of Archives and History, 1923), 6:442–45; *Richmond Daily Examiner*, January 9, 1865; *Richmond Daily Whig*, January 17, 1865; Jefferson Davis, *Jefferson Davis: Private Letters, 1823–1889*, ed. Hudson Strode (New York: Harcourt, Brace, and World, 1966), 140; Kean, *Inside the Confederate Government*, 186–87; Akin, *Letters of Warren Akin*, 74.

23. *Milledgeville (GA) Confederate Union*, February 28, 1865; *Richmond Daily Whig*, January 25, 1865; OR, Ser. I, 46: pt. 2, 1118, Ser. IV, 3:1046–48; Kean, *Inside the Confederate Government*, 189–92; Jones, *Rebel War Clerk's Diary*, 2:422; Robert Toombs to G. W. Smith, March 25, 1865, Toombs Letter, Special Collections, University of Georgia, Athens.

24. *Richmond Daily Sentinel*, January 27, 1865; Gorgas, *Journals of Josiah Gorgas*, 155; Edmondston, "*Journal of a Secesh Lady*," 683; *Rome (GA) Weekly Courier*, March 19, 1865.

25. *Milledgeville (GA) Confederate Union*, January 31, 1865; Taylor, *Lee's Adjutant*, 230; Josiah Turner Jr. to Kemp P. Battle, February 11, 1865, Battle Family Papers, SHC; Ruffin, *Diary of Edmund Ruffin*, 3:737; Gorgas, *Journals of Josiah Gorgas*, 148; Jones, *Rebel War Clerk's Diary*, 2:399.

26. *Richmond Sentinel*, January 7, March 6, 1865; *Richmond Daily Dispatch*, January 12, 1865; *Milledgeville (GA) Southern Recorder*, March 28, 1865; *Raleigh (NC) Daily Confederate*, April 1, 1865; Woodward, ed., *Mary Chesnut's Civil War*, 698. See, for example, the brilliant analysis of patriotism and combat motivation in

James M. McPherson, *For Cause and Comrades: Why Men Fought in the Civil War* (New York: Oxford University Press, 1997).

27. Berkeley, *Four Years in the Confederate Artillery*, 114–15; William Pitt Chambers, *Blood and Sacrifice: The Civil War Journal of a Confederate Soldier*, ed. Richard A. Baumgartner (Huntington WV: Blue Acorn Press, 1994), 191.

28. Abbie Brooks Diary, February 8, 1865, Atlanta Historical Society; *Edgefield (SC) Advertiser*, March 15, 1865; Kate Cumming, *Kate: The Journal of a Confederate Nurse*, ed. Richard Barksdale Harwell (Baton Rouge: Louisiana State University Press, 1959), 248, 257; McGuire, *Diary of a Southern Refugee*, 328–29; Taylor et al., eds., *South Carolina Women in the Confederacy*, 1:279; Sallie C. Bird to Sarah Hamilton Yancey, January 8, 1865, Benjamin C. Yancey Papers, SHC; House, *Very Violent Rebel*, 152. For a contrasting account arguing that Confederates linked slavery (and the guilt flowing from that particular sin) to the military collapse of their nation, see Richard E. Beringer, Herman Hattaway, Archer Jones, and William N. Still Jr., *Why the South Lost the Civil War* (Athens: University of Georgia Press, 1986), 336–67. For an excellent analysis of how Confederate clergy called people to account for wartime sins, see Drew Gilpin Faust, *The Creation of Confederate Nationalism* (Baton Rouge: Louisiana State University Press, 1988), 41–57.

29. For summaries of a vast literature along with recent research on the influence of wishful thinking in shaping voters' expectations, see Elisha Badad, Michael Hills, and Michael O'Driscoll, "Factors Influencing Wishful Thinking and Predictions of Election Outcomes," *Basic and Applied Social Psychology* 13 (1992): 461–76; Elisha Badad and Eitan Jacobus, "Wish and Reality in Voters' Predictions of Election Outcomes," *Political Psychology* 14 (1993): 37–53; Elisha Badad, "Can Accurate Knowledge Reduce Wishful Thinking in Voters' Predictions of Election Outcomes?" *Journal of Psychology* 129 (1995): 285–300. From my reading of the sources, it seems that wishful thinking was much more pervasive than the "cognitive dissonance" that has been used to explain Confederate attitudes and even explain Confederate defeat. Cf. Beringer et al., *Why the South Lost*, 280–93 and passim.

30. Woodward, ed., *Mary Chesnut's Civil War*, 698; *Richmond Daily Whig*, January 9, 1865; *Journal of the Congress of the Confederate States of America, 1861–1865*, 7 vols. (Washington DC: U.S. Government Printing Office, 1904–05), 4:458, 7:643; "Proceedings of Congress," 289–93, 300–306; Petition of Confederate Senators to Robert E. Lee, February 4, 1865, Louis T. Wigfall Papers, typescripts, Century for American History, University of Texas, Austin; *Laws of the State of Mississippi, Passed at a Called Session of the Mississippi Legislature, Held in Columbus, February and March 1865* (Meridian MS: J. J. Shannon, 1865), 60–61; Allan D. Candler, ed., *The Confederate Records of Georgia*, 5 vols. (Atlanta: Charles P. Byrd, 1909–11), 2:867–70.

31. OR, Ser. I, 46: pt. 2, 1192, 47: pt. 2, 1304–11; Jones, *Rebel War Clerk's Diary*, 2:393; Chesnut, *Private Mary Chesnut*, 225; Wade Hampton to Louis T. Wigfall, January 20, 1865, Joseph E. Johnston to Wigfall, February 12, March 14, 1865, Wigfall Papers; Woodward, ed., *Mary Chesnut's Civil War*, 700, 710, 725, 730; Cuttino, ed., *Saddle Bag and Spinning Wheel*, 309. Johnston's most recent biographer has perceptively and succinctly described the pressure for restoring the general to command: "This outcry from the public and the ranks of the military was genuine, but it was rooted in a sense of desperation; the country needed a savior." See Craig L. Symonds, *Joseph E. Johnston: A Civil War Biography* (New York: Norton, 1992), 340.

32. Jones, *Rebel War Clerk's Diary*, 2:380, 392; *Journal of the Confederate Congress*, 4:453–58; Akin, *Letters of Warren Akin*, 84; OR, Ser. I, 46: pt. 2, 1084, 1091–92; Kean, *Inside the Confederate Government*, 190; Dowdey and Manarin, eds., *Wartime Papers*, 884–85. "Lee is about all we have & what public confidence is left rallies around him," Josiah Gorgas noted sadly. "He it seems to me fights without much heart in the cause. . . . I don't think he believes we will or can succeed in this struggle" (Gorgas, *Journals of Josiah Gorgas*, 153). See also the provocative revisionist account of Lee's attitudes and actions in the final months of the war in Alan T. Nolan, *Lee Considered: General Robert E. Lee and Civil War History* (Chapel Hill: University of North Carolina Press, 1991), 112–33. For a useful diary-like summary of Lee's activities from the beginning of 1865 to the fall of Richmond, see Emory M. Thomas, *Robert E. Lee: A Biography* (New York: Norton, 1995), 347–49.

33. *Richmond Daily Whig*, January 23, 1865; *Richmond Daily Dispatch*, February 3, 1865; Riley, *Grandfather's Journal*, 232; "Townsend's Diary—January–May, 1865," *Southern Historical Society Papers* 34 (1906), 101.

34. Jones, *Rebel War Clerk's Diary*, 2:398; OR, Ser. IV, 3:1007–8, 1012–13, Ser. I, 46: pt. 2, 1229. For documentary evidence on all aspects of this debate, see Robert F. Durden's outstanding collection *The Gray and the Black: The Confederate Debate on Emancipation* (Baton Rouge: Louisiana State University Press, 1972).

35. Francis A. Shoup, *Policy of Employing Negro Troops* (Richmond: N.p., 1865), 1–4; *Richmond Daily Enquirer*, February 18, March 13, 1865; *Richmond Daily Whig*, February 20, 1865; Akin, *Letters of Warren Akin*, 117.

36. *Richmond Daily Dispatch*, February 20, 1865; John Cunningham to Alexander H. Stephens, February 18, 1865, Stephens Papers, Library of Congress; Mills Lane, ed., *"Dear Mother: Don't grieve about me. If I get killed I'll only be dead": Letters from Georgia Soldiers in the Civil War* (Savannah: Beehive Press, 1990), 345; Ulrich B. Phillips, ed., *The Correspondence of Robert Toombs, Alexander H. Stephens, and Howell Cobb* (Washington DC: American Historical Association, 1913), 356–58;

OR, Ser. IV, 3:1010–11; Durden, ed., *The Gray and the Black*, 200–201; *Edgefield (SC) Advertiser*, January 18, 1865.

37. *Annual Message of Governor Henry Watkins Allen to the Legislature of the State of Louisiana, January, 1865* (Shreveport: Office of the Caddo Gazette, [1865]), 17–18; *Lynchburg Virginian*, February 18, 1865; *Richmond Daily Sentinel*, March 7, 1865; *Richmond Daily Whig*, March 3, 1865.

38. Thomas S. Gholson, *Speech of Hon. Thos. S. Gholson, of Virginia, on the Policy of Employing Negro Troops . . . Delivered in the House of Representatives . . . 1st of February 1865* (Richmond: George P. Evans, 1865), 3–20.

39. *Milledgeville (GA) Confederate Union*, March 7, 1865; OR, Ser. IV, 3:1009–10; *Charleston Mercury*, January 25, February 3, 1865; *Raleigh (NC) Weekly Standard*, January 18, 1865; "Proceedings of Congress," 282–83, 322–24. Congress narrowly approved a bill authorizing the enlistment of slaves less than a month before the evacuation of Richmond, and soon all the arguments made in these debates became moot.

40. Kean, *Inside the Confederate Government*, 183; OR, Ser. I, 48: pt. 1, 1319–20, Ser. IV, 3:1067–70, 1160; Patrick, *Reluctant Rebel*, 250; Kate Mason Rowland Diary, January 23, 1865, Museum of the Confederacy, Richmond; ORN, Ser. II, 3:1259. Davis's excuse about state sovereignty was made after it was apparent that there was no European interest in the idea. For details of Louisiana congressman Duncan Kenner's mission to sound out the British and French on the possibility of exchanging emancipation for diplomatic recognition, see Frank Lawrence Owsley, *King Cotton Diplomacy: Foreign Relations of the Confederate States of America* (Chicago: University of Chicago Press, 1959), 532–41. Even during the final months of the Confederacy's brief existence, many traditional elements of the proslavery argument still appeared in public discourse—including the inextricable link between slavery and Southern identity, the harmony of interests between rich and poor, slavery as a divinely ordained institution, the fear of turning the Southern states into another Santo Domingo, and the economic superiority of slave labor. In January 1865, a South Carolina officer even suggested that a relative invest in slaves because Confederate independence would greatly increase their value. Should the Yankees prevail, the paper money would be worthless anyway. See *Charleston Daily Courier*, January 24, 1865; *Richmond Daily Dispatch*, January 30, 1865; *Richmond Daily Whig*, February 8, 1865; Ruffin, *Diary of Edmund Ruffin*, 3:770–83; McPherson, *For Cause and Comrades*, 108.

41. *Richmond Daily Dispatch*, January 18, 24, 1865; LeConte, *When the World Ended*, 19; Patrick, *Reluctant Rebel*, 252; Jones, *Rebel War Clerk's Diary*, 2:428; Lane, ed., *Dear Mother*, 345; Heartsill, *Fourteen Hundred and 91 Days in the Confederate*

Army, 231; Kate Stone, *Brokenburn: The Journal of Kate Stone, 1861–1868*, ed. John Q. Anderson (Baton Rouge: Louisiana State University Press, 1955), 312–13; Edmondston, *"Journal of a Secesh Lady,"* 662, 667, 672.

42. *Macon* (GA) *Daily Telegraph and Confederate*, January 25, 1865; Patrick, *Reluctant Rebel*, 253; *Richmond Daily Dispatch*, January 7, 1865; Jones, *Rebel War Clerk's Diary*, 2:422; Charles Minor Blackford, *Letters from Lee's Army*, ed. Charles Minor Blackford (New York: A. S. Barnes, 1947), 279.

43. "Proceedings of Congress," 260; *Lynchburg Virginian*, January 30, 1865; *Wilmington* (NC) *Daily Journal*, January 30, 1865; Jones, *Rebel War Clerk's Diary*, 2:403.

44. OR, Ser. I, 46: pt. 2, 1037–39; Akin, *Letters of Warren Akin*, 77, 84; *Richmond Daily Whig*, January 14, 1865; *Lynchburg Virginian*, January 21, 1865; Jones, *Rebel War Clerk's Diary*, 2:396; Gorgas, *Journals of Josiah Gorgas*, 149; *Wilmington* (NC) *Daily Journal*, January 28, 1865.

45. *Journal of the Confederate Congress*, 7:451–52, 606–7; Kean, *Inside the Confederate Government*, 187; Gorgas, *Journals of Josiah Gorgas*, 149; Graham, *Papers of William A. Graham*, 6:217–18; ORN, Ser. II, 3:1261; Rowland, ed., *Jefferson Davis*, 6:461–62. For the politics of the peace question, see George C. Rable, *The Confederate Republic: A Revolution Against Politics* (Chapel Hill: University of North Carolina Press, 1994), 278–81, 292–94.

46. Akin, *Letters of Warren Akin*, 72, 83–84; OR, Ser. I, 53:393–94; *Milledgeville* (GA) *Southern Recorder*, January 17, 1865; *Journal of the Senate at the Extra Session of the General Assembly of the State of Georgia, Convened by Proclamation of the Governor, at Macon, February 15th, 1865* (Milledgeville GA: Boughton, Nisbet, Barnes and Moore, 1865), 33–34.

47. Andrew G. Magrath to William H. Trescott, January 9, 1865, Magrath Papers; OR, Ser. I, 53:395–96, 46: pt. 2, 1093–94.

48. *Macon* (GA) *Daily Telegraph and Confederate*, January 16, 1865; *Acts Passed by the Seventh Legislature of the State of Louisiana, at its Second Session, Held and Begun in the City of Shreveport, on the 16th Day of January, 1865* (Shreveport: Printed at the "South-Western," [1865]), 6–8; "Proceedings of Congress," 257–58; Lane, ed., *Dear Mother*, 345.

49. *Atlanta* (*Macon* GA) *Southern Confederacy*, February 3, 1865; Jones, *Rebel War Clerk's Diary*, 2:407; Edmondston, *"Journal of a Secesh Lady,"* 659, 661; House, *Very Violent Rebel*, 142; Akin, *Letters of Warren Akin*, 106; Riley, *Grandfather's Journal*, 231.

50. Akin, *Letters of Warren Akin*, 89, 105; Chris E. Fonvielle Jr., *The Wilmington Campaign: Last Rays of Departing Hope* (Campbell CA: Savas, 1997), 329; *Macon*

(GA) *Daily Telegraph and Confederate*, January 31, 1865; J. Michael Welton, ed., "*My Heart Is So Rebellious*": *The Caldwell Letters, 1861–1865* (Warrenton VA: N.p., n.d.), 260; *Lynchburg Virginian*, January 31, 1865.

51. House, *Very Violent Rebel*, 143; Gorgas, *Journals of Josiah Gorgas*, 150; LeConte, *When the World Ended*, 22; *Richmond Daily Enquirer*, January 18, 1865; *Macon* (GA) *Daily Telegraph and Confederate*, February 3, 1865. A letter written by "A Virginia Woman" denied that women were faltering in their devotion to the cause and still extolled the virtues of the Spartan mother. See *Richmond Daily Sentinel*, January 24, 1865.

52. *Richmond Daily Whig*, January 20, 30, 1865; *Edgefield SC Advertiser*, February 1, 1865; *Richmond Daily Sentinel*, January 30, 1865; Jones, *Rebel War Clerk's Diary*, 2:402.

53. Jones, *Rebel War Clerk's Diary* 2:409; Kean, *Inside the Confederate Government*, 198; Stone, *Brokenburn*, 320; Graham, *Papers of William A. Graham*, 6:232–36; Rozier, *Granite Farm Letters*, 244.

54. Fonvielle, *Wilmington Campaign*, 329; *Macon* (GA) *Daily Telegraph and Confederate*, February 7, 9, 1865; *Richmond Daily Sentinel*, February 6, 1865; *Richmond Daily Dispatch*, February 7, 1865; Jones, *Rebel War Clerk's Diary*, 2:410; *Richmond Daily Whig*, February 6, 1865; *Journal of the Senate of the State of Mississippi, Called Session at Columbus, February and* March *1865* (Meridian MS: J. J. Shannon, 1865), 13–14; *Atlanta* (*Macon* GA) *Southern Confederacy*, February 7, 1865.

55. Jones, *Rebel War Clerk's Diary*, 2:411; Gorgas, *Journals of Josiah Gorgas*, 151; *Wilmington* (NC) *Daily Journal*, February 6, 1865; House, *Very Violent Rebel*, 146; *Macon* (GA) *Daily Telegraph and Confederate*, February 16, 1865; Lane, ed., *Dear Mother*, 345; *Richmond Daily Dispatch*, March 29, 1865; Abbie Brooks Diary, February 15, 1865.

56. Jones, *Rebel War Clerk's Diary*, 2:411, 415; Durden, ed., *The Gray and the Black*, 188–90; *Richmond Daily Sentinel*, February 8, 1865; Gorgas, *Journals of Josiah Gorgas*, 151; *Richmond Daily Dispatch*, February 10, 1865; *Richmond Daily Whig*, February 10, 1865.

57. *Richmond Daily Whig*, February 19, 1865; *Lynchburg Virginian*, February 8, 1865; *Richmond Daily Dispatch*, February 9, 1865; Akin, *Letters of Warren Akin*, 110; Taylor, *Lee's Adjutant*, 221; *Edgefield* (SC) *Advertiser*, February 14, 1865.

58. Jones, *Rebel War Clerk's Diary*, 2:416, 426, 429; Clemson, *Rebel Came Home*, 75; Chambers, *Blood and Sacrifice*, 202–3; John Dooley, *John Dooley, Confederate Soldier: His War Journal*, ed. Joseph T. Durkin (Notre Dame IN: University of Notre Dame Press, 1963), 173; Gorgas, *Journals of Josiah Gorgas*, 152.

59. Stone, *Brokenburn*, 316–17; *Macon* (GA) *Daily Telegraph and Confederate*,

February 6, 1865; *Richmond Daily Sentinel*, February 7, 1865; *Richmond Daily Dispatch*, February 18, 1865.

60. Abbie Brooks Diary, February 6, 1865; OR, Ser. IV, 3:1079; Jedediah Hotchkiss, *Make Me a Map of the Valley: The Civil War Journal of Stonewall Jackson's Topographer*, ed. Archie P. McDonald (Dallas TX: Southern Methodist University Press, 1973), 255; Riley, *Grandfather's Journal*, 232; Lane, ed., *Dear Mother*, 345; *Richmond Daily Dispatch*, February 24, 1865.

61. OR, Ser. I, 47: pt. 2, 1187–92, 1312; Graham, *Papers of William A. Graham*, 6:247–50; *Raleigh (NC) Weekly Standard*, February 22, 1865; Edmondston, *"Journal of a Secesh Lady,"* 666.

62. *Richmond Daily Whig*, February 14, March 4, 1865; *Montgomery (AL) Advertiser*, March 3, 1865; Woodward, ed., Mary *Chesnut's Civil War*, 722; *Lynchburg Virginian*, February 11, 1865; *Richmond Daily Dispatch*, March 6, 1865; *Appeal to the People of Virginia* (Richmond: N.p., 1865), 1–4.

63. Speech of William E. Smith in Confederate Congress, n.d., 1865, Smith Papers, Duke University; *Richmond Daily Dispatch*, January 17, 1865; *Lynchburg Virginian*, January 7, 1865; *Richmond Daily Sentinel*, January 20, 1865; *Atlanta (Macon GA) Southern Confederacy*, January 24, 27, 1865; *Annual Message of Henry Watkins Allen*, 18–19.

64. *Richmond Daily Whig*, January 2, 1865; *Edgefield (SC) Advertiser*, January 11, 1865; *Richmond Daily Dispatch*, January 19, 1865; Williamson S. Oldham, *Speech of Hon. W. S. Oldham of Texas, on the Resolutions of the State of Texas, Concerning Peace, Reconstruction, and Independence* (Richmond: N.p., 1865), 12.

65. *Richmond Daily Whig*, February 12, 1865.

66. Henry Watkins Allen to the "Ladies of Natchitoches," January 26, 1865, unidentified newspaper clipping in Fielding Y. Doke Papers, Department of Archives and Manuscripts, Louisiana State University; LeConte, *When the World Ended*, 21, 67; *Macon (GA) Telegraph and Confederate*, February 28, 1865; *Richmond Daily Sentinel*, March 3, 1865.

67. Woodward, ed., *Mary Chesnut's Civil War*, 733; *Richmond Daily Dispatch*, March 9, 1865; Chambers, *Blood and Sacrifice*, 204; Robert Manson Myers, ed., *The Children of Pride: A True Story of Georgia and the Civil War* (New Haven: Yale University Press, 1972), 1244; *Richmond Daily Dispatch*, March 8, 1865; *Richmond Daily Whig*, March 10, 1865; Grace B. Elmore Diary, March 1, 4, 1865; Cornelia McDonald, *A Diary with Reminiscences of the War and Refugee Life in the Shenandoah Valley, 1860–1865* (Nashville: Hunter McDonald, 1934), 247–48; Taylor, *Lee's Adjutant*, 233.

68. OR, Ser. IV, 3:1037; McGuire, *Diary of a Southern Refugee*, 332–33; *Edgefield (SC) Advertiser*, February 8, 1865; *Richmond Daily Sentinel*, March 9, 1865; Jones,

Rebel War Clerk's Diary, 2:444; Gorgas, *Journals of Josiah Gorgas*, 156; Walters, *Norfolk Blues*, 205; *Lynchburg Virginian*, March 14, 1865.

69. *Richmond Daily Dispatch*, January 13, 1865; Jones, *Rebel War Clerk's Diary*, 2:414; *Richmond Daily Sentinel*, January 4, 1865; Abbie Brooks Diary, January 25, 1865; *Lynchburg Virginian*, March 24, 1865; *Richmond Daily Whig*, January 6, February 4, March 2, April 1, 1865.

70. *Macon (GA) Daily Telegraph and Confederate*, January 7, 1865; *Richmond Daily Dispatch*, February 2, 1865; *Richmond Daily Whig*, February 21, March 10, 1865; *Richmond Daily Sentinel*, January 14, 1865; Susan Bradford Eppes, *Through Some Eventful Years* (Gainesville: University of Florida Press, 1968), 257. Of course, not all comparisons augured well for the Southern cause. One editor believed that the second-raters of the Confederate Congress would never measure up to the stalwart patriots of the Continental Congress (*Richmond Daily Dispatch*, January 17, 1865).

71. *Lynchburg Virginian*, March 20, 1865; *Macon (GA) Daily Telegraph and Confederate*, March 24, 1865; *Richmond Daily Whig*, January 10, 1865; *Edgefield (SC) Advertiser*, April 5, 1865; *Richmond Daily Dispatch*, January 3, February 9, 22, March 8, 1865.

72. *Richmond Daily Whig*, March 22, 1865; Cumming, *Journal*, 266; *Richmond Daily Dispatch*, March 8, 1865; OR, Ser. I, 46: pt. 2, 1295; *Macon (GA) Daily Telegraph and Confederate*, March 10, 1865; Gorgas, *Journals of Josiah Gorgas*, 157.

73. Gorgas, *Journals of Josiah Gorgas*, 154, 157, 158; Heartsill, *Fourteen Hundred and 91 Days in the Confederate Army*, 234; Edmondston, *"Journal of a Secesh Lady,"* 682, 684; Ruffin, *Diary of Edmund Ruffin*, 3:812; House, *Very Violent Rebel*, 153, 155, 156; *Richmond Daily Whig*, March 25, 27, 1865.

74. House, *Very Violent Rebel*, 151, 153, 154; Jones, *Rebel War Clerk's Diary*, 2:418, 421, 440, 447; OR, Ser. I, 46: pt. 2, 1242, 1252–53; Gorgas, *Journals of Josiah Gorgas*, 153; *Richmond Daily Dispatch*, January 14, 1865; *Richmond Daily Sentinel*, March 4, 9, 1865.

75. Taylor, *Lee's Adjutant*, 225; Jones, *Rebel War Clerk's Diary*, 2:453; Gorgas, *Journals of Josiah Gorgas*, 158; *Richmond Daily Dispatch*, March 30, 1865; *Richmond Daily Sentinel*, March 30, 1865; *Richmond Daily Whig*, March 30, 31, 1865; Dooley, *John Dooley, Confederate Soldier*, 176; McGuire, *Diary of a Southern Refugee*, 342.

76. Edmondston, *"Journal of a Secesh Lady,"* 689, 692; Clemson, *Rebel Came Home*, 81; Eppes, *Through Some Eventful Years*, 270.

77. OR, Ser. I, 46: pt. 3, 1382–83; *Macon (GA) Daily Telegraph and Confederate*, April 5, 13, 1865.

78. *Macon* (GA) *Daily Telegraph and Confederate*, April 6, 1865; *Edgefield* (SC) *Advertiser*, April 12, 1865; Edmondston, "*Journal of a Secesh Lady,*" 694; Heartsill, *Fourteen Hundred and 91 Days in the Confederate Army*, 240.

79. House, *Very Violent Rebel*, 160; LeConte, *When the World Ended*, 90; Clemson, *Rebel Came Home*, 81; Stone, *Brokenburn*, 330; Edmondston, "*Journal of a Secesh Lady,*" 694–95.

80. House, *Very Violent Rebel*, 161–62; McGuire, *Diary of a Southern Refugee*, 353–54; Heartsill, *Fourteen Hundred and 91 Days in the Confederate Army*, 240; Dowdey and Manarin, eds., *Wartime Papers*, 939; OR, Ser. I, 47: pt. 3, 813–14; LeConte, *When the World Ended*, 85.

81. Stone, *Brokenburn*, 326–27; House, *Very Violent Rebel*, 159, 162; OR, Ser. I, 49; pt. 2, 1263–64; Jones, *Rebel War Clerk's Diary*, 2:464; Edmondston, "*Journal of a Secesh Lady,*" 699; Holmes, *Diary of Emma Holmes*, 436.

82. House, *Very Violent Rebel*, 165; Badad, Hills, and O'Driscoll, "Factors Influencing Wishful Thinking," 471.

Jean V. Berlin

Did Confederate Women Lose the War?

Deprivation, Destruction, and Despair on the Home Front

The collapse of the Confederacy was disastrous for Confederate women. Women who had invested their hopes, their money, and their menfolk in the cause found that in a few short months they lost homes, crops, and worldly goods, as well as the husbands, sons, brothers, and sweethearts who were fighting and dying. Under the successful and increasingly stern leadership of generals such as William T. Sherman, Ulysses S. Grant, and Philip H. Sheridan, Federal troops respected the private property and rights of women less and less. Sherman's Atlanta campaign, Sheridan's Valley campaign, and Grant's activities in Virginia in 1864 served notice that the nature of the war had changed. What followed would alter forever the lives of Southern women while it brought about the end of their nation.

What role did these women play in the collapse of their country? The recent growth of gender studies and women's histories of the Civil War has reawakened interest in this question. While white Southerners have always honored the struggle of their foremothers during the darkest hours of the South, some historians began to question whether women were the subversive agents of their own undoing. Women, they asserted, expected much the same results from war as the men, but both experienced it and contributed to it in different ways. Exploring these differences and their implications for Confederate women's loyalty to their cause has become a growing segment of historiography.

Early writings on women and the Confederacy, often by Southerners themselves, focused on the unselfish support and sacrifice of women, echoing the words chiseled on the monument to South Carolina women in Columbia: "In This Monument Generations Unborn Shall Hear the Voice of a Grateful

People to the Sublime Devotion of the Women of South Carolina in Their Country's Need."[1] Historians began to attempt a more dispassionate view of the experiences of Confederate women in the 1950s and 1960s, notably with the work of Mary Elizabeth Massey. Massey, herself a Southerner, was able to stand back and criticize Confederate women, while preserving a firm sense of their accomplishments.[2] But the most innovative and far-reaching work has been done in the last ten or fifteen years, with the exponential growth in women's history and gender studies.[3] Many of these works focus on the explosion of opportunity that the war offered and ponder implications for the postwar period in the absence of an active women's movement in the South.

Recent studies on Confederate nationalism and ideology also have addressed the attitudes of white Confederate women to the war.[4] Drew Gilpin Faust's dense and careful explication of the structure of Confederate nationalism explains why it failed. Based as it was on the notion of the individual households as the building blocks of society and the sanctity of the liberty of those households, the signal failure of the nation and its armies to protect these units by the end of the war undermined the very foundation of Southerners' support for their country: "Confederate nationalism prescribed change in the service of continuity, but then proved able neither to contain nor explain the ensuing transformations. . . . Confederate ideology was defeated in large measure by the internal contradictions that wartime circumstances brought so prominently to the fore." Also, the wartime need for national and united action by the new government and its adherents struck at another notion dear to the hearts of Southerners: states' rights. "The logic of Confederate ideology prescribed an effort to build a social consensus that would have implied a significant transformation in southern life," she concluded.[5] Paul Escott's earlier work on Confederate nationalism also addressed many of these issues, offering insights into the role of class conflict and states' rights in hampering the formation of an effective national government that could win a war. George Rable's work on the Confederate republic in turn offers ideas on how the dynamics of republicanism and party politics created conflicts that also hindered an effective war effort.[6]

Two historians who have written most recently and directly on Confederate women and the war are George Rable and Drew Gilpin Faust, whose expertise in Confederate politics and ideology give them great insight into women, war, and the republic. Rable's *Civil Wars: Women and the Crisis of Southern Nationalism* was the first such survey to appear in many years and certainly the first to use the methodologies and theories of the new generation of historians of women and gender. He focused on the impact of the war on Southern white women, whom he saw as the custodians of a fundamentally conservative social order that was challenged internally and externally by war. He wrote of Sherman's troops and their devastating effect on women's morale during the closing months of the war: "They struck at the heart of the home, tearing at the sinews of memory that bound families together and to past generations. In ransacking houses, they in effect ravaged habit and tradition, destroyed the commonplace, and left lasting scars, on the land and the people." Such catastrophes left women dispirited, and their invective against the invaders in their diaries and letters began to reflect weary resignation rather than active resistance. Many women, he added, fell silent, as the evangelical Protestantism they espoused led them to interpret the events around them as a divine indictment of their lives, prompting agonizing, if silent, soul-searching. And he observed that the war exacerbated the already existing rift between the planter, yeoman, and poor classes.[7]

Drew Gilpin Faust's well-received *Mothers of Invention* centers on the enormously articulate white women of the upper, planter class and how the war affected them. She corroborated Rable's findings that these women wished to uphold a very conservative social order that had benefited them both singly and collectively. But the war to defend this order, she observed, required increasing efforts from them and ones that often forced them into men's roles. Tired of their new positions and responsibility by the end of the war, the women boldly asserted their own self-interest and helped to bring about the end of the war by urging their men to desert and undermining the armies. The war, she concluded, left women unsure of whether their menfolk could uphold this order for them but still supporting much of the necessary postwar rehabilitation of the patriarchy, rather than embracing the changes and opportunity which the war had brought them.[8] Unfortunately, she never explicitly addresses the failure of Confederate nationalism, or the fact that the men responded in droves to their women's pleas to come home, arguing a more complex dialogue between husbands and wives, mothers and sons, sisters and brothers, than a mere assertion of female self-interest. By deserting, men acknowledged not only the futility of the Confederate cause but also the justice of women's arguments, indicating that there was a common perception of home and hearth. Southern men are awkward, silent partners in her story.

This essay will not so much challenge the work of Rable, Faust, and others but will try to use their findings as well as those of recent political and military historians to try to understand the interplay of the events of the closing months of the war between the military and domestic fronts. All too often in this time, women found themselves on or near the front line of the battles and campaigns, and this proximity could not help but shape their view of their country and the war and lead them to actions that would shape the course of military and political history. Rarely in history did political commanders assess women so seriously as a military threat and take direct action to thwart them. No one, however, has linked women's attitudes to the war and defeat to the political and military situation of late 1864 and 1865 and the ideals on which the Confederacy was founded.

By late 1864, Southerners' faith in the ability and willingness of their government to win the war had begun to flag, and women were as discontented as the men. As early as August, one prominent Richmond matron had written to a friend: "There is a strong feeling among the people I meet that the hour has come when we should consider the lives of the men left to us. Why let the enemy wipe us off the face of the earth? . . . I am for a tidal wave of peace— and I am not alone." She pointed out another danger—the widening gap between the white classes—when she spoke of the suffering of the yeomen and the poor: "These are the people who suffer the consequence of all that talk about slavery in the territories you and I used to hear in the House and Senate Chamber."[9] Lincoln's reelection dashed the hopes for peace raised by McClellan's nomination as the Democratic candidate for president. "This is a dark hour in our country's history. Lincoln has been elected by 300,000 majority," wrote Ella Gertrude Clanton Thomas.[10]

Some hopes were raised anew with the word of the peace talks at Hampton Roads, but they were quickly dashed with the news that Lincoln and the North insisted that the Confederate states must and would return to the Union. Mary Chesnut commented, "Why not? He has it all his way now."[11] Women who had kept diaries now wrote much less regularly, and, if they gave a reason, cited their anxiety about the political and military situation: "I can't keep a regular diary now, because I do not like to write all that I feel and hear," Judith Brockenbrough McGuire lamented, while Ella Gertrude Clanton Thomas confided that "I know I will regret hereafter that I have made no record of time and events which are fraught with so much interest, record of events which are hourly making history—but I cannot. I shrink from the task."[12]

Battles between Jefferson Davis and the state legislatures over the draft demonstrated the failure of the national government. As the military crisis grew, the Confederate Congress, state legislatures, and governors took it upon themselves to try to limit their losses in the defense of what they suspected to be a lost cause. Davis's attempts to increase the conscription powers of the central government were frustrated when Congress restored exemptions from military service and states declared that all able-bodied men would first go to the state militia ranks. Some political leaders lobbied for the removal of Hood and the reinstatement of Joe Johnston. The appointment of Lee as general in chief in February 1865 reflected the country's disillusionment with Davis's military leadership.[13]

But the debate that perhaps most signified the death of the Confederacy and all it stood for was the long-simmering argument over whether to use blacks as soldiers, offering them emancipation for military service. In early November 1864, Davis had first proposed that more slaves be used as army laborers, with freedom the reward for faithful service. This idea provoked a firestorm of controversy. At first the notion was met with revulsion and violent opposition; after all, "Confederate leaders could never separate slavery from national identity or their political culture."[14] The women soon weighed in with their opinions. "I take a woman's view of the subject but it does seem strangely inconsistent, the idea of our offering to a Negro the rich boon—the priceless reward of freedom to aid us in keeping in bondage a large portion of his brethren, when by joining the Yankees he will instantly gain the very reward which Mr Davis offers to him after a certain amount of labor rendered and danger incurred. Mr Davis to the contrary, the Negro has had a great deal to do with this war," Ella Gertrude Thomas observed.[15] In December, a Miss Rhett told Mary Chesnut, " 'Now, we feel that if we are to lose our negroes, we would as soon see Sherman free them as the Confederate government. Freeing negroes seems the last Confederate government craze.' "[16] Slavery was the basis of states' rights; it was the essential defining element of Southern republicanism—in contrast to the blacks, all whites, at least, were free. Women seemed well aware of this fact. Military considerations won out, however, especially when Lee came out in favor of enlisting blacks, and politicians reluctantly concluded that victory without slavery was better than defeat and slavery for all whites. In March, the Confederate Congress passed a bill allowing a limited form of slave conscription—only 25 percent of eligible males between eighteen and forty-five in each state could enlist, contingent on their masters' assent.[17] Many saw this act as the end of the Confederacy, a subversion of the principles on which their republic had been founded.

The very nature of Southern society militated against a strong, effective federal government. The basic unit of Southern society was the household, as befitted a largely agrarian region. Thus Confederate nationalism had to call on the devotion of Southerners to their home and its protection. But ironically, the very sacrifices required by Southerners to meet this goal went against their grain: universal conscription, national taxation, conscription of black labor—all were met with stubborn opposition. The Confederacy's dire situation in late 1864 and 1865 cried out for national unity, for Southerners to band together, as Americans had allegedly done during the Revolution, and to sacrifice their individual rights and liberties for the good of the nation. But this price seemed too high to a nation predicated on the supremacy of each man in his own household, his inviolate right to control his property as he saw fit. Southern women complained as stridently about perceived abuses by their national government as about the Yankees. The notion of the home as the basic unit of the society spoke strongly to women, reinforcing their sense of self-importance as the domestic rulers of the foundation of the Confederacy. When they felt their government could no longer protect them and thus could no longer protect the very basis, as they saw it, of the government, their loyalty faltered and died. The most heartfelt and stirring professions of patriotism are framed to the countryside, to the region, to the land itself. The women had watched the unraveling of Confederate ideology and saw that little was left—and its ultimate component, the sanctity and safety of home and hearth, was coming under a sustained and purposeful attack that would erode their will to fight and render their nation impotent.

Furthermore, the Confederate nation had very little to offer poor white women. One historian has shown how the war in North Carolina "turned poverty into a desperate struggle for survival." The Confederacy could not offer these women anything to win their support and could not control them, losing a crucial portion of the Southern population and weakening the war effort.[18] Shortages of food and clothing were particularly hard on those with no reserves on which to rely. The worsening situation in the closing months of the war made life unbearable for them. Another historian observed that the "triple evils of inflation, scarcity, and destruction" were particularly hard on yeomen and poor women, those who would become most likely to urge their husbands, sons, fathers, and brothers to desert.[19] These women, like their sisters responsible for the 1863 bread riots in Richmond, found that their government had promised them much and given them little. Hit hard by the impressment of men and supplies, isolated from the markets, albeit inflated ones, of urban areas, these poor farm women "worked hard and had little to show for it, and they came to hate the government as they did the foe."[20] " 'I hate Yankees, and I hate niggers too,'" one yeoman woman had remarked in 1862, accurately conflating the war with slavery, an institution that had little to do with her own life.[21]

And in the fall of 1864, Union military policy had shifted to commanders who instinctively understood their enemy. Ulysses S. Grant and William T. Sherman were aware of both the need to weaken the morale of Southerners by making them feel their government could not guarantee their safety and the complete impossibility of invading and subduing the South by traditional military means.[22] As early as September 1863, Sherman told Halleck that to win the war, "we will remove & destroy every obstacle, if need be take every life, every acre of land, every particle of property, everything that to us seems proper, that we will not cease till the end is attained, that all who do not aid are enemies, and we will not account to them for our acts."[23] Phil Sheridan's Shenandoah Valley campaign of 1864 and 1865 left no doubt that he, too, ascribed to the school of hard, destructive war. These military commanders were aware of Southern feelings and acted on them in a way calculated to raise all Southerners' anxieties about the safety of their families, their homes, and their property.

Sherman in particular, who had spent much time in the South before the war and who had hoped to spend the rest of his life there, understood how Southerners felt and how he could use this to his military advantage and suffer very few losses. The destruction of all materials that Federal troops could not carry with them that could possibly be used by the enemy, as well as his willingness to exempt women from the treatment prescribed by the traditional rules of war, recognizing them as the powerful enemies they could be, became the hallmarks of all his major campaigns from the summer of 1864 through to the end of the war. His conduct of the Atlanta campaign gave Confederate women the first inkling of what the war could and would mean to them.

On July 6, 1864, Brig. Gen. Kenner Garrard, a cavalry commander in the Army of the Cumberland, captured the town of Roswell, Georgia, including its highly productive textile factories. One of them, a particularly large and prosperous installation, had been producing thread, cotton, and rope exclusively for the Confederate government. Following earlier instructions, Garrard burned all the factories and reported that while all "citizens of property" had already left, the employees and management of the factories remained, including four hundred female workers. Sherman approved his actions and ordered him to go even further: "To make the matter complete you will arrest the owners & employees & send them under guard charged with Treason, to Marietta," adding, "I repeat my orders that you arrest all people male & female connected with those factorys no matter what the clamor & let them foot it under guard to Marietta, whence I will send them by cars to the North. . . . Useful laborers, excused by reason of their skill as manufacturers, from conscription are as much prisoners as if armed. The poor women will make a howl. Let them take along their children & clothing providing they have the means of hauling or you can spare them. We will retain them until they can reach a country where they can live in Peace & Security." He would restate these views in his report to Halleck later that day.[24]

These four hundred women, joined later by another large number of mill operatives from the Sweetwater Factory in Sweetwater, Georgia, spent a miserable, short detention in Marietta before being sent north to Nashville and thence over Federal lines in Indiana and elsewhere along the Ohio River. The care and support of these women and their children were left to towns and countryside already flooded with refugees. Women all over the South put themselves into their sisters' shoes and shuddered at the thought of what might happen to them when the Yankees came.

But what happened in Roswell was as nothing compared to the debacle of the Atlanta campaign. When Sherman arrived with his troops in Atlanta on September 7 after a long summer of advancing, retreating, and outwaiting the enemy, he found a city reeling from the effects of months of siege warfare. Inhabitants were further staggered by his announcement the next day in Special Field Orders No. 67 that he would evacuate all civilians from the city to avoid shedding innocent blood. Despite the vehement and angry protests of Confederate commander John Bell Hood and the mayor and citizens of Atlanta that such an evacuation was unnecessary and would unduly harm women and children, Sherman stuck to his guns.[25] His letter to the mayor and city council became the source of his famous "War is hell" quote: "You cannot qualify war in harsher terms than I will. War is cruelty, and you cannot refine it: and those who brought war into our Country deserve all the curses and maledictions a people can pour out."[26] The reaction of his wife, Ellen, to the expulsion of the women and children of Atlanta echoed his own feelings and those of many other Northerners: "I am charmed with your order expelling the inhabitants of Atlanta as it has always seemed to me preposterous to have our Government feeding so many of their people—their insolent women particularly for they are responsible for the war and should be made to feel that it exists in sternest reality."[27]

Southern women understood what the loss of Atlanta meant. Judith Mc-Guire lamented from Richmond that "General Hood telegraphs that the inhabitants of Atlanta have been ordered to leave their homes, to go they know not whither. Lord, how long must we suffer such things?"[28] Mary Chesnut concluded, "Atlanta gone. Well—that agony is over. Like David when the child was dead, I will get up from my knees, will wash my face and comb my hair. No hope."[29] On being told that Atlanta was lost, Mary Ann Harris Gay recalled: "Dumbfounded we stood, trying to realize the crushing fact. Woman's heart could bear no more in silence, and a wail over departed hopes mingled with the angry sounds without."[30] In October, Mary Mallard wrote to her mother: "Everything seems very dark with us now, and we are anxiously awaiting the next telegraphic intelligence. . . . We have a rumor today from some 'reliable gentleman' that General Hood's army has been surrounded, and our loss very great . . . if we lose our army, our state is at Sherman's mercy."[31]

This fear and anxiety felt by Southern women, rich and poor, would be brought to a fever pitch by the successful march of Sherman's army across Georgia to the sea. He and his men traveled without a supply line, living off the land and taking whatever they found wherever they found it. Most women had expected that their sex and civilian status would guarantee them a degree of safety and respect. Instead they found on their doorstep an enemy who took all their food and often destroyed their household goods, despite official orders to the contrary. When they complained to the Union commanders, little was done, and they even found that they themselves were blamed for the men's behavior, accused of reckless and provoking speech or leaving liquor where thirsty soldiers could find it. Sherman had observed earlier to his wife that Confederate women would curse him and his cause in one breath and in the next throw themselves on his mercy; this complaint would be a common refrain of his in the years to come.

Like Sherman, many Union officers found their sympathies strained from listening to Confederate women reciting a continual litany of the evil of their men and their cause, and they hardened their hearts toward women's pleas for protection and supplies. Many quickly grasped Sherman's idea that by leaving women and families hungry and vulnerable they were weakening the Confederate army in two ways: Southern soldiers became more concerned about their families than their brothers in arms and their armies while the destruction of crops deprived the Southern troops of much needed supplies. The Federal commanders' high evaluation of the women's effect on their men's morale was a well-gauged and a perverse compliment. Most Union leaders thought that Confederate women and the support they offered their army were vital to the South's ability to continue fighting when all seemed lost. The women were not prepared for Union commanders to take them and their contributions to the war cause seriously, to find they were expected to face consequences for supporting their new nation. The compliment implicit to their strength in the campaigns of 1864 and 1865 was one they could do without.[32]

Before Sherman embarked on his infamous March to the Sea, he explained to the skeptical Henry Wager Halleck: "This movement is not purely military or strategic, but it will illustrate the vulnerability of the South. They don't know what war means, but when the rich planters of the Oconee and Savannah see their fences and corn and hogs and sheep vanish before their eyes they will have something more than a mean opinion of the 'Yanks.' "[33] After the successful conclusion of the march, he reassured George Henry Thomas that his proposed march to the Carolinas would not mobilize the civil populace: "It is nonsense to Suppose that the People of the South are enraged or united by such movements. They reason very differently. They see in them the Sure and inevitable destruction of all their property, they realize that the Confederate armies cannot protect them, and they see in the repetition of such raids the inevitable result of starvation & misery."[34] Sherman had always disliked the way Confederate women used their gender as an excuse to beg him for protection from "bummers" and other "lawless" elements in his command. He had written to his wife in June 1863 that he had come across some social connections from his days at the Louisiana State Seminary of Learning and Military Academy and how the women upbraided him: "Do, oh do General Sherman spare my son, in one breath and in another, that Lincoln was a tyrant and we only Murderers, Robbers, plunderers and defilers of the houses and altars of an innocent & outraged People. She and all the women were real secesh, bitter as gall & yet O do General Sherman protect my son. The scene set all the women crying, and Dolly [his horse] & I concluded to go into the more genial atmosphere out in the Fields & Woods." He concluded, "I doubt if History affords a parallel of the deep & bitter enmity of the women of the South."[35]

Some of the worst fears of women in the path of Sherman's army were realized when the "bummers" or stragglers helped themselves to supplies indiscriminately. One woman remonstrated that they were taking food meant for herself, her daughters, and grandchildren, but to no avail; "they said they meant to starve us to death."[36] But in spite of their terror and rage, some Southern women found ways to adapt themselves to the invaders and to evade the worst depredations and deprivations. A suspiciously large number of women claimed to be widows because "a frail and defenseless appearance" could "evoke feelings of sympathy among the bluecoats who descended upon their home."[37] From the start of the war, women throughout the South had shown a willingness to accept food and supplies from the Yankees and to exploit sympathetic officers for whatever indulgences they could get.[38] Sherman himself noted how many women turned to him for help and defense, and, in spite of his angry words, he obliged them more often than not. Women thus showed a streak of practical, self-preserving behavior that indicated there were indeed limits to their support for the Confederacy and foreshadowed their nation's demise. Above all, Southern women valued the integrity and safety of their own households, one of the central tenets of Confederate nationalism. But Federal guards were usually posted too late to prevent the worst of the looting and served rather to protect what had not been thought worthy of capture and to reassure women that no bodily harm would come to them or their families. But the majority of women who sought and were granted this protection were well-to-do—the poor women and even the moderately prosperous yeoman farmer women lost far more.

The effects of campaigns such as Sherman's on a civilian population were dramatic and long-lasting; one contemporary observer visiting Georgia in late December found that the people no longer cared about the Confederacy but worried about survival—they had been defeated.[39] Even the fire-eating Emma LeConte recorded that after Sherman's visit to Columbia, "I feel at times an entire and apathetic indifference as to what should transpire."[40] Some women blamed Confederate men for the defeat: Hood for following a doomed plan and the soldiers for surrendering rather than fighting. "But say what you will," commented Mary Chesnut, "this movement of the western army is against common sense." It would, she reflected, send the Yankees "lighthearted and rejoicing, into the Carolinas."[41] Grace Brown Elmore was outraged that men were planning to take the oath of allegiance, while Judith McGuire was convinced that if the Georgians had had the experience of the Virginians, they would have made short work of Sherman and his legions.[42]

While Sherman was laying siege to Atlanta and cutting a swath to the sea, Philip Sheridan was fulfilling Grant's desire that his men in the Shenandoah Valley "eat out Virginia clear and clean as far as they go, so that Crows flying over it for the balance of this season will have to carry their provender with them."[43] In August, about a month before Sheridan's victory at the battle of Winchester ensured his control of the strategic Valley, Grant had instructed him: "Do all the damage to rail-roads & crops you can. Carry off stock of all discreptions [*sic*] and negroes so as to prevent further planting. If the War is to last another year we want the Shenandoah valley to remain a barren waste."[44] Sheridan's Valley campaign was brutal and unremitting, marked by atrocities on both sides, and it scarred the women of the region. To have lost only foodstuffs or livestock was to be counted lucky.[45] Burning of property and summary executions were common reprisals in late September and October as all the Valley went up in smoke. "These stories of our defeats in the Valley fall like blows upon a dead body," mourned Mary Chesnut.[46] By October 7, Sheridan was able to report to Grant that his men had destroyed all grain and forage from the Blue Ridge to North Mountain: "This destruction embraces the Luray valley and Little Fort valley as well as the main valley," adding, "Tomorrow I will continue the destruction of wheat, forage Etc., down to Fisher's Hill. When this is completed the valley from Winchester up to Staunton 92 miles, will have but little for man or beast." "The people here are getting sick of the war, Heretofore they have had no reason to complain because they have been living in great abundance," he concluded.[47] These clearings would continue through the winter, when an abnormally bitter season would make things worse for those women in the Valley. "It was, I suppose, the most cruel and desolating raid upon record— more lawless, if possible, than Hunter's," wrote one Virginia woman. "His soldiers were allowed to commit any cruelty on non-combatants that suited their rapacious tempers."[48] On December 2, "owing to the incompetency of the Confederate Army upon which we depend for defence," one group of women proposed forming a ladies' regiment in the Army of the Shenandoah.[49] Although Confederate authorities did not act on this radical proposal, it did reflect a growing opinion among Confederate women that their armies and government could not or would not defend them.

Grant's campaign in Virginia in the summer and fall of 1864 may have been less spectacular than Sherman's and Sheridan's, but it was at least as important as theirs, demonstrating as it did the weaknesses of that demigod of the Confederacy, Robert E. Lee, and intimating to women that Lee would be defeated. In early June, when Grant had been seemingly defeated before the defenses of Petersburg, a central railroad point for supplying what remained of the Confederacy, he did not back down. Rather, he settled in with his troops for a long siege, knowing that time, resources, and strategy were on his side. Even when the daring scheme to dig a tunnel under the Confederate defenses and use mines to blow a hole in the ramparts failed miserably, Southern women were astonished at Federal audacity and began to sense they were up against a different kind of commander. "He has the disagreeable habit of not retreating before irresistible veterans," commented Mary Chesnut, later adding, "Grant's dogged stay about Richmond very disgusting and depressing to the spirits."[50] It would be a long winter for women in Virginia, fearing Sheridan in the Valley and Grant at Petersburg.

Military and political events would further converge on Confederate women in November. Lincoln's reelection in early November, owing in no small part to Sherman's victory at Atlanta, increased the political malaise among the Confederate public. Mary Chesnut observed that "time is short now. We have lost nearly all of our men, and we have no money. And it looks as if we had taught them to fight since Manassas. . . . Here we stand—despair in our hearts . . . and our houses burnt, or about to be, over our heads."[51] A cold and bleak winter worsened the supply problems that had plagued what was left of the Confederacy since the fall campaigns. Women became increasingly desperate, and their fear and rage deepened in the New Year.

The national government did nothing to alleviate shortages, and, in reality, could not do anything. Many policies ended by having precisely the opposite effect than intended. Impressment of supplies and livestock by the army was administered under a system Southern citizens found particularly odious because it relied on the judgment of military commanders and the "tithing" system, which called on all farmers to give up one-tenth of their farm produce in lieu of taxes. When the Confederate government tried to act as a national government and seize what it needed, its citizens cried foul and pleaded the doctrine of states' rights against the very government formed to support them.[52] The shortages of food were particularly acute for women, who needed the labor of men to help them sow and harvest crops properly. Hunger was rampant on the home front, and all households faced shortages of coffee, tea, and salt, the latter posing a particular problem for the preservation of meat. Firewood and clothing were particularly prized; thieves often broke into woodsheds or brazenly stole clothes from the lines where they were drying; many soldiers realized a lucrative business in selling their clothes and rations to desperate civilians, leading Adjutant General Samuel Cooper to make the selling of rations an offense in the fall of 1864 and reminding soldiers of the penalties (jail time and fines) for selling their clothes in March 1865.[53]

Cornelia McDonald, living as a refugee in Lexington, Virginia, recorded in detail what little she subsisted upon: "With all I could do we had barely enough food to keep from actual want; and that of a kind that was often sickening to me. I generally went all day with a cup of coffee and a roll." It would particularly gall her that her children went hungry or poorly clothed, often without shoes.[54]

Such conditions provoked a religious crisis in many women. A "Confederate theology" had always been an important part of Confederate ideology.[55] The Christian community and church gatherings, whether for services or social functions, were vitally important for Southern society. The clergy threw their support behind the new nation, and their fire-eating sermons, published as pamphlets and in newspapers, were widely read and influential. For those women who could not read or did not have the money to buy such publications, the clergyman in their local pulpit reinforced their fire-eating message. Women's hopes were high at the start of the war, and they invoked God's aid, confident they were his chosen people. Southerners, under the clergy's auspices, saw themselves as the new Israel, separating from an unjust and oppressive ruler. "We all have such entire reliance in the justice of our cause and the valor of our men, and, above all, on the blessing of Heaven!" wrote Judith McGuire, the wife of a clergyman.[56] But as the war raged on, and menfolk were killed or returned home maimed in body or spirit, women found their faith severely tested. For a while, they found comfort in the notion that God was testing them and that they and their nation would emerge purified and strengthened by the crucible of war. Southerners had sinned, they reasoned, and would have to suffer for the reward of freedom. Even mourning, a peculiarly female prerogative during the war, was burdened with political meaning; women were expected to show resignation, a willingness to sacrifice their loved ones to the greater good. At the same time, they were to carry on at home to fulfill their end of the covenant.

But this resolve began to falter in the face of mounting losses. How much suffering and death were enough? At times it seemed as if the very world they were fighting for had ended, and they questioned the price they were paying. God seemed to be against them; were they in the wrong? Were the Yankee invaders truly the servants of God? While few women uttered their thoughts in quite these words, they were thinking them. Self-examination and fault-finding became common. If they were the justified and virtuous, women reasoned, victory should be theirs. Instead, they faced an enemy whose numbers and strength grew, whose depredations on the Southern landscape would have seemed unthinkable just three and a half years before, who had unlimited supplies but still confiscated foodstuffs and livestock at will. "God has been good to us in deferring our trial so long, but now it has come, 'tis a trial of fire. There is not a spot to which we can flee & find safety," exclaimed Grace Brown Elmore in December 1864. She speculated that the war was God's way of making blacks deserving of freedom, comparing them to the Israelites.[57]

Conflating God and the government, Confederate women saw that supreme authority was unwilling or unable to help them: "Neither God nor Jefferson Davis was attending to women's desperate needs," Drew Gilpin Faust remarked, echoing George Rable's comment that "the contradictions between personal and national salvation became unmanageable. To still believe in a covenant between God and the Southern people required more faith than many women could muster."[58] Unlike Christ, Southern women found that when they asked God why he had forsaken them, their lamentations were met with silence. "Defeat seemed such a calamity as was never known, and as no people ever survived, it would be so for us; our enemies were implacable, and defeat would be utter ruin to us all. How hard it was to say 'Thy will be done'; how hard to feel that God knew best," one woman recalled in sorrow.[59] In the end, wrote Ellen Renshaw House, "We have depended too much on Gen Lee too little on God, & I believe God has suffered his surrender to show us he can use other means than Gen Lee to affect his ends."[60]

At the end of January, General Sherman turned his attention to the Carolinas. During these dying days of the winter, Sherman would confide to his wife: "I fear the People along our Road will have nothing left wherewith to Support an hostile army, but as I told them their sons & brothers had better stay home to take Care of the females instead of running about the Country playing soldiers. The same brags and boasts are Kept up, but when I reach the path where the lion crouched I find him slinking away."[61] The women had apparently taken his advice to heart. Desertions among Confederate ranks increased sharply, and Sherman observed to one of his brothers-in-law on April 9, "My march through Georgia and South Carolina, besides its specific fruits actually produced a marked effect on Lee's Army, because fathers & sons in his Ranks felt a natural solicitude about children or relations in the regions through which I had passed with Such relentless Effect."[62] The march through the Carolinas was more vindictive than the March to the Sea and the women in its path were even more vociferous in their lamentations and complaints. Both officers and men were eager to punish South Carolina, the home of secession and the author, as the Federals saw it, of all their nation's troubles since 1861. "The importance of this march exceeds that from Atlanta to Savannah," Sherman told his wife. "South Carolina has had a visit from the West that will cure her of her pride and boasting."[63]

The anticipation and fear among South Carolina women that had risen steadily during the March to the Sea became hysteria after the bluecoats captured Savannah. "Georgia has been desolated. The resistless flood has swept through that state, leaving but a desert to mark its track. . . . They are preparing to hurl destruction upon the State they hate most of all, and Sherman the brute avows his intention of converting South Carolina into a wilderness," raged young Emma LeConte from her home in Columbia.[64] Malvina Black Gist, a young Confederate widow working for the Confederate treasury in Columbia, began by dismissing the rumors that Sherman would come ("I marvel at the ease with which some people lose their heads") but soon began to think differently: "The dawning of a doubt is a troublesome thing, for if a doubt does not out and out destroy faith, it assuredly chastens it to an uncomfortable degree. Is he coming, that terrible Sherman, with all his legions?"[65] Several of Mary Chesnut's correspondents wrote to her of events in South Carolina, explaining that they had burned the first drafts of their missives: Sally Rutledge wrote only briefly of the "red-hot wrath which consumed her—indignation, disgust, despair," leading her to burn her work for fear it would fall into enemy hands. Louisa Cheves McCord was "cool and businesslike," explaining in a postscript that "she had written a letter in her first futile rage at the senseless destruction &c&c, but that letter she thought it wisest to destroy." Harriot Horry (Mrs. St. Julien) Ravenel explained that she was not sending her letter on the burning of Columbia for reasons she would explain later.[66] Emma LeConte mourned the destruction of Columbia, "a night of horrors": "The sun rose at last, dim and red through the thick, murky atmosphere. It set last night on a beautiful town full of women and children— it shone dully down this morning on smoking ruins and abject misery."[67] The complaints of the diary keepers and correspondents, who lost most of their provisions, are written by women far better off than the average white woman in South Carolina, and it is painful to imagine just how devastating a visit from the Yankees was to a poor household. Just as disheartening to these women was the realization that the Federal forces were more numerous and better equipped than their own: "The sight of that army was enough to make the weak faint, they were so robust, so splendidly equipped no tattered garments, no well worn cloths, all perfect, all as it should be."[68] The women in their path, most of whom had already sacrificed the presence, if not the lives, of their menfolk, had no recourse, no rich friends or relatives, no hope of avoiding the stark poverty that Sherman's men brought. While Sherman could cavalierly tell them that their menfolk should come home to protect them, these women faced hard choices. Without their men at home, they faced certain destitution, illness, and perhaps death. Encouraging their men to come home would put the soldiers in more direct danger and ask them to defy the very government they were fighting to support. What followed is instructive.

Desertion rates, which had been high, began to skyrocket as the news of Sherman's marches reached Lee's Army of Northern Virginia. The perils of desertion began to pale in comparison to the needs of the soldiers' households. With no end to the war in sight and inadequate militia companies searching for deserters, it should be no surprise that half of the underfed, underclothed, underarmed, and unpaid Army of Northern Virginia disappeared during the retreat from Richmond and Petersburg. More than seventy thousand men had already deserted between October 1, 1864, and the early winter of 1865.[69] Many of them were getting letters such as one received by a soldier in Pickett's command in December 1864: "Christmus is most hear again, and things is worse and worse." The family was down to their last change of clothes, and those were badly worn and patched. The children had to stay in bed to try to keep warm for they had so few clothes. They were nearly out of food and had broken up the rail fence for fuel. "I don't want you to stop fighten them yankees till you kill the last one of them," the wife explained, "but try and get off and come home and fix us all up some and then you can go back and fight them a heep harder than you ever fought them before." She ended with a warning: "but, my dear, if you put off a-comin' 'twon't be no use to come, for we'll all hands of us be out there in the garden in the old graveyard with your ma and mine." Another woman was heard crying to her husband as the provost guard dragged him off: " 'Take it easy, Jake—you desert agin, quick as you kin—come back to your wife and children. . . . Desert, Jake! desert agin, Jake!"[70] " 'And before God, Edward, unless you come home, we must die,' " wrote another woman.[71] By such actions, Southern women changed the moral complexion of desertion from cowardice to courage, to the moral imperative of defying a government that had failed to protect their families. "Lee's army must be melting like a Scotch mist," commented Mary Chesnut.[72]

The increasingly desperate attempts of the government to fill its ranks with new conscripts reflected many of these problems, and the anger with which

Confederate civilians met these attempts showed their disillusionment with their government. Cornelia McDonald recorded in her diary/memoir that the agents had taken one mountain man, aged forty-five, leaving his wife alone and desperate. Yet another man had deserted when a new conscript arrived in the trenches and told him that his family at home was starving. "The conscription had forced many unwilling ones to go to the army, leaving unprotected wives and children in lonely mountain huts to abide their fate whatever it might be, freezing or starvation," she wrote, concluding that the government had reached new heights of despotism in the closing months of the war.[73]

Confederate commanders had not failed to see the problem. Lee focused on "the alarming frequency of desertions from this army" in a letter to the secretary of war urging him to work harder at supplying his troops. On February 9, the day he assumed the position of general in chief, Lee wrote to Davis, proposing an amnesty for deserters with the proviso that no further pardons would be issued. He further suggested that the pardons be issued under his signature because Davis had issued pardons before and his threats would have little weight. "It is the only method that I can propose to cause the return of our absentees," he concluded. Two weeks before his surrender at Appomattox he issued an order rebuking his soldiers for joking about deserting and reminding them of the penalties for such an act. He knew that conditions at home and the news thereof were largely responsible for the defection: "It seems that the men are influenced very much by the representations of their friends at home, who appear to have become very despondent as to our success. They think the cause desperate and write to the soldiers, advising them to take care of themselves, assuring them that if they will return home the bands of deserters so far outnumber the home guards that they will be in no danger of arrest."[74]

An insidious loss of morale grew during these hard months. One young woman thought of cutting her hair and selling it to raise money for the purchase of a new gunboat to defend Richmond in the closing months of the war but decided upon reflection that "the sacrifice would be in vain." The end of the war, wrote Cornelia McDonald, brought much relief with defeat: "they were glad to bury pride, patriotism, all, if they could see an end to destruction and bloodshed" and "others were happy at the thought of being released from danger, hunger and weariness, and of seeing their homes again, even if they were robbed of so much that had made them happy and though death had left its shadow there."[75] One diarist in Georgia noted that people around her "acknowledged themselves whipped" by the start of the New Year.[76]

Scared and troubled women panicked, and many feared they were going insane while anxiety crippled them. Ella Gertrude Clanton Thomas's mother sent her a note in late November, asking her to visit: "'I don't know what to do. I laugh awhile and cry awhile—The reflection is awful as I begin to realise poverty and starvation staring me in the face.'"[77] In October, Varina Davis wrote to her friend Mary Chesnut, "I am so constantly depressed that I dread writing—even four lines betray the feeling."[78] Drew Gilpin Faust wrote about these fears in *Mothers of Invention*, commenting that "material deprivation" played a large part in these reactions.[79] Ellen Renshaw House, who had been sent from her home in Knoxville behind Confederate lines in Georgia, noted with regret that she lost her temper several times because of her worries, even injuring a man on one occasion.[80]

The final, symbolic blow to the Confederate cause was the fall of Petersburg to Federal forces on April 2 and the taking of Richmond the following day. "Richmond has fallen—and I have no heart to write about it," mourned Mary Chesnut.[81] One diarist in Richmond had earlier stopped keeping her journal regularly "because I do not like to write all that I feel and hear." Judith McGuire did not believe the Confederate government's assurances that Richmond would be given up to the Yankees only to serve larger strategic goals: "I know that we ought to feel that whatever General Lee and the President deem right for the cause must be right, and that we should be satisfied that all will be well; but it would almost break my heart to see this dear old city, with its hallowed associations, given over to the Federals." Like many, she understood the symbolic value of the capital and that its abandonment marked the end of the Confederacy. When the worst came to pass, it would be as bad as she feared: "All Bedlam let loose could not have vied with them in diabolical roarings."[82]

Defeat did not come easily for Confederate women, although they tried to bow to the inevitable. The widespread destruction necessary to bring the Confederacy to its knees created a legacy of poverty and destitution for all, bringing the experience of all women to a level many of the well-bred would have believed impossible four years before. Less than a year later, a Northern schoolteacher and former Union army nurse wrote from Charleston: "Poverty means more here than in the North. It means destitution and a destitution that forbids any hope of anything better."[83] The bitterness remarked on by so many began soon after Appomattox and continues, in some quarters, to this day. "It is impossible not to feel rebellious and bitter," exclaimed Emma LeConte, while Sarah Morgan agonized, "'Never! let a great earthquake swallow us up first! Let us leave our land and emigrate to any desert spot of the earth, rather than return to the Union, even as it Was!' "[84] "Grief and despair took possession of my heart, with a sense of humiliation that till then I did not know I could feel," wrote Cornelia McDonald wearily, but her anger was replaced by resignation and concern for the future.[85] "We are almost paralyzed here by the rapid succession of strange and melancholy incidents that have marked the last few weeks," wrote a Georgia woman at the end of April.[86]

It was not so much that Southern women had failed as that the Southern armies and the Confederate nation had failed them. Because they had no political language of sacrifice or a definition of nation that allowed them to make sense of their sufferings and their losses, they could not cope when the North and its generals brought their superior numbers and resources directly to bear on those things they held most dear—family and home. The men may have hated the Yankees, but when these crucial days of the war arrived, they heeded women's pleas and returned to protect and help them. The fact that the South's society was based on the household became part of its downfall.[87] In contrast, their more united enemy could and did invoke the spirit of the Constitution and of the Union to overcome their internal differences. With hindsight, the legends of the self-sacrificing, selfless, and ingenious Southern women who persevered in the face of overwhelming odds and allowed Southern men to keep on fighting long after the nation's resources had run out can also be read as explanations of why, in the end, most beleaguered Southern women wanted the war to end and to return to some semblance of a normal life. Let the Confederacy die, they would say; we have done more than our share.

Southern women, like Southern men, were defeated by the superior military and economic force of the North. By the time Sherman began his March to the Sea, most women and men in the South knew that the war was over. When a foreign army can march through enemy countryside largely unmolested, a government and an army have failed their people. "The patriotism women had so enthusiastically embraced in 1861 began to erode before seemingly endless—and increasingly purposeless—demands for sacrifice," Drew Gilpin Faust wrote, adding, "Commitment to the Cause was not unbounded but had to be calculated in a balance sheet on which the burden of further hardship and the growing likelihood of ultimate defeat figured large."[88]

Southern women may have, to some degree, welcomed and even rationalized defeat, but they recognized it and suffered accordingly. They wondered if they had sacrificed enough, if God had found them wanting; and in trying to sort out the reasons for their failure, they searched their own conduct for blameworthy behavior. The simple facts that the North had had more men, superior resources, and commanders who understood the nature of civil war in profound ways were unpalatable, for they rendered the South ultimately powerless. And that was anathema to many women, especially those of the upper classes. It was better to blame defeat on their own error or omission than to acknowledge the enemy's superiority.

But for many women, especially those of the lower classes, defeat was probably greeted with relief, with the hope that missing menfolk might return to help with planting crops and with the belief that the bluecoated scourge would now leave them and their modest properties in peace. For some, peace came too late; they had lost everything and faced a bleak future of dire and unrelenting poverty. The price of defeat was indeed high for white Southern women; but by the fall of 1864 victory was no longer theirs to snatch from the jaws of defeat. When Sherman began marching, Sheridan began burning, and Grant started tightening his grip on Petersburg, Appomattox was only a matter of time.

The surrenders of Lee and Johnston in 1865 were ultimately efforts to preserve what was left of the society that had gone to war in 1861. There was no other point to the Confederacy in 1865. Surrender was, in fact, the best that could be done, a way to avoid even more catastrophic devastation. Most Confederate women knew this as well as or better than the men. To suggest that they hastened or postponed defeat is to ignore the complex interplay of Confederate ideology, religion, domestic politics, and military events in late 1864 and 1865. In the end, Confederate women were let down by their government and the principles for which it stood, defeated by an alien army, and devastated by the military policies of both Northern and Southern armies. But they focused their rage and disappointment solely on the North, not on the institutions that failed them at home. And it would be this preoccupation with defeat at the hands of a demonized North, combined with a refusal to examine the failures of their beloved Confederacy, that would keep these women trapped among the ghosts of the past.

Notes

1. See, for example, Matthew Page Andrews, ed., *The Women of the South in War Times* (Baltimore: Norman Remington, 1920); Francis W. Dawson, ed., *Our Women*

in the War: The Lives They Lived, the Death They Died (Charleston: Walker, Evans, and Cogswell, 1887); Francis Butler Simkins and James Welch Patton, *Women of the Confederacy* (Richmond: Garrett and Massie, 1936); and Mrs. Thomas Taylor et al., eds., *South Carolina Women in the Confederacy*, 2 vols. (Columbia: State, 1907). Two late examples of this type of work can be found in H. E. Sterks, *Partners in Rebellion: Alabama Women During the Civil War* (Rutherford NJ: Fairleigh Dickinson University Press, 1970), and Bell Irvin Wiley, *Confederate Women* (1975; rpt. New York: Barnes & Noble, 1994). The monument's inscription is reproduced in full in Edward D. C. Campbell Jr. and Kym S. Rice, eds., *A Woman's War: Southern Women, Civil War, and the Confederate Legacy* (Charlottesville: University Press of Virginia, 1996), 173.

2. See, for example, Mary Elizabeth Massey, *Refugee Life in the Confederacy* (Baton Rouge: Louisiana State University Press, 1964), 204–24. Her other works, still sound and used by scholars today, are *Ersatz in the Confederacy* (Columbia: University of South Carolina Press, 1952), and *Bonnet Brigades* (New York: Knopf, 1966), reprinted as *Women in the Civil War* (Lincoln: University of Nebraska Press, 1994).

3. Anne Firor Scott, *The Southern Lady: From Pedestal to Politics, 1830–1930* (Chicago: University of Chicago Press, 1970); Catherine Clinton, *Plantation Mistress: Women's World in the Old South* (New York: Pantheon, 1982); Elizabeth Fox-Genovese, *Within the Plantation Household* (Chapel Hill: University of North Carolina Press, 1988); Victoria E. Bynum, *Unruly Women: The Politics of Social and Sexual Control in the Old South* (Chapel Hill: University of North Carolina Press, 1992); Catherine Clinton and Nina Silber, eds., *Divided Houses: Gender and the Civil War* (New York: Oxford University Press, 1992); Catherine Clinton, *Tara Revisited: Women, War, and the Plantation Legend* (New York: Abbeville Press, 1995); George C. Rable, *Civil Wars: Women and the Crisis of Southern Nationalism* (Urbana: University of Illinois Press, 1989); Drew Gilpin Faust, *Mothers of Invention: Women of the Slaveholding South in the American Civil War* (Chapel Hill: University of North Carolina Press, 1996); and Campbell and Rice, eds., *Woman's War*.

4. Drew Gilpin Faust, *The Creation of Confederate Nationalism: Ideology and Identity in the Civil War South* (Baton Rouge: Louisiana State University Press, 1988), and George C. Rable, *The Confederate Republic: A Revolution Against Politics* (Chapel Hill: University of North Carolina Press, 1994).

5. Faust, *Creation of Confederate Nationalism*, 84, 83.

6. Paul D. Escott, *After Secession: Jefferson Davis and the Failure of Confederate Nationalism* (Baton Rouge: Louisiana State University Press, 1978); Rable, *Confederate Republic*.

7. Rable, *Confederate Republic*, ix–xii, 173, 215–18, 5–6, 245–48.

8. Faust, *Mothers of Invention*, 238–43, 6–7, 248–54.

9. Katharine M. Jones, *Heroines of Dixie*, vol. 2, *Winter of Desperation* (1955; rpt., Marietta GA: Mockingbird Books, 1975), 119–20.

10. Ella Gertrude Clanton Thomas, *The Secret Eye: The Journal of Ella Gertrude Clanton Thomas, 1848–1889*, ed. Virginia Ingraham Burr (Chapel Hill: University of North Carolina Press, 1990), 243.

11. C. Vann Woodward, ed., *Mary Chesnut's Civil War* (New Haven: Yale University Press, 1981), 706–7, 710.

12. Judith W. McGuire, *Diary of a Southern Refugee During the War* (1867; rpt., Lincoln: University of Nebraska Press, 1995), 332; Burr, ed., *Secret Eye*, 257.

13. Rable, *Confederate Republic*, 282–87.

14. Rable, *Confederate Republic*, 290.

15. Thomas, *Secret Eye*, 243.

16. Woodward, ed., *Mary Chesnut's Civil War*, 696.

17. Rable, *Confederate Republic*, 287–92.

18. Bynum, *Unruly Women*, 111–29; quote on 112.

19. Suzanne Lebsock, *Virginia Women, 1600–1945: "A Share of Honour"* (Richmond: Virginia State Library, 1987), 86.

20. Massey, *Bonnet Brigades*, 208.

21. McGuire, *Diary of a Southern Refugee*, 78.

22. Brooks D. Simpson, *Let Us Have Peace: Ulysses S. Grant and the Politics of War and Reconstruction* (Chapel Hill: University of North Carolina Press, 1991), 24–25, 33, 47–48; Mark Grimsley, *The Hard Hand of War: Union Military Policy Toward Southern Civilians* (New York: Cambridge University Press, 1995), 162–66; John F. Marszalek, *Sherman: A Passion for Order* (New York: Free Press, 1993), 230, 288, 309–10; Michael Fellman, *Citizen Sherman: A Life of William Tecumseh Sherman* (New York: Random House, 1995), 140–43, 171–73, 180–85.

23. William T. Sherman to Henry Wager Halleck, September 17, 1863, in Brooks D. Simpson and Jean V. Berlin, eds., *Sherman's Civil War: Selected Correspondence of William T. Sherman, 1860–1865* (Chapel Hill: University of North Carolina Press, 1999), 547–48.

24. Garrard to Sherman, July 6, 1864, in *War of the Rebellion: A Compilation of the Official Records of the Union and Confederate Armies*, 128 vols. (Washington DC: U.S. Government Printing Office, 1880–1910; hereafter OR), Ser. I, 38: pt. 5, 68; Sherman to Garrard, July 7, 1864, OR, Ser. I, 38: pt. 5, 76; Sherman to Halleck, July 7, 1864, OR, Ser. I, 38: pt. 5, 73.

25. Marszalek, *Sherman*, 285–86.

26. William T. Sherman to James M. Calhoun et al., September 12, 1864, in Simpson and Berlin, eds., *Sherman's Civil War*, 708.

27. Ellen Ewing Sherman to William T. Sherman, September 17, 1864, Sherman Family Papers, University of Notre Dame, Notre Dame IN.

28. McGuire, *Diary of a Southern Refugee*, 304–5.

29. Woodward, ed., *Mary Chesnut's Civil War*, 642.

30. Jones, *Winter of Desperation*, 143.

31. Robert Manson Myers, ed., *The Children of Pride: A True Story of Georgia and the Civil War*, 2 vols. (1972; rpt. New York: Popular Library, 1979), 2:1213.

32. For a good discussion of gender in the controversy between Ben Butler and the women of New Orleans, which includes most of the issues Union commanders would face with hostile women throughout the war, see Mary P. Ryan, *Women in Public: Between Banners and Ballots* (Baltimore: Johns Hopkins University Press, 1990), 143–45, and George Rable, "Missing in Action": Women of the Confederacy," in *Divided Houses*, eds. Clinton and Silber, 134–46; Marszalek, *Sherman*, 288–316.

33. William T. Sherman to Henry Wager Halleck, October 19, 1864, in Simpson and Berlin, eds., *Sherman's Civil War*, 736.

34. William T. Sherman to George Henry Thomas, January 21, 1865, in Simpson and Berlin, eds., *Sherman's Civil War*, 808.

35. William T. Sherman to Ellen Ewing Sherman, June 27, 1863, in Simpson and Berlin, eds., *Sherman's Civil War*, 492.

36. Myers, *Children of Pride*, 2:1227.

37. Lee Kennett, *Marching Through Georgia: The Story of Soldiers and Civilians During Sherman's Campaign* (New York: HarperCollins, 1995), 305.

38. For example, Anne Frobel of Fairfax, Virginia, and her sister Lizzie were vehement supporters of the Confederacy who found themselves under nearly constant Union occupation and developed a talent for identifying officers sympathetic to their plight and obtaining their protection. See Anne S. Frobel, *The Civil War Diary of Anne S. Frobel* (McLean VA: EPM Publications, 1992), 121–22, 135, 200–201.

39. Kennett, *Marching Through Georgia*, 312.

40. Emma LeConte, *When the World Ended: The Diary of Emma LeConte*, ed. Earl Schenck Miers (1957; rpt. Lincoln: University of Nebraska Press, 1987), 65.

41. Woodward, ed., *Mary Chesnut's Civil War*, 652, 657.

42. Grace Brown Elmore, *A Heritage of Woe: The Civil War Diary of Grace Brown Elmore*, ed. Marli F. Weiner (Athens: University of Georgia Press, 1997), 139; McGuire, *Diary of a Southern Refugee*, 317–18.

43. Ulysses S. Grant to Henry Wager Halleck, July 14, 1864, in John Y. Simon et al., eds., *The Papers of Ulysses S. Grant*, 24 vols. (Carbondale: Southern Illinois University Press, 1967–), 11:242–43; hereafter cited as *PUSG*.

44. Ulysses S. Grant to Philip H. Sheridan, August 26, 1864, *PUSG*, 12:97.

45. Ray Morris Jr., *Sheridan: The Life and Wars of General Phil Sheridan* (New York: Crown, 1992), 205–9; Jeffry D. Wert, *From Winchester to Cedar Creek: The Shenandoah Campaign of 1864* (New York: Simon & Schuster, 1987).

46. Woodward, ed., *Mary Chesnut's Civil War*, 648.

47. Sheridan to Grant, October 7, 1864, *PUSG*, 12:270.

48. McGuire, *Diary of a Southern Refugee*, 340.

49. Campbell and Rice, eds., *Woman's War*, 95.

50. Woodward, ed., *Mary Chesnut's Civil War*, 520, 637.

51. Woodward, ed., *Mary Chesnut's Civil War*, 678.

52. For a good discussion of these policies, see Massey, *Ersatz in the Confederacy*, 33–53.

53. Massey, *Ersatz in the Confederacy*, 55, 57, 42, 166.

54. Cornelia Peake McDonald, *A Woman's Civil War: A Diary with Reminiscences of the War, from March 1862*, rev. ed., ed. Minrose C. Gwin (Madison: University of Wisconsin Press, 1992), 222, 210.

55. See Faust, *Creation of Confederate Nationalism*, 22–40; Rable, *Civil Wars*, 203–17; Faust, *Mothers of Invention*, 179–84, 187–95.

56. McGuire, *Diary of a Southern Refugee*, 12.

57. Elmore, *Heritage of Woe*, 87, 107–8.

58. Faust, *Mothers of Invention*, 194; Rable, *Civil Wars*, 213.

59. McDonald, *Woman's Civil War*, 223.

60. Ellen Renshaw House, *A Very Violent Rebel: The Civil War Diary of Ellen Renshaw House*, ed. Daniel E. Sutherland (Knoxville: University of Tennessee Press, 1996), 161–62.

61. William T. Sherman to Ellen Ewing Sherman, March 12, 1865, in Simpson and Berlin, eds., *Sherman's Civil War*, 832–24.

62. William T. Sherman to Philemon Boyle Ewing, April 9, 1865, in Simpson and Berlin, eds., *Sherman's Civil War*, 852.

63. William T. Sherman to Ellen Ewing Sherman, March 12, 1865, in Simpson and Berlin, eds., *Sherman's Civil War*, 823. See also Marszalek, *Sherman*, 320–21, and Lloyd Lewis, *Sherman: Fighting Prophet* (New York: Harcourt, Brace, 1932), 488–89.

64. LeConte, *When the World Ended*, 3–4.

65. Jones, *Winter of Desperation*, 171.

66. Woodward, ed., *Mary Chesnut's Civil War*, 777. Harriot Ravenel's daughter's account of the Yankees' visit to her family reveals that black troops, unsupervised by officers, reached them first and treated her grandfather roughly. The white troops were a welcome contrast as a result, and she had little bad to say about the white

officers. See Charlotte St. Julien Ravenel, "The Enemy Comes to Our Plantation," in Jones, *Winter of Desperation*, 186–91.

67. LeConte, *When the World Ended*, 48.

68. Elmore, *Heritage of Woe*, 103.

69. Steven A. Channing, *Confederate Ordeal: The Southern Home Front* (Alexandria: Time-Life Books, 1984), 160.

70. Jones, *Winter of Desperation*, 159–60; Woodward, ed., *Mary Chesnut's Civil War*, 773; Faust, *Mothers of Invention*, 243.

71. Letter quoted in Massey, *Ersatz in the Confederacy*, 209 n. 68.

72. Woodward, ed., *Mary Chesnut's Civil War*, 777.

73. McDonald, *Woman's Civil War*, 214, 224–45.

74. Robert E. Lee to James A. Seddon, January 27, 1865, Robert E. Lee to Jefferson Davis, February 9, 1865, Robert E. Lee to John C. Breckinridge, February 24, 1865, and General Orders No. 8, March 27, 1865, in Clifford Dowdey and Louis H. Manarin, eds., *The Wartime Papers of Robert E. Lee* (1961; rpt. New York: Da Capo Press, 1987), 886–87, 892–93, 910–11, 918.

75. McDonald, *Woman's Civil War*, 229, 232.

76. House, *Very Violent Rebel*, 139.

77. Thomas, *Secret Eye*, 246.

78. Woodward, ed., *Mary Chesnut's Civil War*, 664.

79. Faust, *Mothers of Invention*, 235–36.

80. House, *Very Violent Rebel*, 148, 150, 152.

81. Woodward, ed., *Mary Chesnut's Civil War*, 782.

82. McGuire, *Diary of a Southern Refugee*, 332, 334, 346.

83. Henrietta Stratton Jaquette, ed., *South After Gettysburg: Letters of Cornelia Hancock, 1863–1868*, 2d ed. (New York: Thomas Y. Crowell, 1956), 213.

84. LeConte, *When the World Ended*, 98; Sarah Morgan, *The Civil War Diary of Sarah Morgan*, ed. Charles East (Athens: University of Georgia Press, 1991), 606.

85. McDonald, *Woman's Civil War*, 232.

86. Myers, ed., *Children of Pride*, 2:1268.

87. For two recent accounts emphasizing the role of community in the Confederate war effort, see Daniel E. Sutherland, *Seasons of War: The Ordeal of a Confederate Community, 1861–1865* (New York: Free Press, 1995), and Stephen V. Ash, *When the Yankees Came: Conflict and Chaos in the Occupied South, 1861–1865* (Chapel Hill: University of North Carolina Press, 1995).

88. Faust, *Mothers of Invention*, 238–39.

Index

African Americans: as Confederate soldiers, 7–8, 140–42, 172; as runaway slaves, 55; as Union soldiers, Confederate treatment of, 88
Akin, Mary, 140
Akin, Warren, 133, 144
Allen, Henry Watkins, 150
American Revolution, 2, 114–17, 122, 151–52
"American Victory, American Defeat" (McPherson), 4
Anderson, "Bloody Bill," 112
Appomattox campaign, 91–96, 100
Appomattox Court House VA, surrender at, 1, 10, 62, 63, 75, 96, 98, 117, 120, 185, 186, 188
Army of Northern Virginia, 41, 69, 86, 90, 91, 92, 95, 110, 117, 129, 154, 184; condition of, in Feb. 1865, 49–50
Army of Tennessee, 41, 46, 87, 105, 121, 139; condition of, in Feb. 1865, 42, 51, 58; rail transfer of, 42–43, 45, 52, 70–71; reorganized, 60
Army of the Cumberland, 174
Army of the James, 6, 95
Army of the Potomac, 6, 93, 95
Army of the Shenandoah, 179

The Art of War (Jomini), 112
Atlanta Campaign, 168, 175, 178
Atlanta GA: captured, 1, 22, 85; evacuated, 175–76
Averasboro NC, battle of, 55

Badeau, Adam, 100
Banks, Nathaniel P., 86
Barnum, P. T., 151
Beauregard, P. G. T., 9, 13, 118, 154; and Carolinas campaign, 41–45, 46, 47, 48, 51, 52, 72, 135; and surrender, 62, 64, 70, 71, 119
Benjamin, Judah P., 13, 30, 31, 67, 140, 147
Benning, Henry L., 30
Bentonville NC, battle of, 56–58, 60, 71, 73, 152
Beringer, Richard E., 3, 70
Blair, Francis Preston, Sr., 8, 26–27, 28, 30, 82, 83, 99
Blair, Frank, 27
Blair, Montgomery, 27
Blair initiative. *See* peace initiatives, proposals, and negotiations
"Bleeding Kansas," 108
blockade, 81, 134